The Basic Fault
Therapeutic Aspects of Regression

The Basic Fault

Therapeutic Aspects of Regression

MICHAEL BALINT

With a Foreword by Paul H. Ornstein

NORTHWESTERN UNIVERSITY PRESS
Evanston, Illinois

NORTHWESTERN UNIVERSITY PRESS
Evanston, Illinois 60208-4210

Printed in the United States of America

Second paperbound printing 1994

ISBN 0-8101-1025-3

Library of Congress Cataloging-in-Publication Data

Balint, Michael.
    The basic fault: therapeutic aspects of regression / Michael
Balint; with a foreword by Paul Ornstein.
        p. cm.
    Originally published: New York : Brunner/Mazel, c1979, in series:
Brunner/Mazel classics in psychoanalysis.
    Includes bibliographical references and index.
    ISBN 0-8101-1025-3 (paper : alk. paper)
    1. Regression (Psychology) 2. Psychoanalysis. I. Title.
RC489.R42B35 1992
616.89'17—dc20   92-9641
                                                              CIP

The paper used in this publication meets the minimum requirements of the
American National Standard for Information Sciences—Permanence of Paper
for Printed Library Materials, ANSI Z39.48-1984.

Contents

How to Read *The Basic Fault*

*An Introduction to Michael Balint's Seminal Ideas on the
Psychoanalytic Treatment Process*

SOME PERSONAL REFLECTIONS

I still remember vividly the excitement and enthusiasm I felt when reading *The Basic Fault* for the first time in 1969, just one year after its publication. I read it in anticipation of one of Michael and Enid Balint's regular visits from London to Cincinnati. On many of these visits I was their host, and it was again my privilege on this occasion to propose that he discuss the new book with the faculty and residents of the Department of Psychiatry at the University of Cincinnati (where both Michael and Enid Balint were Visiting Professors). I recall that Balint was somewhat skeptical of the project at first, wondering whether it was a good idea to discuss such a complex, psychoanalytic text, which raised many of the core questions of clinical psychoanalysis, with an audience consisting predominantly of psychiatrists and psychiatry residents in training. I insisted that we all had grappled with the text, that under the influence of his, by then, more than a decade of teaching in Cincinnati we were ready to move on to try to understand *The Basic Fault,* with his help. As usual, he accepted the challenge, and the session was both inspiring and highly informative.

The main impact of Balint's freewheeling responses was a lessening of our exclusive indoctrination in our brand of ego psychology and, for some of us, a broadening of our perspective in psychoanalysis—to object relations theory. Interestingly, Balint never used this term with us; he never labeled his innovative ideas as anything but psychoanalysis, although in his psychoanalytic writings he focused on object relations from the very beginning. Balint's approach clearly enhanced the therapeutic leverage of the psychoanalytic psychotherapies and offered us an alternative to our drive-theory-based ego psychology, an alternative that explicitly focused on the treatability of "sicker" patients. Balint's visits in general, but on this occasion in 1969 in particular, were a unique opportunity to witness his mode of thinking in relation to clinical as well as theoretical issues that occupied him throughout his professional life; to enjoy his overall, exemplary clarity and forcefulness, coupled with his openly expressed uncertainty about some recurring questions in psycho-analysis; and to appreciate his willingness to leave those questions unanswered and point toward the need for further empirical observations.

As I reflect on that discussion now, a little less than twenty-five years later, I realize that our excitement and enthusiasm were much greater than our ability to grasp the far-reaching implications of Balint's pioneering work. We did understand some of the major clinical and theoretical issues from prior reading of his major works (Balint 1952 [1965], 1956) and from our current reading of *The Basic Fault* (Balint 1968); from his previous teaching of psychotherapy; and now from his explication of his ideas in response to questions that arose from our reading and our own clinical work.

A few of us have already been deeply affected in our approach to psychotherapy and psychoanalysis—ever since his first visit to Cincin-nati in 1956—by Michael Balint's particular emphasis on the centrality of the many facets of the therapist-patient relationship, including trans-ference. This emphasis—rare at that time in teaching psychotherapy—stressed the fact that the therapist's interpretive activity depends on his/her grasp of the manifestations of the therapeutic process (i.e., the subtle details of the evolving and deepening experiences of both participants in their relationship), rather than merely on the content of what the patient presents in the sessions.

In his dramatic and affect-laden clinical teaching, Balint would abhor speculations about the "dynamics" and "genetics" of the patients' psychopathology, especially when the speculations were based on the history rather than on what patient and therapist experienced with one another—namely, their "object relationship." He thus focused on "how patient treated doctor" and on "how doctor treated patient" as entry points to understanding and characterizing the nature of each unique therapeutic endeavor. To put it even more sharply: Balint's focus was on the dynamics (and, later on in the treatment, also on the genetics) *of the relationship*, and only then on the nature of the patient's specific psychopathology—as the latter emerged from what went on in the therapist-patient relationship. Such a focus on the relationship—as we gradually understood this in the course of our own growing clinical experience—has turned out to be a highly reliable guide for the treatment process. It discouraged speculative inferences about the patient's psychopathology and yielded instead experience-near, observable, clinical data. It also offered us ways of checking on the adequacy of our grasp of the patients' therapeutic experiences, since we could now gain more or less direct empirical evidence for some consensual validation of our understanding and interventions. What was most impressive in all of this was Balint's readiness to *experiment* and to *predict* outcome, so as to study the efficacy of his interventions.

An odd phenomenon occurred during the decade and a half of the Balints' visiting professorship in Cincinnati. During Michael and Enid Balint's various teaching sessions (clinical conferences, demonstrations of group therapy through the one-way mirror, sessions with internists and general practitioners, the presentation of formal papers, etc.), the excitement and enthusiasm of the entire faculty and all the residents was extraordinary. Yet, after the Balints left Cincinnati, and during the interval between their yearly visits, it was as if they had never been teaching in Cincinnati. There appeared to be no lasting impact of their teaching on most members of the faculty and many residents in training, with the exception of a tiny minority. Balint's object-relations-theory-based clinical teaching had made no noticeable, significant inroads into the dominant ego psychology of the faculty. Why was this so, despite everyone's profound excitement and enthusiasm during the visits themselves, and the fact that everyone seemed impressed by the obvious increase in understanding and therapeutic leverage which the Balints' approach demonstrated? This question belongs in the larger context of what enables psychoanalysts and psychotherapists to expand their vision and what obstacles (internal and external) prevent such an expansion. What kinds of experiences (clinical or otherwise) do psychoanalysts and psychotherapists require to convince themselves that they need to change their approaches to treatment, and consequently their theories?

Without attempting to answer these complex questions here, I can identify one powerful obstacle on the basis of my observations: Michael and Enid Balint's approach demanded a more flexible, emotional presence of the therapist in the treatment situation, an acknowledgment of the therapist's contributions to the treatment process, and thus a recognition of the significance of the input of both participants for the outcome of treatment. The fact that the therapist could no longer focus on the patient's psychopathology alone as the obstacle to ure, but would also have to include his/her own treatment approach as a contributing factor, created a powerful resistance among those who were more comfortable with drive-theory-based ego psychology, which permitted—perhaps even prescribed—only a shadowy presence of the therapist behind an (often misconstrued) "neutrality" and "abstinence" in the therapeutic setting. Without a supportive atmosphere in the setting and a mutual commitment of the faculty to grapple with new ideas in an ongoing way, few members of our group had the courage to join an innovator such as Balint, who was too far ahead of the pack and was viewed as an iconoclast. His progressive ideas had not yet found an audience willing to suspend disbelief long enough to come to grips with the clinical-theoretical problems and solutions he was proposing. For reasons to be discussed shortly, Balint's work could not break through this barrier in the United States in his lifetime.

The response of those at the University of Cincinnati, to Balint's teaching in general and to *The Basic Fault* in particular, was not only a local, provincial phenomenon. It reflected the minimal attention paid to, or the outright dismissal of, his psychoanalytic contributions by the larger psychoanalytic community in the mainstream in this country (see, for example, Evans 1955, Ruddick 1959 and Baudry 1970). Balint shared his fate in the United States at that time with all other British object relations theorists: scant knowledge of their work and silent dismissal or vehement repudiation—the latter being reserved for Melanie Klein and her followers.

Perhaps here a brief characterization of Michael Balint and his work will enable us to put his ideas on the psychoanalytic treatment process of severely regressed patients into a proper perspective. To do this I shall examine how we might read *The Basic Fault* in the context of the time of its first publication, in 1968, and how we might read it now, in 1992.

THE MAN AND HIS WORK

For those who had known him personally, were familiar with his writings and had experienced his teaching in many contexts, or those who now take the trouble to study his works carefully, Michael Balint emerges as a towering figure in psychoanalysis in post-World War II Europe. As an analysand and student of Sandor Ferenczi (also his literary executor

PNC BANK

www.pncbank.com

PNC BANK

www.pncbank.com

PNCBANK™

060
SOUTH ORANGE (059)
76 SOUTH ORANGE AVENUE
SOUTH ORANGE NJ 07079
Cashbox 13

Deposit Multi/Mix
1:59   JAN 9 2006

Account Number   8101221802
Tran Amount $1,483.71
Cash Amount $0.00

T/S ID WWSEO597 Sequence Number 00075
Batch 302

and successor), Balint approached clinical and theoretical problems in psychoanalysis with the same courage and independent spirit but with a scientifically more disciplined mind than had his analyst, teacher, colleague, and friend. He burst on the European psychoanalytic scene (and, later, on the international, and still later, after he moved to England in 1939, on the British scene) with original contributions of his own, shortly after he qualified as a psychoanalyst in Budapest in 1926.

Michael Balint (originally Bergsmann) was born in Budapest, Hungary, on December 3, 1896, the son of a general practitioner, who influenced his son's ultimate career choice of medicine. Balint grew up in a very rich cultural milieu, was highly educated and broadly knowledgeable on almost any topic that came up in conversation: history, sociology, cultural anthropology, politics, geography, philosophy, literature, poetry and drama, the arts, and of course the literature and history of psychoanalysis itself. We always marveled at him as a specimen of the vanishing breed of the old-time Renaissance man in psychoanalysis. Balint was originally drawn to the sciences, studied chemistry, biochemistry, and mathematics—he even studied linguistics at one point—and then went to medical school at the University of Budapest and completed his studies by 1918 but did not receive his M.D. degree until 1924. He married soon after he graduated from medical school and, with his wife, Alice (who later also became a psychoanalyst and was Balint's closest coworker until her untimely death in Manchester, England, in 1939), moved to Berlin. There he worked as a biochemist for a while, acquired a Ph.D. in biochemistry, and practiced internal medicine while embarking on his psychoanalytic training. During that period he combined his interest in medicine and psychoanalysis by analyzing patients with medical (psychosomatic) illnesses—thus becoming the first person in history to have done so.

Balint's analytic training (as well as that of his wife, Alice) began with Hanns Sachs in Berlin. After about two years, both he and Alice found their analyses unsatisfactory and moved back to Budapest in 1924, to continue with Ferenczi. That second experience (also lasting for about two years) was much more felicitous for Michael Balint (presumably, lso for Alice) and, despite some additional forays into internal medicine in Budapest, decisively influenced his turning to psychoanalysis as his life's work. He then rose rapidly in the ranks of Hungarian psychoanalysts, becoming the director of the Psychoanalytic Clinic in Budapest after Ferenczi's death in 1933 at the age of thirty-seven. (For additional biographical data, see Sutherland 1980; Whitman 1977; and Harmat 1988; and for a more systematic presentation of both the biographical data and a recent assessment of Balint's scientific contributions, see Haynal 1988, who also established the Balint Archives at the University of Geneva, Switzerland; and Bacal 1990.)

Balint collected his most significant papers in psychoanalysis written from 1930 to 1953 in *Primary Love and Psychoanalytic Technique* (Balint 1952; enlarged 1965) and in *Problems of Human Pleasure and Behavior* (Balint 1956). In the former, Balint arranged his writings under three headings: "Instincts and Object Relations" (ten chapters); "Problems of Technique" (eight chapters); and "Problems of Training" (two chapters)—reflecting major areas of his scientific interests in the core areas of psychoanalysis. In the latter, Balint also arranged his papers under three headings: "The Individual and the Community" (seven chapters); "Clinical Problems" (six chapters); and "Men and Their Ideas" (seven chapters)—reflecting applications of his clinical-theoretical approach to well-delineated, wide-ranging, concrete problems.

These collections were then followed by the monograph on *Thrills and Regressions* (Balint 1959)—essentially Balint's contributions to psychoanalytic characterology—a way station toward the book that became his magnum opus in psychoanalysis: *The Basic Fault* (Balint 1968).

In addition, Balint's contributions to medicine—via his training method called the "Balint Groups"—jointly with his wife, Enid (whom he married in 1953), are the best known all over the world. In these Balint Groups a number of physicians (mainly general practitioners, but also internists and others) would gather weekly to discuss their ongoing clinical experiences. It was testimony to Balint's pedagogic philosophy and educational skill that he could refrain from "teaching" and instead facilitated the "learning" of the group members from their own experiences. The discussion of these daily clinical experiences included—and this was the crux of Balint's approach—careful attention to the nature of the doctors' own participation in the diagnostic and treatment process. It was the latter, the focus on the atmosphere the doctors created, the specific interventions they used (and their motives for them) that made these group sessions unique emotional-intellectual learning experiences.

The Doctor, His Patient, and the Illness (Balint 1957; revised and enlarged 1964), a distillate of that work, has long since become a classic and, along with *Psychotherapeutic Techniques in Medicine* (Balint and Balint 1961) and other, smaller monographs written with various collaborators of Balint Groups, attest to the enormous impact of the groups on the field of general medical practice.

Another area of psychotherapy in which Balint was a pioneer is *Focal Psychotherapy—An Example of Applied Psychoanalysis* (Balint, Ornstein, and Balint 1972)—an effort to successfully shorten the treatment process for suitable patients, without necessarily sacrificing depth, by formulating a focus early on in the evaluation and restricting subsequent interpretive work (as much as possible) within that chosen focus. This, too, received less attention in this country than it deserved, perhaps because it eschewed manipulative responses or other shortcuts in favor of an analytic, interpretive approach—one that is more difficult to learn to do without analytic, or at least intensive, long-term psychotherapeutic experience.

This sketchy overview portrays Balint's wide-ranging interests and calls attention to his major contributions. Knowledge of the content of the two volumes of his collected papers would undoubtedly have enhanced the readers' appreciation of his two subsequent monographs at the time of their publication. Thorough familiarity with his work in the Balint Groups, and the published papers and books that arose from that work, would have allowed the reader to recognize that Balint was a psychoanalytic thinker and practitioner par excellence, irrespective of the setting in which he happened to be working—whether behind the couch doing analysis (on the average, six hours daily), or in Balint Groups, or doing group or focal psychotherapy. Significantly, all of Balint's work was of a piece—permeated by his fundamental psychoanalytic attitude, sensitivity, knowledge, and skill. English psychoanalysts have recognized this, having known about his contributions to psychoanalysis proper (especially to object relations theory and to training psychoanalysts) throughout his professional life in England and recognizing his devotion to progress in psychoanalysis during the last two years of his life as president of the British Psychoanalytical Society—which finally placed him at the center of British psychoanalysis. This is what J. D. Sutherland said about him in his obituary: "As a contributor to psychoanalytic thought, Balint may well be rated in the future amongst the first-rank original minds after Freud and his immediate circle. He published several books and many papers on basic psychoanalytical theory. An appraisal of his work would be a major task . . . " (Sutherland 1971).

German analysts have also recognized Balint as a formidable psychoanalyst, since he had actively participated in rebuilding psychoanalysis in post-World War II Germany and had analyzed (in London) a number of the subsequently most influential psychoanalysts in that country. Some German analysts have also gained firsthand experience of his approach in Balint Groups (as did the Swiss and French) before these spread to other countries. But, in the United States, Balint of the "Balint Groups' fame" was for a long time unfairly discounted as a leading psychoanalyst. He was viewed mainly as having become a popularizer of psychoanalysis in general medicine, without recognition of his enormous original contributions to the psychology of medical practice. While he was undoubtedly a "popularizer" of psychoanalysis among physicians, this was by no means the whole story, as his writings demonstrate and as the remainder of this introductory essay will show.

A 1968 READING OF *THE BASIC FAULT*

The majority of psychoanalysts in this country were not yet sufficiently receptive to *The Basic Fault* in 1968. Balint had shared with the psychoanalytic community his developing ideas in his papers on "Instincts and Object Relations" as well as "Problems of Technique" (Balint 1952; reprinted 1959; and enlarged 1965) at frequent intervals after 1930. But these collections—dealing with his ideas on human sexuality, object relations, and the treatment of deep regression in patients—curiously enough, did not awaken a sufficiently wide-spread interest within the analytic community. (See, for example, a lukewarm review by Evans 1955, and Ruddick 1959).

The years 1930, 1932, and 1935 were landmark years in Balint's unfolding analytic career. These were the years in which he presented some important precursors of his fundamental ideas, which progressively matured and were later more comprehensively, and somewhat more systematically, formulated in *The Basic Fault*. Early in his career as a psychoanalyst Balint began to focus on sexuality, object relations, and analytic technique and worked on them steadily for the remainder of his professional life. (It would be instructive to follow his clinical experiences, his mode of theorizing, and the observational data on which these were based, leading up to *The Basic Fault*, step by step—which cannot be done in this context—and thereby to appreciate more fully Balint's creative genius and also recognize more clearly where we cannot follow him.)

The first of the three papers that started him on his clinical investigative journey was "Psychosexual Parallels to the Fundamental Laws of Biogenetics" (Balint 1930 [1965]), presented at the Second Conference of the German Psycho-Analytic Society, in Dresden, in which he introduced the term "New Beginning." His second paper was on "Character Analysis and New Beginning" (Balint 1932 [1965]), presented at the Twelfth International Psycho-Analytical Congress (Wiesbaden, Germany), a prestigious forum with great visibility. This paper elaborated more extensively the concept of the "new beginning," which later became an indispensable experience for the patient, enabling him/her to emerge from a deep regression to the level of the basic fault, and thus a precondition for cure. The third paper was on "Critical Notes on the Theory of the Pregenital Organization of the Libido" (Balint 1935 [1965]), presented to the Vienna Psychoanalytic Society—hardly a less significant audience. The presentation of this paper in Vienna required great courage, since it contradicted important elements of Freud's libido theory.

In Vienna Balint introduced the idea that the sustained, noisy, visible manifestations of pregenital sexuality are not the expressions of biological, partial instincts, as Freud claimed them to be, but are the consequences of faulty, traumatic responses on the part of the infant's primary objects. All three of these papers thus contained significant kernels of Balint's later clinical concepts and theories, as well as his emerging technical recommendations. These three papers also introduced Balint as a startlingly innovative analyst, who was—as we now recognize—way ahead of his time, though clearly following in the footsteps of Ferenczi, which may have made the mainstream in this country somewhat suspicious of his work. American psychoanalysts were especially leery of his recommendation that patients, at the end of the analysis, in the phase of the new beginning, often require some form of symbolic act (such as touching, or holding a finger, etc.). From Balint's perspective, this symbolic act made a great deal of sense, because he viewed the experiences at the level of the basic fault as preverbal, as having originated in a two-person matrix, and thus as being incapable of expression in adult language, hence requiring other means of communication—silent pres-

Foreword

ence and/or symbolic acts. His subsequent contributions (the remainder of the papers in the two collections) continued in the same innovative spirit, close to clinical observation and well reasoned. Yet, in this country, these too had a mixed reception.

A majority took little notice, since most analysts could not fit Balint's observations with their own clinical experiences. The American psycho-analytic vision was by and large restricted by a somewhat rigid concern about "analyzability," as if this were exclusively a definable character-istic of the patient and did not also depend on the analyst. Balint focused, not on analyzability, but on the "fit" between patient and analyst, and he therefore struggled with the question of what kind of clinical atmosphere (i.e., what kind of an object relationship) and analytic responsiveness was called for at what stage of the analysis. The extremes of regression he portrayed were also unfamiliar to those who worked only with so-called analyzable neurotic patients. And, short of detailed analytic reports, one could not really have an adequate picture of what Balint actually did, no matter how much he *described*, rather than *illustrated*, what he did. But perhaps even illustrative clinical details would not yet have aroused sufficient receptivity and interest without some matching clinical expe-rience, or less prejudice against the experimental spirit of Ferenczi and Balint.

Another possible reason for a lack of interest might have been Balint's way of theorizing: his idiosyncratic, new language was somewhat confusing, since he simultaneously insisted that he remained within the Freudian paradigm. The two could not easily be reconciled. His notion of "The Three Areas of the Mind" (Balint 1957)—the "oedipal area," "the area of the basic fault," and "the area of creation"—all within the realm of the ego, was too vague on the one hand and perhaps too rigidly drawn on the other, and might well have put off his American colleagues, who could not see sufficient heuristic value in his conception. Soon thereafter, Balint expanded his new theory of the mind in a paper entitled "Primary Narcissism and Primary Love" (Balint 1960), claiming that "primary narcissism" was untenable. He replaced the concept with the idea of a "primary, archaic, object relatedness" or "primary love"—the corner-stone of all his later ideas. These two theoretical papers were then followed by two clinically focussed progress reports, in "The Regressed Patient and His Analyst" (Balint 1960) and in "The Benign and Malignant Forms of Regression" (Balint 1965), where he detailed his technical principles and correlated them with his recently articulated theory of the mind. These four papers (with some modifications and expansions) constitute the bulk of *The Basic Fault.*

Only a small minority of analysts (I count myself among them), those working with "sicker" patients (later on referred to as suffering from narcissistic and borderline conditions), recognized the significance of Balint's work and reacted with a greater degree of openness and receptivity (Ornstein 1971; Ornstein and Goldberg 1973a and 1973b). Balint's theory of the mind (the three "areas") and the fuzziness of certain features of the new beginning—which few observed and even fewer knew how to bring about—notwithstanding, many aspects of his ideas and approach to treatment were nevertheless clinically significant. His notion that the basic fault reflects the consequences of actual, early, traumatic experiences in a two-person situation; that these can be revived and analytically healed (even if the healing leaves a scar); that the area of basic fault is not characterized by specific conflicts—that it reflects a "fault" that has to be put right; that the trauma occurred at the hand of archaic objects—these were worthy of further scrutiny. However, admittedly, these conceptions and technical principles could not easily be accommodated within our American ego psychology paradigm. They demanded a shift to an object relations theory, which was then still barely considered necessary or acceptable in this country. Those acquainted with patients who belonged to the "widening scope of psychoanalysis" were beginning to be less satisfied with the theoretical confines of ego psychology but were not yet ready, in the late sixties and early seventies, to embrace more openly ideas of the British object relations theorists who had significantly widened the scope of psychoanalysis, both clinically and theoretically.

Balint was in the forefront of British object relations theorists, having brought his key ideas with him from Hungary, where object relations theory originated with Ferenczi. He showed us that there were alternative ways of thinking and working—and he therefore commanded our attention. And even if his theories and technical recommendations were not adequately illustrated with clinical details and therefore not easily translatable by us into actual practice, he did free us to search for a better understanding and an empirically more justifiable approach. His work prepared us for the emerging self psychology of Heinz Kohut, some of whose crucial ideas Balint, in a very different theoretical context, nevertheless anticipated (see also Bacal 1990).

Foreword

In summary, in this country the early reading of Balint's work, including *The Basic Fault*, was animated by two contradictory attitudes toward expanding the narrow definition of psychoanalysis as a method of treatment and discouraging too rigid an adherence to the ego psychology paradigm. Under the banner of the "widening scope of psychoanalysis" technical alterations ("parameters") were acceptable, but a change in the basic paradigm was not. Such a paradigm change was deemed unwarranted, since ego psychology was encompassing enough—so the claim went—and able to accommodate all clinically desirable changes. Those who remained unconvinced about the adequacy of introducing parameters (and were then hoping to make them unnecessary at a later point, via interpretation of their meaning) and who were searching for a better solution to their clinical problems, welcomed Balint's refreshing, open, empirically sensible approach. This is what his approach offered: an increase in clinical sensitivity, a chance to learn how "to be with the patient," and a gradual acquisition of how to be "emotionally present" in the treatment situation. All this accrued to those who could enter Balint's clinical-theoretical world after overcoming group pressure and the stranglehold of a dominant paradigm.

There were certain problems. The idea of creating a "suitable atmosphere" or "offering a particular form of object relation"—as if the latter were to be shaped and dosed, rather than spontaneously unfold or develop—was not always easy to translate into therapeutic or analytic activity if one was not inclined to follow Balint into symbolic action. Another problem arose from his notion that the experiences at the level of the basic fault could not be expressed in adult language (with conventional meaning); yet he described these experiences so evocatively that his descriptions of archaic states are to this day unsurpassed (see especially Balint 1959). And he enabled us to talk to our patients even in the midst of their archaic experiences (as these come alive in the consulting room) in the very language in which he portrayed these experiences. Balint had an uncanny ability to describe the communicative aspects of regression, showing that even without adult language a great deal could be learned from patients in the treatment situation. Balint's sharp delineation of the three "areas"—the oedipal area with adult language, the area of the basic fault without adult language (preverbal), the area of creation without language (largely inaccessible)—had become somewhat schematized and concretized. This indicated, perhaps, that, with all that Balint's theory offered, a more reliable guide to treatment was still missing in his approach. He would have been the first to acknowledge this. In time he might have developed such a guide, since he was constantly searching for one. For a growing number of patients, however, a "repair" of ego psychology (its expansion or modification) would not be sufficient. Psychoanalysis seemed destined for a major overhaul.

This takes us to the current reading of *The Basic Fault*. But first, a number of Balint's specific terms, such as "primary love" (or "primary, archaic object relatedness"), the "basic fault," and "the new beginning" have been used so far in this essay with only cursory allusions to their fuller meaning and specific clinical-theoretical position in Balint's work. The reader will, of course, encounter them repeatedly in Balint's own exposition, but I shall add a set of definitions of these terms here to provide an orientation to a strange land which, to the contemporary reader in 1992, is no longer so strange.

Primary Love. A fundamental assumption underlies Balint's developmental-theoretical innovation, which is that "the aim of all human striving is to establish—or, probably, to re-establish—an all embracing harmony with one's environment, to be able to love in peace" (Balint 1968, 65). In suggesting the replacement of the theory of primary narcissism (which assumes that no object exists at the beginning of extrauterine life) by the theory of primary love (which assumes an immediate, primitive, or primary form of object relatedness), Balint, true to his methodologic commitment of focus on empirical data, had this to say: "clinical experiences with patients should be employed to construct a new theory that could replace primary narcissism and that might be more suitable for verification or refutation by direct observation" (ibid.). This is a leitmotiv in Balint's work and gives the idea of intense, primary relatedness its compelling power over primary narcissism. He goes on: "A common feature of all these primitive forms of object relationship is that in it the object is taken for granted. . . . In this harmonious two-person relationship only one partner may have wishes, interests, and demands on his own; without any further need for testing, it is taken for granted that the other partner, the object or the friendly expanse, will automatically have the same wishes, interests, and expectations" (ibid., 70). This, then, is primary love, or primary object relatedness, and it forms the cornerstone of Balint's ideas. An important conclusion is that sadism and hate are secondary phenomena, consequences of inevitable frustrations, that manifestations of narcissism are always secondary (since there is no such state as primary narcissism).

The Basic Fault. This is a level of experience, or an area of the mind, that in Balint's view results from the variety of possible disturbances of the primary object relationship. He writes: "In my view the origin of the basic fault may be traced back to a considerable discrepancy in the early formative phases of the individual between his bio-psychological needs and the material and psychological care, attention, and affection available during the relevant times. This creates a state of deficiency whose consequences and after-effects appear to be only partly reversible. The cause of this early discrepancy may be congenital, i.e., the infant's bio-psychological needs may have been too exacting . . . or may be environmental, such as care that is insufficient, deficient, haphazard, over-anxious, over-protective, harsh, rigid, grossly inconsistent, incorrectly timed, over-stimulating, or merely un-understanding or indifferent" (ibid., 22).

The basic fault has an interrelated clinical and theoretical position in Balint's work. Clinically it encompasses the various disturbances of secondary narcissism (previously viewed as pregenital or preoedipal disturbances), and theoretically it assigns these to the above-mentioned disturbances in object relations, rather than considering them as primarily biological, partial-drive-related phenomena. This is a significant departure from previous conceptualizations but in keeping with Ferenczi's views. Balint describes the basic fault in his patients' language and imagery: "The patient says that he feels there is a fault within him, a fault that must be put right. And it is felt to be a fault, not a complex, not a conflict, not a situation. Second, there is a feeling that the cause of this fualt is that someone has either failed the patient or defaulted him; and third, a great anxiety invariably surrounds this area, usually expressed as a desperate demand that this time the analyst should not—in fact must not—fail him" (ibid., 21).

New Beginning. The curative process in the basic fault hinges on the patient's capacity to regress to that level in the treatment process, as well as on the analyst's capacity to create the requisite climate and allow the patient to find the level to which he has to regress in order to reemerge with a capacity for a different, more mature, object relationship. Thus the new beginning is the clinical-technical correlate of the basic fault. "New beginning means: (a) going back to something 'primitive' to a point before the faulty development started, which could be described as a regression, and (b) at the same time discovering a new, better suited, way [of relating to objects of love and hate] which amounts to progression" (ibid., 132).

Regression is another key concept in the treatment process, a prerequisite to reach the basic fault and then to achieve the new beginning. Its possible forms, "regression in the service of recognition" and "regression in the service of gratification," play an important role in Balint's conception of success or failure in the treatment process.

A 1992 READING OF *THE BASIC FAULT*

During the twenty-four-year interim, the atmosphere in American psychoanalysis changed considerably. The change was slow in coming and occurred on two related fronts. Kohut's self psychology shook up the psychoanalytic establishment in the late sixties and early seventies. It offered a new psychoanalytic paradigm—it accomplished the necessary overhaul—that soon evoked a great deal of controversy and debate. Partly in response to the increasing acceptance of Kohut's ideas, the slowly and cautiously increasing interest in the British object relations theories just then gained momentum, apparently as an antidote. The object relations theories including those which began to develop in this country—did not seem to threaten the leading paradigm; they could be viewed as extensions of it. This increasing interest in object relations theories—broadly motivated by a wider and more open search for approaches to narcissistic and borderline conditions—had a salutary impact on attention being paid to *The Basic Fault*. A reprint of the book in this country in 1979 already showed this increasing interest in Balint's work in the wake of cultural changes that foreshadowed the current theoretical pluralism in psychoanalysis. (It is highly instructive in this connection to read Lagache 1953 and to study Masud Khan's assessment of Balint's work soon after the publication of *The Basic Fault* [Khan 1969], which offers a very different reading. So does a later one by Haynal in 1988 and by Bacal in 1990.)

While such pluralism had already existed in the British Psychoanalytical Society, for us in this country it was a newly developing phenomenon that created the ambience in which Balint's work could be reexamined. It was now possible to tease out the clinically relevant aspects of Balint's contributions, and to recognize how he theorized about them, without having to follow him in every theoretical or technical detail. Balint's work is particularly suited to this exercise, because he tells us with admirable clarity which clinical observation evoked which technical approach and which consequence of that approach led him to which theoretical proposition, even if his actual creative process was not so neatly linear and was greatly affected a priori by his fundamental humanism and optimism, as well as by his experimental spirit and inordinate curiosity.

Seen in this light, even the theory of the three areas of the mind seems less abstract and more closely linked to Balint's technical principles, as was so elegantly portrayed by Masud Khan (1969). Even the headings of Khan's essay will convey some of the essence and core of Balint's ideas regarding the treatment process throughout the clinical spectrum: "The area of the oedipal level" is linked to "the provision of frustration" (ibid, 242-43); "the area of the basic fault and the 'new beginning' is linked to "the provision of recognition" (ibid., 243-47), and, finally "the area of creation" is linked to "the provision of failure" (ibid., 247-48).

Kohut's description of the selfobject transferences—the remobilization of archaic needs and forms of relatedness in the treatment situation—and their systematic clinical as well as theoretical elaboration, opened for us a new way to appreciate Balint's work. The observational and developmental elements of "primary love," aspects of the "new beginning," the pathogenic impact of early traumata in the archaic relationships that give rise to the "basic fault," although differently conceptualized—once stripped of their theoretical baggage, if such is at all possible—show kinship to and can be fitted into the broader framework of self psychology. In fact, it appears that in this new context Balint's ideas gain added specificity and a clinically usable language for the treatment process. And as Bacal astutely observed, this fits in well with an early demand of Balint himself, which Bacal quotes: "what we need . . . is a theory that would give us a good description of the development of object relations comparable to, but independent of, our present, biologizing, theory of the development of instincts" (Balint 1949, 217, Bacal 1990, 122.). Bacal notes, and I agree with him, that Kohut's self psychology provides just such a developmental theory. I would further add that this new theory gave to many of Balint's descriptions of archaic states (the basic fault) a more specific meaning within the conception of the mirror transference, the idealizing and twinship transference. Kohut made the basic fault thereby more accessible to psychoanalytic treatment, with a new language that can, through the analyst's empathic immersion in the patient's transference experiences, offer a further increase in therapeutic leverage.

Both Balint and Kohut considered psychoanalysis an empirical science. Each of them prided himself for starting in the clinical context and giving precedence to observation and to what worked, being willing to drop outmoded preconceptions and ineffective technique. But, most importantly, each of them was willing to be swayed by his observational data (combined with some inexplicable inner readiness) to change theory. Reluctance to let go of theories that have lost their erstwhile heuristic value must be a special psychoanalytic predilection, otherwise Freud would not have insisted (Freud 1914) that theory is only the dispensable superstructure of psychoanalysis whereas the observational data are its foundation. Kohut and Balint were exemplary in that they could make the necessary changes their respective experiences demanded.

It is my fervent hope that the reader of this edition of *The Basic Fault* will be aided by this introduction to enter Balint's clinical and theoretical world with an open mind and to retrn from that journey amply rewarded. I can find no more eloquent way to conclude than to quote Masud Khan, whose 1969 essay on Balint I greatly admire and whose closing comment expresses my own feelings: "I undertook to write this essay from a wish to pay homage to the researches of a distinguished and creative analyst, whom I have enjoyed the privilege of knowing both as my teacher and as my friend."

PAUL H. ORNSTEIN
1992

REFERENCES

Bacal, H. A., and Newman, K. M. 1990. *Theories of Object Relations: Bridges to Self Psychology,* chap. 6, "Michael Balint," pp. 121-134. New York: Columbia University Press.
Balint, M. 1958. "The Three Areas of the Mind." *Int. J. Psycho-Anal.,* 39:328-340.
------. 1959. *Thrills and Regressions.* London: Hogarth; New

York: International Universities Press.

------. 1960. "The Regressed Patient and His Analyst." *Psychiatry,* 23:231-243.

------. 1960. "Primary Narcissism and Primary Love." *Psychoanal. Q,* 29:6-43.

------. 1968. *The Basic Fault: Therapeutic Aspects of Regression.* London: Tavistock Publications.

------. 1969. "Trauma and Object Relationship." *Int. J. Psycho-Anal.,* 50:429-35.

Balint, M.; Ornstein, P. H.; and Balint, E. 1972. *Focal Psycho-therapy--An Example of Applied Psychoanalysis.* London: Tavistock Publications; Philadelphia: J. B. Lippincott.

Baudry, F. 1970. "Book Review of M. Balint, *The Basic Fault.*" *Psychoanal. Q.,* 39:129-3.

Evans, W. N. 1955. "Review of Primary Love and Psychoanalytic Technique." *Psychoanal. Q.,* 24:438-39.

Harmat, P. 1988. "Freud, Ferenczi und die ungarische." *Psychoanalyse.* Tübingen: Edition Discord.

Haynal, A. E. 1988. *The Technique at Issue. Controversies in Psychoanalysis from Freud and Ferenczi to Michael Balint.* London: Karnac.

Khan, M. M. R. 1969. "On the Clinical Provision of Frustrations, Recognitions, and Failures in the Analytic Situation. An Essay on Dr. Michael Balint's Researches on the Theory of Psychoanalytic Technique." *Int. J. Psycho-Anal.,* 50:237-48.

Lagache, D. 1953. "Review of Primary Love and Psychoanalytic Technique." *Int. J. Psycho-Anal.,* 34:328-29.

Morse, S. J. 1972. "Structure and Reconstruction: A Critical Comparison of Michael Balint and D. W. Winnicott." *Int. J. Psycho-Anal.,* 53:487-500.

Ornstein, P. H. 1971. "In Memoriam Michael Balint 1896-1970." *Amer. J. Psychiat.,* 127:133.

Ornstein, P. H. and Goldberg, A. 1973a. "Psychoanalysis and Medicine: I. Contributions to Psychiatry, Psychosomatic Medicine and Medical Psychology." *Dis. Nerv. Sys.,* 34:143-147.

------. 1973b. "Psychoanalysis and Medicine: II. Contributions to the Psychology of Medical Practice." *Dis. Nerv. Sys.,* 34:278-283.

Ornstein, P. H., and Ornstein, A. 1972. "Focal Psychotherapy:

Its Potential Impact on Psychotherapeutic Practice in Medicine."
Psychiatry in Medicine, 3:311-25.

Ruddick, B. 1959. "Book Review. *Thrills and Regressions.*"
Psychoanal. Q., 28:401-402.

Shaw, P. M. 1971. "Book Review. *The Basic Fault.*" *British
Journal of Social and Clinical Psychology,* June 1971.

Sutherland, J. D. 1971. "Obituary. Michael Balint (1896-1970)."
Int. J. Psycho-Anal., 52:331-33.

------. 1980. "The British Object Relations Theorists: Balint,
Winnicott, Fairbairn, Guntrip." *J. Amer. Psychoanal. Assn.,*
28:829-60.

Whitman, R. M. 1977. "Balint, Michael (1896-1970)." *International
Encyclopedia of Psychiatry, Psychoanalysis, and Neurology,* pp.
279-80.

Preface to the 1979 Reprint

The ideas put forward and the questions raised in this book were important ten years ago; some of them are, perhaps, even more important today. I am very glad to have been given the opportunity to write the preface for the second edition.

Michael Balint, in his preface to the first edition, wrote, in April 1967, exactly twelve years ago, that the problems discussed in the book had occupied him for the past ten years or so. It is my impression that they had occupied him for much longer: perhaps for all of his working life. In spite of that, when we had discussion together about the matters raised in the book, discussion which invariably arose out of clinical problems, Balint would not allow any preconceived ideas, or earlier theories, to block his observations and thinking. He tolerated long periods of doubt and uncertainty brought about by his new observations and thus avoided being content with false solutions which would have evaded the problems and the understanding he was trying to reach. His honesty of mind was impressive to me then as it is today.

Perhaps some of Balint's precise descriptions of different techniques—of a mythical 'correct' technique—are less central to our work than they were ten years ago. Their description, however, is a valuable and necessary stage in the development of our thinking. Balint, like all good theoreticians, changed as he thought and as he worked and wrote. We had together planned to re-write certain parts of this book and to add a chapter to it. On re-reading it I am glad that we were never able to do so. It stands well in its present form, and gives the reader insight in a lucid way into some of the, until then, undescribed ways that patients relate to their analysts and analysts to their patients in the two-person relationship originally created and described by Freud. These relationships must continue to be re-observed and re-defined in order to elucidate not only problems for psychoanalysts but for all workers for whom the study of human relationships is relevant.

April 1979   ENID BALINT

Preface

The problems discussed in this book have occupied me for the last ten years or so. On several occasions during this time I wrote down and published this or that part which I thought sufficiently mature. In chronological order these were: 'The Three Areas of the Mind' (1957), 'Primary Narcissism and Primary Love' (1960), 'The Regressed Patient and his Analyst', also in 1960, and 'The Benign and the Malignant Forms of Regression' in 1965.

All these independent publications had to be rearranged and parts of them rewritten to accommodate them in this book. The one that was altered most is 'The Regressed Patient and his Analyst'. It was extended considerably and the first half of it became Part III while the second half formed the nucleus of Part V.

I wish to acknowledge the courtesy of the Editors of the *International Journal of Psycho-Analysis*, the *Psychoanalytic Quarterly*, *Psychiatry: Journal for the Study of Interpersonal Processes*, as well as of Grune & Stratton, New York, for allowing me to use material previously published by them.

As in every other of my books, in this one too I wish to record my indebtedness to my wife, without whose help the compilation of this book would have taken still more time. On more than one occasion when I was hopelessly bogged down in my ideas, it was a discussion with her that enabled me to find my way out of the morass and continue my work.

I am greatly indebted to my friend and colleague Dr Mary Hare, and to Miss Ann Hutchinson, our Library Secretary at the Institute of Psycho-Analysis, for reading the proofs and for their valuable comments. I also owe thanks to Miss Hutchinson for preparing the Index.

April 1967   MICHAEL BALINT

PART I

The three areas of the mind

Chapter 1

The therapeutic processes
and their localization

Part I of this book consists almost wholly of self-contained chapters, and this will not make the main argument easy to follow. I had to adopt this structure because on several occasions I had to clear away some established ways of looking at, and thinking about, well-authenticated clinical observations before I could start on the next stage of my train of thought.

Before beginning our journey, let us agree that all of us, the readers as well as the writer, are fairly reliable analysts who do not make elementary mistakes; that is, all of us give fairly correct interpretations at fairly sensible times and work through the material produced by our patients, as far as possible, on several, both genital and pre-genital, levels, both in the transference and in reality.

Having agreed on this, perhaps we may also admit that all of us occasionally have difficult patients *vis-à-vis* whom we feel puzzled and uncertain and that – according to rumours circulating in every Branch Society of our International Association – even the most experienced and most skilled analysts among us have occasional failures.

How can this be so; and what is the explanation of this unpleasant fact? On the whole the reasons for our difficulties and failures may be grouped under three headings. They may be due (a) to our inadequate technique, (b) to the difficulties inherent either in the patient's personality or in his illness, and (c) to a bad 'fit' between our otherwise adequate technical skill and the otherwise curable intrinsic qualities of the case.

The first question we have to deal with is why some patients are more difficult to treat than others, or why some analyses are less rewarding to the analyst – and to his patients – than others. Let us

3

formulate the same question in a different way which might enable us to tackle it better. What are the therapeutic processes; in which part of the mind do they take place; and what in them is responsible for the various difficulties experienced by us analysts?

After more than sixty years of research the problem is still largely unresolved as to which parts of the mental apparatus are accessible to psychoanalysis, and to what extent; or, to use our formulation, which parts of the mind are those in which the therapeutic processes take place. Though these two formulations do not describe exactly the same problem, they overlap considerably.

It is generally agreed that influencing the super-ego should be, and in fact is, one of the desirable aims of therapy. We even have ideas about what happens in that part of the mind, ideas, that is, about the therapeutic processes involved and the changes that take place.

We know, for instance, that the super-ego has been built up chiefly of introjections, the most important sources being the stimulating but never fully satisfying sexual objects of early infancy, childhood, and puberty; in a way one may say that the super-ego is the sum total of the mental scars left by these objects. On the other hand, the super-ego can be changed by new introjections as late as in mature life; a convincing instance of such change is analytic treatment during which the analyst becomes partly or even wholly introjected. I would like to differentiate between introjection and another process – most important in building up the super-ego – identification, which can be thought of as a secondary step after introjection: the individual not only takes in the stimulating but frustrating sexual object, but henceforth feels it an integral part of himself. Often identification is preceded by, or intimately associated with, idealization; on the other hand a high degree of idealization may be a serious obstacle against identification with the introjected object. All this is fairly well known, but we have hardly any knowledge about the processes that are needed to *undo* introjection, idealization, or identification. To sum up, we have some idea of the processes that lead to new introjections and identifications, but hardly anything is known about the ways that undo an established introjection or identification. This is regrettable because it would be highly important for our technical efficiency to know how to help the patient to get rid of parts of his super-ego.

4

There is also fair agreement that analytic therapy as a rule ought to aim at making the ego stronger, although our ideas of the exact nature of the strengthening and the techniques for achieving it are as yet rather vague. What we do know about this aspect of our therapy might be summed up as follows: the ego in closest contact with the id should be strengthened; I refer to that part of the ego that can enjoy instinctual gratifications, can endure a considerable increase of tensions, is capable of concern and consideration, can contain and tolerate unsatisfied desires, as well as hatred, and tries to accept, and can test, both internal and external realities. Whereas that part of the ego that cannot, and dare not, enjoy intense instinctual gratification, that must defend itself against any increase of emotional tension by denial, inhibition, and turning into the opposite, or by reaction formations – i.e. that part which is adapted to external reality and to super-ego demands at the expense of internal reality – should not be strengthened; on the contrary, its role should be made less dominant.

The question whether this strengthening of the ego and the previously discussed modifications of the super-ego mean only two aspects of the same process or are two processes, more or less independent, has not been explicitly stated, nor properly discussed. The formula used most frequently states that the ego has to mediate at the behest of the super-ego between the demands of the external reality and the id. It is still an open question as to whether the mediator has, or has not, any power of its own to influence the compromise and, further, as to what are the therapeutic processes that have any effect on this power.

There is still greater uncertainty about the possibility and the means of influencing the id. We have hardly any idea whether this can be done at all and, if it can, how it should be done. Those who accept the existence of primary death instinct and with it primary sadism, primary narcissism, and destructiveness, are forced to the conclusion that by our therapy the id must be changed too. One aspect of this possible change has been described already by Freud, in 'Analysis Terminable and Interminable' (1937), as 'taming of the instincts'. In the special case of primary sadism this means that the vehemence of the destructive urges – sometimes called *destrudo* – must be mitigated during and through analytic treatment – or upbringing – either by changing them at their source, i.e. in the id, or at any rate

5

by 'fusing' them with more libido. As the two theoretical concepts of 'fusion' and 'defusion' are very vague, it is almost impossible to place them with confidence either in the id or in the ego; moreover, apart from their names we have not been able to form any idea of the mechanisms and processes involved in them. Perhaps the only hint we have is that possibly defusion and frustration are fairly closely linked; whether the same is true of the technically highly important counterpart, gratification and fusion, is rather uncertain.

In these circumstances it is small wonder that nobody has been able to describe reliable methods for influencing these two processes. If 'fusion' and 'defusion' are amenable to influence by analysis at all, the only thing we can state with certainty is that this influence occurs through the transference, i.e. essentially through an object relationship. Conversely it means that processes initiated in the analytic situation must be conceived of as being powerful or intensive enough to penetrate into deep layers of the mind and achieve fundamental changes in them. How this happens and what sort of object relationship, of what intensity, would achieve this task, have not been properly discussed in our literature.

Thus we have arrived at one answer to the puzzle with which we began our journey: why it is that even the most experienced among us have difficult cases and occasional failures? We have some theoretical conceptions about possible processes in the mind during psychoanalytic therapy, but as yet there is no direct link, of sufficient reliability, between these theoretical conceptions and our technical skill. In other words, on the basis of our theoretical conceptions about the therapeutic processes and their localizations, we are not yet in the position to state what particular technique is advisable and what technical measures are better avoided. This fact is the *raison d'être* for the co-existence of various schools in analysis, each of them with its own technique differing considerably from that of the others, but each accepting the same basic ideas about the structure of the mind. It is important to add that analysts of all schools – without exception – have their successes, their difficult cases, and their fair share of failures. It is highly probable that the protagonists of the differing schools succeed – or fail – with different patients; moreover that the mode of success – or failure – may be different with the different techniques. Thus, an impartial but critical study of this field would be most revealing for our theory of technique.

Unfortunately no such independent survey exists; the story of the statistical survey attempted by the American Psychoanalytic Association – a most cautious, even over-cautious, attempt – which had to be abandoned, shows well the amount of anxiety and resistance stirred up by a research of this sort.

Chapter 2

Interpretation and working-through

As I have attempted to show, the topical point of view does not seem to offer much help towards a better understanding of our technical difficulties and, in particular, does not place in our hands criteria reliable enough to decide whether any one individual therapeutic step is correct in the given circumstances or not. This, however, could have been expected. We must not forget that the last revision of our theory of the mental instances and localities was undertaken by Freud in the early twenties, some forty years ago. Since then no essentially new idea about the mental apparatus has been put forward (though cf. the new ego psychologies by Fairbairn, Hartmann, and Winnicott). On the other hand, it is unquestionable that since that time our technical potential, our actual skill, and, together with them, our technical problems, have increased considerably. I surveyed these new developments in a paper I presented at the Zürich Congress (1949), in which I tried to show that Freud's technique and his theoretical conceptions were interdependent.

Freud himself stated in his two great monographs, *The Ego and the Id* (1923) and *Inhibitions, Symptoms, and Anxiety* (1926), that he based both his technique and his theory on his clinical experiences with obsessional and melancholic patients because – I use his own words – in these patients both the mental processes and the conflicts are considerably 'internalized' (*verinnerlicht*). That means that the original conflicts, as well as the defensive mechanisms and processes mobilized for coping with them, have become – and largely remain – internal events in these patients. Conversely, external objects are only weakly cathected by them. Thus, in the first approximation, all important events with these patients, both the pathological and the therapeutic, can be taken as happening almost exclusively internally. It was this condition that enabled Freud to describe the therapeutic changes in a simpler form. If external events and objects are only weakly cathected, the influence of their variation from one

8

analyst to another, provided the analysts use a 'sensible' analytic technique, will be still smaller, indeed practically negligible. Forgetting that this is true only for this limit case and only as a first approximation, some analysts have arrived at the idea of 'the correct technique', i.e. one that is correct for all patients and all analysts, irrespective of their individuality. If my train of thought proves valid, 'the correct technique' is a nightmarish chimera, a fantastic compilation from incompatible bits of reality.

An important precondition for the internalization is a fairly good ego structure that can withstand, and contain, the tensions caused by internalization without breaking down and without resorting to a different type of defence – which may be called externalization – such as, for example, acting-out, projection, confusion, denial, depersonalization. With patients who are capable of sustained internalization, the famous simile used by Freud gives a fair description of what really happens during analytic treatment. Most of the time the analyst is indeed a 'well-polished mirror' who merely reflects what the patient conveys to him. Moreover, as shown by all case histories published by Freud, the material conveyed to the analyst in this kind of analytic work consists almost exclusively of words, and equally it is words that are used in reflecting the material back to the patient. Throughout this process of conveying and reflecting, each of the two partners – patient and analyst – understands reliably in the same sense what the other says. True, resistances are encountered, which may at times even be highly intense, but one can always count on a reliable and intelligent ego that is able to take in words and then allow them to influence itself. That is, the ego is able to perform what Freud called 'working-through'.

This train of thought leads to the second answer to our problem. First, the description, just given, of our technique, presupposes that interpretations are experienced by both patient and analyst as interpretations and not as something else. This may seem rather like a statement of the obvious, but I hope to show later that it is important to emphasize this fact in so many words.

Psychoanalytic therapy, even in the classic sense of the 'well-polished mirror', is essentially an object relationship; all the events which lead ultimately to therapeutic changes in the patient's mind are initiated by events happening in a two-person relationship, i.e. happening essentially *between* two people and not inside only one of them. This

9

fundamental fact could be neglected only as long as the main objects of study were patients using chiefly internalization, i.e. patients with a fairly strong ego structure. These people can 'take in' what their analyst offers as well as what they experience themselves in the analytic situation, and are able to experiment with their new knowledge. Their ego is strong enough to bear – at any rate for a time – with the tensions thereby created. The tensions and strains caused by the interpretations may be severe at times, but still these patients can carry on. At any rate this is the picture we gain from Freud's published case histories.

Thus we arrive at the second possible cause of difficulties and failures in analysis. Our technique was worked out for patients who experience the analyst's interpretation as interpretation and whose ego is strong enough to enable them to 'take in' the interpretations and perform what Freud called the process of 'working-through'. We know that not every patient is capable of this task, and it is with these patients that we encounter difficulties.

Chapter 3

The two levels of analytic work

In order to describe the characteristic atmosphere of the level of classical therapeutic work, psychoanalytic literature habitually uses the terms 'Oedipal or genital level', contrasted with the 'pre-Oedipal, pre-genital, or pre-verbal level'. In my opinion these latter terms already have a loaded meaning, and I shall presently propose a new, unequivocal term which, I hope, will free us from some latent bias; but before doing so, let us examine the real meaning of these common terms.

The Oedipus complex was one of Freud's greatest discoveries, which he justly described as the nuclear complex of all human development – of health and illness, of religion and art, civilization and law, and so on. Though the Oedipus complex characterizes a fairly early stage of development, Freud had no hesitation in describing the child's mental experiences, emotions, and feelings at this stage in the language of adults. (As I want to keep clear of the vexed problem of chronology, I deliberately leave open the definition of this early age. It suffices for my purpose to state that it is a very early age.) In fact, Freud's assumption was a bold projection, a daring extrapolation. He made the tacit assumption, without further proof, that the emotions, feelings, desires, fears, instinctual urges, satisfactions, and frustrations of the very young are not only closely similar to those of adults, but also that they have about the same reciprocal relation to one another. Without these two assumptions the use of adult language for describing these events would be totally unjustifiable.

I repeat, this assumption was a very bold step, but its results were subsequently fully validated, both by observations of normal children and by clinical experiences during the analysis of neurotic children. Further, it should be emphasized that, although it had started with the analysis of Little Hans (1909), all this validation took place during the same period as Freud's last revision of our

11

theoretical concepts about the mental apparatus, namely in the twenties.

To avoid a possible misunderstanding, I would add that while working on this Oedipal level, pre-genital material is not, of course, disregarded or neglected by the analyst, but is worked with in adult language, i.e. is raised to the Oedipal or 'verbal' level. This is an important point for our technique as it immediately raises the problem of what an analyst should do in a case in which the expression of pre-genital material in adult words is either unintelligible or unacceptable to the patient, i.e. in a case in which there is apparently no simple road for the patient, direct from the pre-verbal to the Oedipal.

Since the twenties our technique has progressed greatly and it is fair to say that today we can treat patients who were then considered untreatable, and we can certainly better understand the average patient, at greater depth and more reliably, than our colleagues of forty years ago. In the course of this development we have collected a rich harvest of clinical observations and of puzzling problems. All of them pertain to events happening, and observed, in the psycho-analytic situation. In the first approximation these events may be described in terms of the Oedipus conflict, and using adult language. However, *pari passu* with our growing experience and our improving powers of observation, we have got hold of events that cause considerable difficulties both for our theoretical descriptions and for our technical skill.

For instance, we have learned that there are some patients who have great difficulty in 'taking in' anything that increases the strain upon them, and there are others who can 'take in' everything in the world because, apparently, their innermost self remains largely uninfluenced by it. As I have just said, these two types create serious theoretical and technical difficulties, perhaps because their relationship to the analyst differs considerably from that which we are accustomed to meet at the Oedipal level.

The two types just mentioned are only a small sample of the many patients who are described usually as 'deeply disturbed', 'profoundly split', 'seriously schizoid', 'having a much too weak or immature ego', 'highly narcissistic', or suffering from a 'deep narcissistic wound', and so on, thereby implying that the root of their illness goes further and deeper than the Oedipus conflict. In this respect, in terms

12

of the oft-discussed theoretical problem, it is immaterial whether they had originally arrived at their Oedipus period already ill, or whether only later traumatic events rendered the defensive mechanisms belonging to this period ineffective, thus forcing them to a regression or deviation beyond the Oedipal level. What is important in the present context is the recognition of the two different levels of analytical work.

To illustrate the kind of problem encountered on this other level, I wish to quote an eternal example from outside our fields. At our research seminars on general medical practice (Balint, M., 1964) doctors often used to report that they had explained to a patient very clearly what certain implications of an illness were; then, when the actual results of the explanation were compared with those intended, surprisingly often it emerged that the explanation was clear only to the doctor; to the patient it was not clear, often it constituted no explanation at all. So now, whenever a doctor reports that he explained something very clearly, the habitual question follows: 'clearly, but to whom?'. The reason for this discrepancy between intention and result is that the same words have a totally different meaning for the sympathetic but uninvolved doctor and his deeply involved patient.

We analysts are often faced with the same experience. We give our patient an interpretation, clear, concise, well-founded, well-timed, and to the point, which − often to our surprise, dismay, irritation and disappointment − either has no effect on the patient or has an effect quite different from that intended. In other words, our interpretation was not clear at all, or was not even experienced as an interpretation. As a rule analysts try to explain away these disappointments, using three self-reassuring trains of thought. The analyst may criticize himself for not succeeding in interpreting the most important anxiety of the situation − that is, being misled to something of secondary importance only; this self-criticism will usually be followed by frantic efforts to divine what in the patient's fantasies had barred the way to his understanding the analyst's interpretations. Or the analyst may revive in himself the eternal controversy about the relative merits and disadvantages of content, defence, or transference interpretations, which can then be continued endlessly. And, last, he might reassure himself that the patient's resistance at the operative moment was too strong, and that

13

consequently he would need considerable time for 'working-through' it. This last formula is the more reassuring as it was used before by Freud.

Unfortunately these reassuring formulas and trains of thought are without relevance here, since all of them belong to the Oedipal level, i.e. they presuppose that the analyst's interpretations are experienced as interpretations by the patient. It was for this situation only that Freud coined the term 'working-through'. Obviously working-through is possible only if, and in so far as, the patient is capable of taking the interpretation in, experiencing it as an interpretation, and allowing it to influence his mind. With the class of 'deeply disturbed' patients this may or may not be the case. But, if the patient does not experience the analyst's interpretation as an interpretation, i.e. a sentence consisting of words with agreed meaning, no working-through can take place. Working-through can come into operation only if our words have approximately the same meaning for our patients as for ourselves.

No such problem exists at the Oedipal level. The patient and his analyst confidently speak the same language; the same words mean about the same for both. True, the patient may reject an interpretation, may be annoyed, frightened, or hurt by it, but there is no question that it *was* an interpretation.

The establishment of the two different levels gives us a third answer to our original question while, at the same time, it points to further interesting problems. But before embarking on these latter, let us survey our route up to the present point. We started with the finding – or truism – that even the most experienced among us have occasionally some difficult or even very difficult patients. We then asked ourselves what the therapeutic processes were, in which part of the mind they took place, what in them was responsible for the difficulties and, last but not least, what technical means we had to influence them. Then we surveyed our present theory of technique but found that the topological approach did not offer us much help. Going further, we realized that all our descriptions of what happens in the patient's mind during our therapy are based on the close study of patients – initiated by Freud himself in the early twenties – who can accept and 'take in' the analyst's interpretations as interpretations and who are capable of 'working-through'. And last, we found that there are at least two levels of analytic work; consequently it is very likely that there are two levels of therapeutic processes, and, further, that one aspect of this difference is the different usefulness of adult language at the two levels.

This important difference with regard to language, which may create a gulf between patient and analyst and obstruct the progress of treatment, was first described by Ferenczi, in particular in his last Congress paper (1932) and in his posthumously published 'Notes and Fragments'. He called it 'The Confusion of Tongues between the Child [singular!] and the Adults [plural!].' Since then – though usually without mentioning his pioneer work – several attempts have been made by various research workers to describe the same phenomenon. Thus, the conclusion arrived at in the previous chapter is only a reformulation of something well known, namely, that the analytical work proceeds on at least two different levels, one familiar and less problematic, called the Oedipal level, and the other, for the description of which terms like pre-Oedipal, pre-genital, and pre-verbal are in use.

I propose to retain the terms Oedipal level, period, conflict, complex, as they denote the most important features of the level to which they relate. There are several characteristics that differentiate clinically the phenomena belonging to this level from those of the other. The first is that everything at the Oedipal level – whether it relates to genital or pre-genital experiences – happens in a triangular relationship, which means that in addition to the subject, there are always at least two parallel objects involved. These two might be two persons, as in the Oedipus situation, or one person and some object, as in the sphere of anal, and almost certainly also of oral, eroticism. In the former the second object is represented by the faeces and their manifold derivatives, while in the latter, at any rate in its later stages, apart from the source or provider of the food there is always the food itself as a further object present. Although these two spheres are pre-genital by definition, the structure of the relevant relationship – certainly at the anal and the later stages of the oral phase – consisting of the subject and at least two parallel objects, brings them into the Oedipal area and raises them to the Oedipal level.

The second important characteristic of the Oedipal area is that it is inseparable from conflict. Apart from a few instances, not well studied, the conflict is caused by ambivalence arising in the complexities of the relationship between the individual and his two

15

parallel objects. Though this conflict is inherent in the situation it can be solved or, at any rate, considerably adjusted. Perhaps the best-studied example of conflict is that in which an authority – external or internal – prescribes, or forbids, a particular form of gratification. Such a conflict leads eventually to a fixation whereby a certain amount of libido is pinned down in a fruitless struggle creating a continuous tension. Analytic treatment then has the task of mobilizing and freeing such amounts of libido either by interpretation or by offering opportunities to the patient in the transference to regress in order to find a better solution. Though no solution is ideal, in that each of them leaves some tension to be borne, it is almost always possible to find one which considerably reduces the tension.

The third important characteristic of this level is that in it adult language is an adequate and reliable means of communication – as we all know, Oedipus was an adult man. Should there ever arise a need to coin a new term for this level, I would propose to call it the level of agreed, conventional, or adult language.

It often happens in science that an unhappy choice of name leads to misunderstandings, or prejudices the unbiased study of the problem. In order to avoid these risks the two mental levels should be called by terms that are independent of each other. Just as the Oedipal level possesses its own name derived from one of its main characteristics, so the other level should have its own, and should not be called pre-something else – certainly not pre-Oedipal, because it may co-exist with the Oedipal level, at any rate as far as our clinical experiences go. For the moment I wish to leave open the question whether or not there are periods when the mind knows only the one level and not the other. On the other hand it must be emphasized that this other level is definitely simpler, more primitive, than the Oedipal level. I propose to call it the level of the *basic fault,* and I wish to stress that it is described as a fault, not as a situation, position, conflict, or complex. I will later explain why.

The chief characteristics of the level of the basic fault are (a) all the events that happen in it belong to an exclusively two-person relationship – there is no third person present; (b) this two-person relationship is of a particular nature, entirely different from the well-known human relationships of the Oedipal level; (c) the nature of the dynamic force operating at this level is not that of a conflict, and (d) adult language is often useless or misleading in describing events

16

at this level, because words have not always an agreed conventional meaning.

Though some of these characteristics will become meaningful only during the discussion in the later chapters, I can state something about the others now. First about the nature of the primitive two-person relationship at this level. In the first approach this can be considered as an instance of primary object relationship or of primary love, which I have described on several occasions (Balint, M., 1932, 1934, 1937, 1959) and in Chapter 12 of this book. Any third party interfering with this relationship is experienced as a heavy burden or as an intolerable strain. A further important quality of this relationship is the immense difference of intensity between the phenomena of satisfaction and frustration. Whereas satisfaction – the 'fitting in' of the object with the subject – brings about a feeling of quiet tranquil well-being which can be observed only with difficulty as it is so natural and soft, frustration – the lack of 'fitting in' of the object – evokes highly vehement and loud symptoms (see also Chapter 16).

Later, in Chapter 4, I shall come back to discuss the nature of the forces operating at the level of the basic fault, but I wish to illustrate here the curious vagueness of language obtaining at this level. This is brought about by the *cluster of associations* which still surrounds each word in adult usage. On the level of the basic fault, however, practically each member of the cluster may have an equal right to the possession of the word. That this is not restricted to the level of the basic fault is shown by the practical impossibility of finding exact definitions, especially in our science of psychology. In order to devise an exact definition one must strip the word of all its unwanted or undesirable associations. Experience shows that this is only very rarely possible, as people obstinately think, or even prove, that the words used imply other meanings than the one intended by the inventor of the definition. (This problem will be discussed further in Chapter 20.)

Chapter 4

The area of the basic fault

Accepting theoretically the existence of the level of the basic fault, we have to ask what kind of events in the course of analytic treatment have to be considered as signals that this level has been reached. Taking a fairly normal case, let us suppose that the treatment has been proceeding smoothly for some time, patient and analyst have understood each other, while the strains and demands on either of them, but especially on the analyst, were only reasonable and, in particular, at all times intelligible. Then at some point, suddenly or insidiously, the atmosphere of the analytic situation changes profoundly. With some patients this might happen after a very short period, or even right from the start.

There are several aspects of what I will call the profound change of atmosphere. Foremost among them is, as discussed in the previous chapter, that interpretations given by the analyst are not experienced any longer by the patient as interpretations. Instead he may feel them as an attack, a demand, a base insinuation, an uncalled-for rudeness or insult, unfair treatment, injustice, or at least as a complete lack of consideration, and so on; on the other hand, it is equally possible that the analyst's interpretations may be experienced as something highly pleasing and gratifying, exciting or soothing, or as a seduction; in general as an irrefutable sign of consideration, affection, and love. It may also happen that common words which until then have had an agreed conventional 'adult' meaning and could be used without any great consequence, become immensely important and powerful, either in a good or a bad sense. At such times, in fact, the analyst's every casual remark, every gesture or movement, may matter enormously and may assume an importance far beyond anything that could be realistically intended.

Moreover – and this is not so easy to admit – the patient somehow seems able to get under the analyst's skin. He begins to know much too much about his analyst. This increase in knowledge does not

18

originate from any outside source of information but apparently from an uncanny talent that enables the patient to 'understand' the analyst's motives and to 'interpret' his behaviour. This uncanny talent may occasionally give the impression of, or perhaps even amount to, telepathy or clairvoyance. (See Balint, M., 'Notes on Parapsychology and Parapsychological Healing', 1955.) The analyst experiences this phenomenon as if the patient could see inside him, could find out things about him. The things thus found out are always highly personal, in some ways always concerned with the patient, and are in a way absolutely correct and true, and at the same time utterly out of proportion, and thus untrue – at least this is how the analyst feels them.

If now the analyst fails to 'click in', that is, to respond as the patient expects him to do, no reaction of anger, rage, contempt, or criticism will appear in the transference as one would expect it at the Oedipal level. The only thing that can be observed is a feeling of emptiness, being lost, deadness, futility, and so on, coupled with an apparently lifeless acceptance of everything that has been offered. In fact everything is accepted without much resistance but nothing makes any sense. Another reaction to the analyst's failure to 'click in' might have the appearance of persecutory anxieties. Leaving on one side that in these states anxiety – in its common-sense clinical form – is usually very slight, hardly existent, the fact remains that at any frustration these patients feel that it was intentionally inflicted upon them. They cannot accept that there exists any other cause for a frustration of their desires than malice, evil intention, or at least, criminal negligence. Good things may happen by chance, but frustrations are unchallengeable proofs of evil and hostile sentiments in their environment.

Remarkably, all this is simply accepted as a painful fact and it is most surprising how little anger, still less a willingness to fight, is mobilized by it. It is still more surprising that a feeling of hopelessness hardly ever develops; it seems that despair and hopelessness belong to the Oedipal level; they are probably post-depressive. Though feelings of emptiness and deadness (cf. Balint, Enid, 1963) may be very strong, behind them there is usually an earnest, quiet determination to see things through. This queer mixture of profound suffering, absence of cheap pugnacity, and an unshakeable determination to get on makes these patients truly appealing – an important

19

diagnostic sign that the work has reached the level of the basic fault.

The analyst's reaction also is characteristic, and is utterly different from his reaction to a resistance at the Oedipal level. I shall return to this in Parts III, IV, and V of this book; here it will suffice to say that everything touches him much more closely; he finds it rather difficult to maintain his usual attitude of sympathetic, objective passivity; in fact, he is in constant danger of subjective emotional involvement. Some analysts allow, or even elect, to be carried away by this forceful current and must then change their techniques accordingly. Others carefully and cautiously stick to their well-proven guns and consistently avoid any risk of becoming involved. There are also those who, in face of this threat, adopt – perhaps as a reaction formation against it – a somewhat omnipotent confidence, constantly reassuring themselves that their technique of interpretation is capable of dealing with any situation.

Another important group of phenomena is centred upon what may be called appreciation of, and gratitude for, the analyst's work. On the Oedipal level, provided the analyst's work has been up to professional standards, these two sentiments – appreciation and gratitude – are powerful allies and, especially during bleak periods, may help considerably. At the level of the basic fault one cannot be certain at all that the patient will bear in mind, still less that he will appreciate, that his analyst was skilful and understanding in the past, whether remote or recent. One reason for this profound change is that at that level patients feel that it is their due to receive what they need. I shall return presently to this important feature.

Thus, if the analyst provides what is needed, this fact is taken for granted and loses all its value as proof of professional skill, of exceptional gift, or of favour, and in due course more and more demands will be produced. In present-day analytical literature this syndrome is called greediness, or even oral greed. I have no objection to calling it greed, but strong objection to calling it 'oral' because this is misleading. It is not the relationship to the oral component instinct that is relevant for the understanding of this syndrome but the fact that it originates in a primitive two-person relationship which may or may not be 'oral'. To cite the range of addictions in which 'greediness' is a most important feature, there are very numerous and unquestionably 'oral' addictions, foremost among

20

them nicotine and alcohol; but there are many that are non-oral, such as morphinism, sniffing cocaine, and not forgetting the various forms of scratching as in pruritus.

At the Oedipal level the analyst is hardly ever tempted out of his sympathetic passivity; if he abandons his passivity at the level of the basic fault, he may start on a dangerous spiral of addiction – because of the peculiar lack of gratitude, or presence of greed; if he remains adamant either the treatment will be broken off by the patient as hopeless, or after a long forlorn struggle the patient will be forced to identify himself with the aggressor, as the analyst is felt to be, i.e. as I heard it described in one of my seminars – the patient is made to acquire an everlasting internal long-playing record. In Chapter 17 I shall have to return to this important technical problem.

All these events belong essentially to the field of two-person psychology and are more elementary than those belonging to the three-person Oedipal level. Moreover, they lack the structure of a conflict. This was one of the reasons why I proposed to call them 'basic'. But why fault? First, because this is exactly the word used by many patients to describe it. The patient says that he feels there is a fault within him, a fault that must be put right. And it is felt to be a fault, not a complex, not a conflict, not a situation. Second, there is a feeling that the cause of this fault is that someone has either failed the patient or defaulted on him; and third, a great anxiety invariably surrounds this area, usually expressed as a desperate demand that this time the analyst should not – in fact must not – fail him.

The term fault has been in use in some exact sciences to denote conditions that are reminiscent of that which we are discussing. Thus, for instance, in geology and in crystallography the word fault is used to describe a sudden irregularity in the overall structure, an irregularity which in normal circumstances might lie hidden but, if strains and stresses occur, may lead to a break, profoundly disrupting the overall structure.

We are accustomed to think of every dynamic force operating in the mind as having the form either of a biological drive or of a conflict. Although highly dynamic, the force originating from the basic fault has the form neither of an instinct nor of a conflict. It is a fault, something wrong in the mind, a kind of deficiency which must be put right. It is not something dammed up for which a

21

better outlet must be found, but something missing either now, or perhaps for almost the whole of the patient's life. An instinctual need can be satisfied, a conflict can be solved, a basic fault can perhaps be merely healed provided the deficient ingredients can be found; and even then it may amount only to a healing with defect, like a simple, painless scar.

The adjective 'basic' in my new term not only means that it relates to simpler conditions than those characterizing the Oedipus complex, but also that its influence extends widely, probably over the whole psychobiological structure of the individual, involving in varying degrees both his mind and his body. In this way the concept of the basic fault allows us to understand not only the various neuroses (perhaps also psychoses), character disorders, psychosomatic illnesses, etc., as symptoms of the same etiological entity, but also – as the experiences of our research into general medical practice have shown – a great number of ordinary 'clinical' illnesses as well (Balint, M., 1957; Balint, M., & Balint, Enid, 1961; Lask, 1966; Greco and Pittenger, 1966). By this I mean that under the influence of various emotional experiences, among them medical treatment, a 'clinical' illness may disappear to give way to a specific psychological disorder and vice versa.

In my view the origin of the basic fault may be traced back to a considerable discrepancy in the early formative phases of the individual between his bio-psychological needs and the material and psychological care, attention, and affection available during the relevant times. This creates a state of deficiency whose consequences and after-effects appear to be only partly reversible. The cause of this early discrepancy may be congenital, i.e. the infant's bio-psychological needs may have been too exacting (there are non-viable infants and progressive congenital conditions, like Friedreich's ataxia or cystic kidneys), or may be environmental, such as care that is insufficient, deficient, haphazard, over-anxious, over-protective, harsh, rigid, grossly inconsistent, incorrectly timed, over-stimulating, or merely un-understanding or indifferent.

As may be seen from my description, I put the emphasis on the lack of 'fit' between the child and *the people* who represent his environment. Incidentally, we started with a similar lack of 'fit' – between the analyst's otherwise correct technique and a particular patient's needs; this is very likely to be an important cause of

22

difficulties, and even failures, experienced by analysts in their practice. This will be discussed in more detail in Part V.

Returning now to our main theme, I wish the reader to be aware of my personal bias, under the influence of which my description of the processes, which eventually may result in some basic fault, will be couched in terms of object-relationship. In my view, all these processes happen within a very primitive and peculiar object-relationship, fundamentally different from those commonly observed between adults. It is definitely a two-person relationship in which, however, only one of the partners matters; his wishes and needs are the only ones that count and must be attended to; the other partner, though felt to be immensely powerful, matters only in so far as he is willing to gratify the first partner's needs and desires or decides to frustrate them; beyond this his personal interests, needs, desires, wishes, etc., simply do not exist. In Chapter 12 I propose to discuss in more detail this essentially two-person relationship and to differentiate it from what I have called primary object love, or primary object relationship.

Chapter 5

The area of creation

Until now I have discussed two possible levels, or areas, in the mind: those of the Oedipus conflict and of the basic fault. To complete the picture I have to mention, though only briefly, a third area before summing up the relevance of my ideas for the psychology of the human mind.

Whereas the area of the Oedipus conflict is characterized by the presence of at least two objects, apart from the subject, and the area of the basic fault by a very peculiar, exclusively two-person relationship, the third area is characterized by the fact that in it there is no external object present. The subject is on his own and his main concern is to produce something out of himself; this something to be produced may be an object, but is not necessarily so. I propose to call this the level or area of creation. The most often-discussed example is, of course, artistic creation, but other phenomena belong to the same group, among them mathematics and philosophy, gaining insight, understanding something or somebody; and last, but not least, two highly important phenomena: the early phases of becoming – bodily or mentally – 'ill' and spontaneous recovery from an 'illness'.

Despite many attempts, very little indeed is understood of these processes. One obvious reason for this paucity of knowledge is the fact that throughout this whole area there is no external object present, and thus no transference relationship can develop. Where there is no transference, our analytic methods are powerless, and thus we are restricted to inferences from observations obtained after the individual has left the boundaries of this area. As soon as an external object appears on the scene, such as a completed work of art, a mathematical or philosophical thesis, a piece of insight or understanding which can be expressed in words, or as soon as the illness reaches the stage at which the individual can complain to someone about it, an external object is there and we can get to work with our analytic methods.

24

The lack of transference also explains why our attempts at understanding these important states of the mind have remained at a rather pedestrian stage. Most of the analytic theories relating to these states – following the example of language – consider the individual as a kind of procreator. All languages, as far as they are known to me, describe these states by words borrowed from conception, pregnancy, and childbirth. The individual conceives an idea, is pregnant, has labour pains, gives birth to something, or miscarries, and so on. Perhaps it is due to the same lack of transference that our psychology of pregnancy and childbirth is comparatively poor. There too we try to turn an evidently one-person situation into a two-person relationship in order to be able to use our well-proved methods and accustomed ways of thinking.

Here we come up again with the difficulties created by our adult, conventional language. We know that there are no 'objects' in the area of creation, but we know also that for most – or some – of the time the subject is not entirely alone there. The trouble is that our language has no words to describe, or even to indicate, the 'somethings' that are there when the subject is not completely alone; in order to be able to talk about them at all, I propose to use the term 'pre-object'; 'object-embryo' would be too definite; in German *Objekt-Anlage* may prove a good term. If I understood Bion (1962 and 1963), he was faced with the same difficulty; his proposition for this special case was to call them α and β elements, and α function.

All this indicates that the 'pre-objects' existing in the area of creation must be so primitive that they cannot be considered as 'organized' or 'whole'. Only after the work of creation has succeeded in making them 'organized', or 'whole', can a proper, 'verbal', or 'Oedipal', interaction between them and external objects take place. It is probable that more primitive interactions – congenial to the levels of the basic fault and of creation – take place all the time; these, however, are difficult to observe and still more difficult to describe adequately (Balint, M., 1959, esp. Chapters 8 and 11).

The only thing we know is that the process of creation – transforming the 'pre-object' into a proper object – is unpredictable. We do not know why it succeeds in some cases and fails in others, why it takes ages in some and happens with lightning speed in others. The history of artistic and scientific creation gives us many interesting anecdotes, but this is about all. We know, for instance, that the

25

problems of Faust occupied Goethe all his life, the *Urfaust* was started when he was twenty-one, and he was working on the Second Part until his death in 1832. Flaubert's usual output was one or two pages a day; he needed seven years to finish *Madame Bovary*. Vermeer and Giorgione were very slow workers and so was Beethoven on the whole. Leonardo worked fifteen years on La Gioconda – to mention a few. On the other hand, Mozart was a fast worker[1] (the most famous example is his Overture to *Don Giovanni*), and so were Haydn and Bach. Balzac was a fast writer, as is Simenon, whose habitual output was at one time one novel per fortnight. A very large part of Van Gogh's *oeuvre* was painted in two years. We have some idea that intense conflicts at the Oedipal level may accelerate or inhibit the speed of the creative process, but it seems that, over and above these conflicts, the individual's mental make-up, the structure of his area of creation, is what really matters.

All this amounts to very little, especially as compared with our knowledge of the unconscious processes and mechanisms operating under the pressure of conflicts. This is the more remarkable as analysts have the unique opportunity of observing people while absorbed in the area of creation. What I have in mind is the silent patient, a puzzling problem for our technique. The pedestrian analytic attitude is to consider the silence merely as a symptom of resistance to some unconscious material stemming either from the patient's past or from the actual transference situation. One must add that this interpretation is nearly always correct; the patient is *running away* from something, usually a conflict, but it is equally correct that he is *running towards* something, i.e. a state in which he feels relatively safe and can do something about the problem bothering or tormenting him. The something that he will eventually produce and then present to us is a kind of 'creation' – not necessarily honest, sincere, profound, or artistic – but none the less a product of his creativity. True, we cannot be with him during the actual work of creation, but we can be with him in the moment just before and

---

[1] 'Two days before the première of his *Don Juan* in Prague, Mozart had not yet started to compose the overture. His friends, the Opera director, and the orchestra, were in excited suspense while the genius himself unconcernedly enjoyed a gay party. Late in the evening he wrote the music without any later correction; he said that the whole musical score suddenly and simultaneously presented itself clearly to his mind' (Weiss, E., 1957, p. 213).

immediately after, and, in addition, we can watch him from the outside during his actual work. Perhaps, if we can change our own approach from that of considering the silence as a symptom of resistance to studying it as a possible source of information, we may learn something about this area of the mind.

Chapter 6

Summary

Thus we seem to have at least three areas of the mind, each of them characterized, as first proposed by Rickman (1951), by a number. One might equally designate these three areas as spaces, spheres, fields, levels, localities, or instances, and perhaps by other terms as well. All of these terms have their own clusters of associations, and I, for one, am rather wary of tying myself down to any one of them as the most suitable. For the time being I prefer to use either 'area' or 'level', but I must admit I am not myself clear why I prefer these two.

The most widely known among these three areas is characterized by the number 3, and may be called *the area of the Oedipus conflict*. This is rightly described as the nuclear complex, for all human development – individual or collective – must pass through it and will then bear for ever the imprint of the solution that the individual or the civilization in question has found in its struggle with the conflicts involved. The whole area is characterized by the fact that everything that happens in it involves in addition to the subject at least two parallel objects. The force operating at this level has the form of a conflict originating, as a rule, from the ambivalence created by the complexities of the relationship between the individual and his two parallel objects.

This level is the one of which we know most. There are two main reasons for it. One is that the relationship between the subject and his objects is very similar to that of an adult's, and the second that adult language is a fairly adequate means of describing what can be observed.

The second area, as I have tried to show in this Part, is profoundly different from the previous one. It is *the area of the basic fault*, characterized by the number 2, which means that in it two, and only two, people are involved. Their relationship, however, is not that obtaining between two adults; it is more primitive. A further

28

difference between the two areas is caused by the nature of the dynamic force operating in each. In the area of the Oedipus complex the form of the force is that of a conflict. Although highly dynamic, the force originating from the basic fault has *not* the form of a conflict. As described in Chapter 4, it has the form of a fault, something distorted or lacking in the mind, producing a defect that must be put right. A number of technical problems arise here, which I propose to discuss in Parts III–V. Perhaps the greatest difficulty facing the attempt at any theoretical description of these phenomena is the comparative uselessness of adult language, as we have already mentioned several times.

And last, we have the *area of creation* which is characterized by the number 1. There is no outside object involved, consequently there is no object-relationship and no transference. That is why our knowledge of these processes is so scanty and uncertain. Our analytic methods are inapplicable in this area and thus we have to resort to insecure inferences and extrapolations.

How far do these areas extend through the mind? A most interesting question, but I have only a very incomplete answer. All three certainly extend through the ego; whether they reach the super-ego or not I cannot say, and the same uncertainty has to be admitted about the id. However, all the recent advances in the theory of the mental apparatus pertain mainly, or even exclusively, to the ego. This is equally true of Fairbairn, Hartmann, and Winnicott; thus in any case I am not in bad company.

Before finishing this part of the book I wish to add certain warnings. The first is about the relevance of our observations for the general theory of human development. Usually it is assumed that the phenomena observed clinically in the psychoanalytic situation can be taken as a representative sample of the whole of human development (Balint, M., 1956). Though hardly ever stated explicitly, this idea in fact colours many of our theoretical propositions. I think it is absolutely false; first, not everything that happens in human development is repeated in the psychoanalytic situation; and second, what is repeated is profoundly distorted by the conditions prevailing there. Freud it is who has already recommended that analytic treatment should be carried out in the state of abstention, that is, frustration. Although perhaps this maxim is not adhered to as unconditionally as its wording suggests, on the whole it is true that the

29

patient must during his treatment accept more frustration than gratification. Whether or not the same disproportion obtains during all human development has first to be examined. Till then it will be safer to assume that what we get to see in our practice is a considerably distorted picture, and that the distortion is brought about by our well-proven technique that imposes frustrations on the patient and at the same time prevents or inhibits his gratifications. By neglecting the effects of this distortion, psychoanalytic theory was inevitably led to exaggerate the importance of frustration and ambivalence for the mind.

True, past and present events belonging to the area of the Oedipus conflict are constantly worked with during analytic treatment, but all this happens chiefly in an indirect way, through the patient's verbal reports. What we observe in a direct form in the analytic situation is a two-person relationship, and thus part of the area of the basic fault. Then, of course, we express our experiences in adult language, which means that we must raise them to the Oedipal level, i.e. to the level of agreed, conventional language. If my ideas are correct, this too must bring about a good deal of distortion, which fact may be one explanation of why our theory and technique have become so widely separated since Freud's last great monographs. In Part I, I have tried to bridge this gap and to use our clinical experiences to develop a new theory of the mind and, in particular, of the ego, which will include Freud's classical ego-psychology as a limiting case.

Second, I wish to stress that as far as this Part of the book is concerned, I have left entirely open the question of chronology, since I do not think that our present knowledge is sufficient to decide this vexed problem. It would be tempting but, I am certain, false to assume that the logically simple is necessarily the chronologically earlier; thus we arrive at a sequence: first, the level of creation, then the level of the basic fault, and last, the level of the Oedipus complex. As we know from embryology, it often happens that during development an early complex structure is gradually simplified or even completely lost at a later stage (cf. Balint, M., 1959, Chapter 7). Thus it is thinkable that the earliest level might be that of primary love and with it the level of the basic fault, out of which, on the one hand, the level of the Oedipus conflict develops in differentiation, and, on the other hand, the level of creation by simplification.

My plan is to adopt this latter idea as a working hypothesis and examine whether we can arrive at a better understanding of some of our puzzling theoretical and technical problems on this basis.

On the theoretical side we have two old and largely interrelated problems, narcissism and regression. Although both have connections with the area of the Oedipus complex, fundamentally they belong to the area of the basic fault. Since this fact could not be properly evaluated, the appearance of narcissistic or regressive features in the transference situation was considered on the whole as an ominous sign. In Parts II and III we shall have to examine how far this generalization was justified and in what sort of cases it has proved incorrect. After having cleared our way, the technical implications will be discussed in the last two parts of this book.

PART II

Primary narcissism and primary love

Chapter 7

Freud's three theories

It is a curious but easily verifiable fact that for many years Freud held three mutually exclusive views of the individual's most primitive relation with his environment. The oldest of these appeared in print in 1905 in his *Three Essays on the Theory of Sexuality* and remained unchanged in all its later editions, though it is worth noting that this book and *The Interpretation of Dreams* were the only ones that Freud tried to keep up to date, revising and amending them with each new edition to include all discoveries in the years since the previous edition. Oddly enough this passage occurs in the last section of the third and final essay which has the sub-title in German: *Die Objektfindung*, a beautifully concise phrase which had to be translated into English rather clumsily as 'The Finding of an Object' (Standard Edition, VII, p. 222).

Freud wrote: 'At a time at which the first beginnings of sexual satisfaction are still linked with the taking of nourishment, *the sexual instinct has a sexual object outside the infant's own body* in the shape of his mother's breast. It is only *later* that the instinct loses that object, just at the time, perhaps, when the child is able to form *a total idea of the person* to whom the organ that is giving him satisfaction belongs. *As a rule the sexual instinct then becomes auto-erotic*, and not until the period of latency has been passed through is the original relation restored. There are thus good reasons why a child sucking at his mother's breast has become the prototype of every relation of love. The finding of an object is in fact a refinding of it.' (The italics are mine.)

I would make two remarks about the otherwise excellent English translation. The last sentence has a real beauty in German: '*Die Objektfindung ist eigentlich eine Wiederfindung*'. The English is a pale rendering of the forceful and categorical German original. Although not quite correct, a somewhat freer — and, to my mind, truer — translation would run as follows: 'All object-discovery is in fact a

35

rediscovery'. My second remark concerns dating. In Freud's version it is the *anfänglichste Sexualbefriedigung* which is incomparably more emphatic than the otherwise correct English translation: 'the first beginnings of sexual satisfaction'; perhaps 'the very first sexual satisfaction' might be a more faithful translation.

As just mentioned, this passage itself remained unchanged, but in 1915 Freud added a footnote to call attention to his discovery of an *additional* method of finding an object, namely, the narcissistic. It is easy to show that for many years after the introduction of the psychoanalytic theory of narcissism Freud did not intend to drop the idea of primary object relationship in favour of primary narcissism.

To prove this assertion I quote two passages from his writings during these years. One is from the Twenty-first Lecture of his *Introductory Lectures* which, as we know, were delivered for the last time in 1916–17 and first published in 1916 and 1917. Freud points out first that certain component instincts of sexuality, such as sadism, scopophilia, and curiosity, have an object right from the start. He continues: 'Others, more definitely linked to particular erotogenic zones of the body, have one to begin with only, so long as they are still attached to the non-sexual functions, and give it up when they become separated from them.' He refers here particularly to the oral component instinct; and then he states: 'The oral instinct *becomes auto-erotic*, as are the anal and other erotogenic instincts from the first. Further development, to put the matter as concisely as possible, has two aims: firstly, the abandonment of auto-erotism, the replacement of the subject's own body once more by an outside object, and secondly, the unification of the various objects of the separate instincts and their replacement by a single object' (Standard Edition, XVI, pp. 328–329).

The other passage is from Freud's article on psychoanalysis in M. Marcuse's *Handwörterbuch der Sexualwissenschaft*, and it is worth mentioning that the passage occurs in the section which has the sub-title 'The Process of Finding an Object'. 'In the first instance the oral component instinct finds satisfaction by attaching itself to the sating of the desire for nourishment, and its object is the mother's breast. It then detaches itself, becomes independent and at the same time *auto-erotic*, that is, it finds an object in the child's own body' (Standard Edition, XVIII, p. 234. Original italics). We know that this article was written in 1922, just before the Berlin Congress, the last that Freud attended, at which he announced his new ideas about the structure of the mind which then led to the development of what is now called ego psychology. Still, as the passage quoted proves, he did not abandon the idea of primary object relationship.

The other two theories about the individual's most primitive relationship with his environment were published for the first time in his paper 'On Narcissism – An Introduction' in 1914, though the older of them had several forerunners in the preceding years.[1] This, the older theory, is stated in the 1914 paper quite categorically, without any qualifications. Freud asks in the first section of that paper 'what is the relation of the narcissism of which we are now speaking, to auto-erotism, which we have described as *an* early state of the libido?' He answers this question as follows: 'I may point out that we are bound to suppose that a unity comparable to the ego cannot exist in the individual from the start; the ego has to be developed. The auto-erotic instincts, however, are there from the very first; so there must be something added to auto-erotism – a new psychical action – in order to bring about narcissism' (Standard Edition, XIV, pp. 76–77. My italics).

We learn further from Ernest Jones (*Sigmund Freud*, II, p. 304) that on the first recorded occasion when Freud used the term 'narcissism', on 10th November, 1909, at a meeting of the Vienna Psycho-Analytic Society, he meant it in the sense quoted above. He stated, 'Narcissism was a necessary intermediate stage in the passage from auto-erotism to allo-erotism'. This is in good agreement with a passage in the Schreber analysis (Standard Edition, XII, pp. 60–61. My italics). 'Recent investigations have directed our attention to a stage in the development of the libido which it passes through on the way from auto-erotism to object love. This stage has been given the name of narcissism . . . *This half-way phase between auto-erotism and object love* may perhaps be indispensable normally; but it appears that many people linger unusually long in this condition, and that many of its features are carried over by them into the later stages of their development.' This passage published in 1911 is, incidentally, the third occasion that Freud used the term 'narcissism' in print,

[1] See the Schreber analysis quoted below and *Leonardo da Vinci* (1910) (Standard Edition, XI, p. 100), and *Totem and Taboo* (1913) (Standard Edition, XIII, pp. 88–90).

the second being the paper on Leonardo. We shall come back presently to the first occasion on which this term was used.

I will discuss two points here. First, Freud's description in these two passages is unequivocal. The most primitive form of the individual's relationship to his environment is auto-erotism. This is followed by the narcissistic stage out of which object relationships then develop. Evidently this is the development which leads to the type of object-choice that later in the paper 'On Narcissism' is described as narcissistic. This development should be considered as an alternative or as a parallel to the one described previously – in the *Three Essays* and in his other writings quoted above – which starts with primary object relationship and leads to an object-choice, later characterized by Freud as anaclitic.

The second point: in the passages just quoted Freud states that narcissism is essentially and inherently a secondary phenomenon – a 'half-way phase'. May I repeat here the relevant sentence: 'There must be something added to auto-erotism – a new psychical action – in order to bring about narcissism.' Note that there is no qualification whatsoever to this statement. This is the more surprising because this quotation comes from the two paragraphs immediately following the passage in which Freud first[1] used his famous metaphor of the amoeba: 'Thus we form the idea of there being an original libidinal cathexis of the ego from which some is later given off to objects, but which fundamentally persists and is related to the object-cathexes, much as the body of an amoeba is related to the pseudopodia which it puts out' (Standard Edition, XIV, p. 76). I shall have to return to the discussion of this contradiction presently after describing Freud's third theory.

It is remarkable that the paper, 'On Narcissism', which introduced this theory does not contain a concise description of primary narcissism. However, as is generally known, primary narcissism became the standard theory for the description of the individual's most primitive relationship with his environment, and Freud referred to it time and again in his later writings. It is a further interesting point that the theory did not change at all during the remaining twenty-five years of Freud's active work. To prove this let me give two quotations. One from an addition to his *Three Essays* on the occasion of its third edition which appeared in 1915: 'Narcissistic or ego-libido seems

[1] Though cf. *Totem and Taboo* quoted above.

to be the great reservoir from which the object-cathexes are sent out and into which they are withdrawn once more; the narcissistic libidinal cathexis of the ego is the original state of things, realized in earliest childhood, and is merely covered by the later extrusions of libido, but in essentials persists behind them' (Standard Edition, VII, p. 218).

The other passage is from Freud's last, unfinished, work, *An Outline of Psycho-Analysis*, written in 1938 and 1939, and is in the second chapter with the sub-title 'The Theory of Instincts': 'It is hard to say anything of the behaviour of the libido in the id and in the super-ego. *All that we know about it relates to the ego, in which at first the whole available quota of libido is stored up. We call this state absolute, primary narcissism.* It lasts till the ego begins to cathect the ideas of objects with libido; to transform narcissistic libido into object libido. Throughout the whole of life the ego remains the great reservoir from which libidinal cathexes are sent out to objects and into which they are also once more withdrawn, just as an amoeba behaves with its pseudopodia. It is only when a person is completely in love that the main quota of libido is transferred on to the object and the object to some extent takes the place of the ego' (Standard Edition, XXIII, pp. 150–151. My italics). The description given here in Freud's own words has become the official version, the one that is taught in all the psychoanalytical institutes all over the world.

Chapter 8

Inherent contradictions

These three theories, *primary object love, primary auto-erotism*, and *primary narcissism*, apparently contradict one another. Still, as far as I know, Freud never discussed this contradiction in writing; on the contrary, there is printed evidence as late as 1923 that he held all these three theories concurrently. This can only mean that he did not feel them to be contradictory or mutually exclusive.

Before starting out on the discussion of this puzzling problem, we ought to remind ourselves that psychoanalysis, faithfully following Freud, uses the term narcissism to describe two similar but far from identical states. One of them – called by Freud primary or absolute narcissism – is a hypothesis, not a clinical observation; we *assume* that in the beginning all libido is stored up in the ego – or in the id. The other, as a rule called simply narcissism, although it should properly be called secondary narcissism, *can be observed clinically*; it denotes a state in which some, or even a very large part, of the libido that has previously cathected external objects, is withdrawn from them and cathects now the ego – definitely *not* the id. This distinction will prove of great importance in the subsequent chapters of Part II.

Freud, without even mentioning the need for resolving or, at least, reconciling the inherent contradictions just mentioned, had attempted a synthesis of all three theories already in his *Introductory Lectures*, in 1917. In the Twenty-sixth Lecture, which has the sub-title, 'Libido Theory and Narcissism', he writes: 'Hitherto I have had very little opportunity of talking to you about the foundations of erotic life so far as we have discovered them, and it is too late now to catch up on the omission. This much, however, I can emphasize to you. Object-choice, the step forward in the development of the libido which is made after the narcissistic stage, can take place according to two different types: either according to the *narcissistic type*, where the subject's own ego is replaced by another one that is as similar as possible, or according to the *attachment type* (*Anlehnungstypus*, which used to be translated into English as 'anaclitic type') 'where people who have become precious through satisfying the other vital needs are chosen as objects by the libido as well' (Standard Edition, XVI, p. 426).

I would add another quotation from the same chapter: 'Auto-erotism would thus be the sexual activity of the narcissistic stage of allocation of the libido' (op. cit., p. 416).

No doubt Freud gave us here an apparently comprehensive theory: the most primitive phase is primary narcissism, out of which all the other organizations of the libido develop as subsequent phases. In spite of all its advantages of simplicity and plausibility, this theory does not solve the fundamental contradictions mentioned above; more-over, it creates unnecessary new problems. To substantiate this point I must mention a curious footnote that Freud added to the third chapter of *The Ego and the Id*, which was first published in 1923 (the same year in which his Encyclopaedia article appeared, restating the primary nature of object-love). The sub-title of the chapter is 'The Ego and the Super-Ego' and the footnote refers to the first part of this chapter. Here Freud describes the changes in the ego that may take place after the id – *not* the ego, as postulated in the above quotation from *An Outline of Psycho-Analysis* – has been forced to give up one of its love objects, these changes being introjection and identification: 'Now that we have distinguished between the ego and the id, we must recognize the id as the great reservoir of libido indicated in my paper on narcissism. The libido which flows into the ego owing to the identifications described above brings about its "secondary narcissism"' (Standard Edition, XIX, p. 30).

Later in the book, in Chapter 4, Freud restates this idea, if possible in a still more unequivocal form: 'At the very beginning, all the libido is accumulated in the id, while the ego is still in process of formation or is still feeble. The id sends part of this libido out into erotic object-cathexes, whereupon the ego, now grown stronger, tries to get hold of this object-libido and to force itself on the id as a love-object. The narcissism of the ego is thus a secondary one, which has been withdrawn from objects' (op. cit., p. 46).

The obvious purpose of these two passages is to clarify an uncer-tain situation in the light of the new discoveries. This it does to some extent – and, as we shall see presently, temporarily only – but at the same time creates further problems and contradictions. We learn that the great reservoir of the libido is the id and not the ego, as stated both previously and subsequently to *The Ego and the Id*; and further that the libidinal cathexes of the ego, in particular of those of its parts that have been changed by introjection and identification, are definitely classified as secondary narcissism, however early in life they may occur. The next question, evidently, would be: Is there then any primary narcissism in the ego? Remarkably, Freud does not raise this question here.

Where then is the place and what is the role of primary narcissism? And can these two passages be integrated with the customary version, such as in the passage quoted from *An Outline of Psycho-Analysis*, according to which all that we know about it (the libido) relates to the ego, in which at first the whole available quota of libido is stored up? We call this state 'absolute, primary narcissism'.

James Strachey attempts a solution of this contradiction in an editorial note to *The Ego and the Id* under the title of 'The Great Reservoir of the Libido'.[1] Strachey suggests there that possibly Freud, without noticing it, used 'The Great Reservoir of the Libido' in two different senses: (a) denoting a function similar to that of a storage tank and (b) another function like that of a source of supply. Evidently the first refers to the ego while the latter to the id. This is a highly plausible hypothesis, very much *à la* Freud and, if accepted, would solve this one contradiction. However, it is a fact that Freud never thought of it and, though it would define the id as the source of primary narcissism, it leaves unsolved what is cathected *by* primary narcissism. This cannot be the ego – in the early stages it is questionable whether there is any ego to cathect; nor can it be the id – this assumption would mix up again the 'source of supply' and the 'storage tank' which Strachey has just neatly separated (Hartmann, H., 1956, p. 433).

Another alternative would be to accept Hartmann's somewhat stern dictum that 'Freud, as did others, sometimes used the term "ego" in more than one sense, and not always in the sense in which it was best defined. Occasionally . . . the term "ego" became interchangeable with "one's own person", or "the self".'

Hartmann then proposes to distinguish between two meanings of the term 'ego': 'the one referring to the functions and cathexes of the ego as a system (in contradistinction with the cathexes of different

---

[1] I wish to express my thanks for the privilege of seeing this note in typescript. It has appeared since in Standard Edition, Volume XIX.

parts of the personality), the other to the opposition of the cathexis of one's own person to that of other persons (object). But the term "narcissism" was used to cover the libidinal cathexis both of the ego and of one's own person. In this usage originated also the frequently found formulation that at the beginning of life all libido is in the ego, part of which is sent out later to cathect the object. In this case it seems perfectly clear that what Freud thought of was the cathexis of one's own person preceding that of the object's – if for no other reason than that, at least at that time, he did not think that anything comparable to the ego was present at birth.' Hartmann then concludes that this 'would mean that, for the definition of narcissism, the distinction of the libidinal cathexis of one's own person, as opposed to that of the objects, is the essential element'.

There are several objections to this proposition. The first is that it avoids the issue by begging the question. The embarrassing fact is that our present theory of the mind and the theory of primary narcissism land us in apparently insoluble contradictions; Hartmann then tries to save the situation by introducing an *ad hoc* concept, instead of examining what is wrong with the two theories or, at any rate, with one of them. We shall have to return to this methodological step presently. In the meanwhile let us examine the meaning of the new concept: 'the libidinal cathexis of one's own person'. Before being able to do so, we must define 'one's own person'. Should it be the sum total of the conscious and the pre-conscious? Does it include the whole of the ego and the super-ego or only those parts of these two instances that are conscious, while totally excluding the id? Or should the id be also included? In this last case, however, we have to ask how this can be made possible as, on the whole, one has no conscious access to the id and thus it is difficult to see how it can be felt as 'self'. I think it is fair to say that 'one's own person' or the 'self' are vague and nebulous concepts like 'character', 'personality', and so on, all of which are ill-defined and hazy terms, most useful in an awkward emergency, but perhaps inadmissible as escape routes out of a theoretical difficulty.

If we accept this new terminology proposed originally by Hartmann, Kris, and Loewenstein, many – though not all – of the internal contradictions in the theory of primary narcissism would disappear. However, we have to ask two questions: Do any new complications arise in the wake of this revised terminology; and secondly, would

Freud have accepted it? Neither of these questions is difficult to answer. A definition of narcissism as the libidinal cathexis of the self would compel us to distinguish in addition to the general form of self-narcissism the special classes of id-narcissism, ego-narcissism, and super-ego-narcissism – possibly each of them in primary and in secondary forms. Though this apparently precise sub-division may prove of advantage in the future – provided the self can be defined adequately to distinguish it from ego, id and super-ego – for the present I see only unnecessary *theoretical* complications from it.

This new terminology does not remove our *clinical* doubts about the primary nature of any of these new types of narcissistic cathexes. Unless we assume that not only the *Anlage* but also some relevant parts of the super-ego are preformed phylogenetically, its cathexis must be secondary, derived from the cathexes of the objects which had to be introjected ontogenetically as described by Freud in *The Ego and the Id*. If we accept Freud's idea that the ego has to be developed by some process of maturation, then its cathexis must develop roughly at the same rate, that is, it cannot be primary. We are left thus with id-narcissism as a possibly primary state. One can imagine, as James Strachey does, without much difficulty, the id as the *source* – or even reservoir – of all libido, but not as its original object. Libido has always been pictured as a current, as a flow; it is difficult to conceive that the source and the target of a stream could be identical unless the stream leaves its source, turns outwards, then changes its direction and returns back from where it started; this picture, however, would fit only what we call secondary narcissism. On the other hand, a source without an outflow would result in an increasing tension, and possibly this was what Freud meant when he wrote: 'in the last resort, we must begin to love in order not to fall ill, and we are bound to fall ill if, in consequence of frustration, we are unable to love' (Standard Edition, XIV, p. 85).

This problem of defining topographically the part of the mental apparatus cathected *by* the hypothetical primary narcissism – in contradistinction to the *source* of all libido – was never solved by Freud and, in my opinion, is only pushed on one side but not really solved by the proposition of Hartmann, Kris, and Loewenstein. True, if we compare the two passages in *The Ego and the Id*, say, with the two passages, one from the *Three Essays* and the other from *An Outline of Psycho-Analysis* quoted above, we must admit that the proposition of Hartmann, Kris and Loewenstein seems to be well founded. In this sense the introduction of the 'self' is a useful proposition as it tidies up – apparently – a rather untidy theory, but we have to ask whether it does anything else. In particular, can we predict on its basis new clinical observations or can it help us to explain well-established clinical phenomena which hitherto have remained inexplicable? The answer to both these questions is in the negative. Furthermore, the introduction of the 'self' does not even make an attempt at solving the important contradiction in chronology discussed in Chapter 11.

In spite of Hartmann's stern criticism, Freud was anything but a careless writer; so there must be some reason why he always returned to the cathexis of the ego when he spoke about narcissism. Thus I concur with Eduardo Weiss in his expression of strong doubts as to whether Freud would ever have agreed to the new propositions of Hartmann, Kris, and Loewenstein. Although it must be admitted that Freud never aspired to be an obsessional theoretician, he was definitely an impeccable clinical observer; and I have found invariably that the more closely one examines his clinical descriptions, the more one is impressed by their verity and profundity. My contention, therefore, is that the cause of this internal contradiction in the theory of primary narcissism is not careless usage or inability to see clearly and define exactly, but Freud's unwillingness to give up or modify clinical observations for the sake of a tidy theory. The reason why he always and invariably returned to the cathexis of the ego by libido when talking about narcissism, is simply that this is *what can be observed*; everything else is speculation, plausible or false, but not observable clinical fact.[1]

[1] It is also possible that the idea of primary narcissism was an attempt at solving a psychological conflict. On innumerable occasions Freud referred in his writings to his intense attachment to his mother – the anaclitic type of object-choice. We know also of his profound attachment to men, a powerful current throughout his life, which had started already certainly at the age of two towards his nephew, John, if not earlier – a narcissistic type of object-choice. There are many indications in Freud's life, among them his long engagement and late marriage, which show that he encountered considerable difficulties when trying to find a satisfactory solution for this conflict. It is thinkable that the theory of primary narcissism, apart from its scientific value, served the additional purpose of pushing those two conflicting strivings into the background and erecting in the place thus vacated a comforting theoretical structure free of conflict, at any rate, for its creator.

45

Chapter 9

Clinical facts about narcissism

Let us follow Freud who, in his paper 'On Narcissism', advised us that speculative or theoretical 'ideas are not the foundation of science, upon which everything rests: that foundation is observation alone. They are not the bottom but the top of the whole structure, and they can be replaced and discarded without damaging it' ('On Narcissism', Standard Edition, XIV, p. 77). Following this advice let us examine the clinical observations that Freud used to prove the existence of narcissism in his paper of 1914. The defenders of the theory will first say, as did Freud, that clinical observations can neither prove nor disprove primary narcissism since it is only a theory; then they, as did Freud, give clinical observations to make the theory *acceptable.* My intention in this chapter is to show that the observations on which Freud, and after him the theoreticians, based the hypothesis of primary narcissism prove only the existence of secondary narcissism. A theory of primary narcissism can be attached to them, but does not follow from them.

Freud enumerated in his paper 'On Narcissism' five clinical facts on which he based his theory of narcissism – though in fact he used eight in his argument. He mentions first the study of schizophrenia and of homosexuality and then continues: 'Other means of approach . . . by which we may obtain a better knowledge of narcissism' are 'the study of organic diseases, of hypochondria and of the erotic life of the sexes' (op. cit., p. 82). The three further facts not mentioned here but used in the argument are: (1) the various – psychotic and normal – overvaluations of self and object, (2) sleep, and (3) observations of young children and infants. There can be no question that in the case of an organic disease or of hypochondria we have to deal with secondary narcissism, that is, with libido withdrawn from objects; but what about the other clinical observations?

I wish to start my discussion with observations concerning homosexuality and the erotic life of the sexes. After referring to his theory

46

of 'the finding of an object' from the *Three Essays*, Freud continues: 'Side by side, however, with this type and source of object-choice which may be called the "anaclitic" or "attachment" type, psychoanalytic research has revealed a *second type*, which we were not prepared for finding. We have discovered, *especially clearly in people whose libidinal development has suffered some disturbance*, such as perverts and homosexuals, that in their later choice of love-objects they have taken as model not their mother but their own selves'. He means here the narcissistic type of object-choice. He finishes the paragraph: 'With this observation we have the strongest of the reasons which have led us to adopt the hypothesis of narcissism' (Standard Edition, XIV, p. 87. The italics are mine).

Which form of narcissism does Freud refer to here? The phrase italicized by me suggests that it is secondary narcissism. It is in good agreement with this assumption that in describing the anaclitic type Freud quotes a development which may be called normal, whereas while describing the narcissistic type he has to use severely pathological conditions. If one accepts primary narcissism as a stage in normal development it is rather strange that no normal type seems to derive from it.

A further argument for my thesis that the narcissistic type of object-choice depends on secondary and not on primary narcissism can be found in the historical passage in which Freud used the word 'narcissism' for the first time in print. This occurred in a footnote added to the *Three Essays* in 1910: '. . . In all the cases we have examined we have established the fact that the future inverts, in the earliest years of their childhood, pass through a phase of very intense but short-lived fixation to a woman (usually their mother), and that, after leaving this behind, they identify themselves with a woman and take *themselves* as their sexual object. That is to say, they proceed from a narcissistic basis, and look for a young man who resembles themselves and whom *they* may love as their mothers loved *them*' (Standard Edition, VII, p. 145. Original italics). This, again, is a categorical statement indeed. Moreover, it is based on clinical observations which have been confirmed by everyone who has analysed homosexuals. It constitutes the strongest possible argument for the secondary nature of the narcissistic type of object-choice.

Then there is another group of clinical observations which,

47

though not mentioned explicitly in the enumeration, is extensively used by Freud to prove the existence of narcissism; this group comprises all sorts of unrealistic over-valuations from psychotic megalomania through over-valuation of oneself or one's love-objects to idealization. It is evident that in every case of over-valuation of an external object the first cathexis is by object-libido which in a second step may be reinforced by narcissistic libido – certainly not a prima facie argument for primary narcissism; the case for the secondary nature of narcissism used in psychotic megalomania is still stronger. Similarly it is easy to show that the formation of the ego-ideal, in fact, any idealization, depends on secondary narcissism.[1] Any ideal starts by the internalization of something derived from and modelled on external objects, usually parental figures. This building up is called introjection; we cannot but admit that only important external objects can be introjected, that is, those strongly cathected by libido.

Closely connected with the phenomenon of idealization is the over-valuation of oneself observed among primitive people and children which in analytic theory is customarily called 'omnipotence'. On occasion this expression is explicitly attenuated by adjectives such as 'illusory' or 'hallucinatory', but this meaning is always and invariably implied whenever the term 'omnipotence' is used. This in itself suggests that this well-authenticated clinical observation is secondary in nature, that is, subsequent to frustration. Moreover, if adults, or for that matter children, exhibiting omnipotent attitudes are analysed, the omnipotence is invariably revealed as a desperate attempt to defend themselves against the crushing feeling of impotence. As far as I know, anthropological data about primitive people are in accord with this explanation. Furthermore, as our ideas about infantile omnipotence were based mainly on extrapolations from facts observed in adults or older children, I think they cannot be used without further proof for the existence of primary, but only for that of secondary, narcissism.

The next clinical phenomenon used by Freud to prove the existence of narcissism is sleep which, remarkably, he did not include in his enumeration quoted above; he referred to it – almost as an afterthought – at the end of his discussion of the changes in the distribution of libido in the course of organic diseases. There he says: 'In

[1] Cf. also *The Ego and the Id*, Chapter III.

48

both states we have, if nothing else, examples of changes in the distribution of libido that are consequent upon the change in the ego' (Standard Edition, XIV, p. 83). This impeccable clinical description suggests that these narcissistic states are secondary in nature.

Unquestionably sleep, both from the biological and the psychological point of view, shows a number of very primitive features. In consequence, ever since the *Interpretation of Dreams* it has been one of the most frequently quoted instances of regression, and it has often been argued that sleep, especially deep, dreamless sleep, should be considered as one of the nearest approximations in a normal individual to the hypothetical state of primary narcissism, the other example being the ante-natal foetal state. Freud, Ferenczi, and many others have noted that these two states exhibit so many similar features that together they constitute a most impressive argument.

Though none can contest the regressive nature of sleep, one must ask what is the fixation point which the sleeper strives to approximate? One answer is primary narcissism, but is this the only possibility? My answer is to quote from a most interesting and stimulating but sadly neglected and almost forgotten book the first paragraph of a chapter entitled 'Coitus and Sleep': 'To the far-reaching analogy between the strivings which are realized in coitus and in sleep we have made reference too often and too insistently to be able to retreat now from the task of examining somewhat more closely into these two biologically so significant adaptations, their resemblances and their differences. In my *Stages of Development of the Reality Sense* the first sleep of the newborn – to which the careful isolation, the warm swaddling by mother or nurse contribute – was described as a replica of the intra-uterine state. The child, frightened, crying, shaken by the traumatic experience of birth, soon becomes lulled in this sleeping state which creates in him a feeling – on a reality basis, on the one hand, and on the other hallucinatory, that is, illusorily – as though no such tremendous shock had occurred at all. Freud (*Introductory Lectures*) has said, indeed, that strictly speaking the human being is not completely born; he is not born in the full sense, seeing that through going nightly to bed he spends half his life in, as it were, the mother's womb' (Ferenczi, 1924, p. 73).

Apparently orgasm in coitus and the act of falling asleep can be achieved only if a state of 'harmony' or, at any rate, peace can be established between the individual and his environment. One condition for this state of peace is that the environment accepts the role of protecting the individual from any disturbing stimulation from the outside and for not inflicting any unnecessarily exciting or distressing stimuli on him itself. In good agreement with this idea is the clinical fact that one of the first symptoms of sexual dissatisfaction is sleeplessness. Thus the point a sleeper tries to approximate in his regression appears to be, perhaps, not that of primary narcissism but a kind of primitive state of peace with his environment in which – to use the modern phrase – the environment 'holds' the individual.

From the very rich literature on sleep may I single out one more author, Mark Kanzer (1955, p. 261), whose observations are relevant to the topic we are discussing. According to him: 'Falling asleep is not a simple narcissistic regression . . . the sleeper is not truly alone, but "sleeps with" his introjected good object. This is evidenced in the habits of sleepers – the physical demands of the child for his parents, of the adult for his sex partner, and of the neurotic for lights, toys and rituals – as preliminary conditions for sleep.' Additional introjective measures among adults enumerated by Kanzer are: eating, drinking, swallowing of pills, or bathing; among children: demands for nursing, rocking, or lullabies. Of course Bertram Lewin's dream screen is equated with the dream partner. Kanzer sums up: 'Sleep is not a phenomenon of primary but rather of secondary narcissism, at least after early infancy, and the sleeper shares his slumbers with an introjected object' (p. 265).

Thus sleep, which at first appeared so impressive, has become rather a doubtful argument for the existence of primary narcissism. True, the individual withdraws from the world of objects when trying to fall asleep and is to all appearances alone. This withdrawal and solitude, which were interpreted as narcissism, revealed on closer examination that the sleeper's true aim was to escape from the strains of his ordinary relationships and to recapture a more primitive, more satisfying form of relationship with objects whose interests were identical with his. Examples of such objects are: comfortable beds, pillows, houses, rooms, books, flowers, toys, and transitional objects (Winnicott, 1951), etc. Of course they are representatives, or symbols, of internal objects which, in their turn, derive from early

50

contacts with the environment, satisfactory feeds, warm soft wrappings, safe 'holding' or cuddling by mother, rocking, and lullabies, etc. The observations quoted show that the sleeper's regression is to this world and not to that of primary narcissism in which there is no environment to which to relate.

Chapter 10

Schizophrenia, addiction, and other narcissistic conditions

The last but one clinical observation used by Freud to justify the introduction of narcissism is schizophrenic regression. Everybody agrees that schizophrenics withdraw their interest from the external world – at any rate that is the impression they make. I have already pointed out that when discussing the dynamics of schizophrenic regressions, Freud invariably started his argument like this: 'The libido that is liberated by frustration does not remain attached to objects in fantasy, but withdraws to the ego' (Standard Edition, XIV, p. 86). This formula was repeated whenever Freud approached the problem of schizophrenia. However, only a few years after the publication of his paper on Narcissism another sentence appeared which more often than not was mentioned together with the previous one. In the *Introductory Lectures*, Freud discusses the fixation points to which the various neuroses regress and then states that in schizophrenia it is 'probably . . . the stage of primitive narcissism, to which dementia praecox returns in its final outcome' (Standard Edition, XVI, p. 421). This is a theoretical statement; moreover, it suffers from all the contradictions inherent in the theory of primary narcissism. What are the clinical observations?

Opinions diverge whether schizophrenics can or cannot be radically cured by psychoanalysis, but there is a general consensus that they are far from inaccessible to it. On the other hand, normal, that is standard, analytic technique has had to be modified considerably to make it applicable to their treatment. Expressed in theoretical terms, this well-established clinical experience means that (a) the impression that schizophrenics are withdrawn from the external world is only partially true; they are withdrawn from the world of normal – that is, triangular or Oedipal – relationships, but (b) they

52

are capable of another kind of relationship which it is the aim of all modifications of technique to provide.

I cannot review here the very rich literature on this subject. Suffice it to say that this kind of relationship – or technique – demands much more from the analyst than the standard technique. This does *not* mean that the analyst must satisfy all the patient's needs immediately and unconditionally but that he must be able to prove that he is capable of understanding the patient and of working in 'harmony', in 'tune', with him.

This, by the way, is true for all regressed patients, not only for schizophrenics. All of them seem to be highly sensitive to the analyst's moods, and the more regressed the patient is, the more sensitive he becomes; what a normal or neurotic patient would not even notice usually affects or, more correctly, disturbs a regressed patient deeply. To avoid this disturbance, the analyst must be 'in tune' with his patient. As long as he can achieve this, the analytic work may proceed steadily, comparable to a steady growth; but if he cannot remain 'in tune' the patient may react with anxiety, with very noisy aggressive symptoms, or with despair.

This harmony, or being in tune, must include the regressed patient's whole life, not merely his relationship with his analyst. It is in the nature of the analytic situation that this harmony can be maintained in it only for short periods; from time to time the analyst must detach himself from his patient to review the situation 'objectively' and perhaps even to give a well considered interpretation. As a rule these patients can stand relationships with a real external object for brief periods only, consequently these periods must be saved for the analytic work. Should the environment, that is, every-day life, make too great demands on the patient, a good deal of his available libido will be drained away and not enough will be left over for the analysis. Hence the, sometimes inordinate, demands by analysts in charge of this kind of patient that the environment should completely 'fall in' with the patient, 'hold' him, in order to enable the patient to concentrate all his remaining libido in a more definite – therapeutic – relationship with his analyst.

Once the importance of this condition is realized, one understands why so many reports on treatment of schizophrenics end with melancholy passages like these: 'At this point, because of external circumstances, the treatment had to be interrupted', or

'Unfortunately the relatives intervened and the treatment had to be discontinued', and so on.

A theoretical aspect of this condition of harmony is the notion of the 'schizophrenogenic mother', that is, a mother who could not be in harmony with her child. A wise and experienced clinician (Hill, 1955, pp. 108–109) writes: 'These mothers love their children who become schizophrenics not only excessively but conditionally. The condition for their love is one that the schizophrenic child cannot meet. . . . These mothers saw only the normal outer shell of the children and were impervious to any impressions as to what went on within them.' A very interesting clinical description of the importance of this harmonious environment for the treatment of schizophrenics is contained in a book by Stanton and Schwarz (1954) in which it is convincingly shown that any disharmony in the environment, that is between the various members of the staff who are concerned with the treatment of any one patient, leads to a deterioration of his condition.

It appears then that the well-established clinical observation of schizophrenic withdrawal cannot be used as proof of a primary narcissistic state. In fact, it would be more correct to say that the schizophrenic has a much closer tie with, and is much more dependent on, his environment than the so-called 'normal' or 'neurotic'. True, a superficial observation of his behaviour will not reveal this close tie and this desperate dependence; on the contrary, it creates the impression of withdrawal and of lack of any contact. In this respect schizophrenic regression may be a counterpart to the infantile or foetal phase in which too we find exactly the same conditions: an outward appearance or narcissistic independence, of no awareness of the external world, of fleeting and seemingly unimportant contacts with part objects, all of which has been shown in modern research, such as that of R. Spitz (1946) on the effects of early deprivation, only thinly to cover a desperate dependence and a very great need for 'harmony'. This topic will be taken up in the next chapter, as well as in Parts III and V.

Having discussed the curious contradictions in the attitude of schizophrenics towards their environment, we may add that this is only an exaggerated form of the attitude found generally in so-called narcissistic people. Although their interest is centred upon their ego – or their own self, to use Hartmann's term – and although apparently they have very little love to give to people, they are anything but secure or independent; equally they cannot be described as stable, self-contained, or self-sufficient. As a rule they are highly sensitive to any failure of their environment in treating them as they expect to be treated; they are easily hurt and offended, and these offences rankle for a long time. Moreover, in real life these narcissistic people are hardly ever found to be able to exist on their own. As a rule they live together with their split-off doublets on the pattern of such famous couples as Faust and Mephistopheles, Don Quixote and Sancho Panza, Don Juan and Leporello, and so on. In all these cases – as has been pointed out many times in the analytic literature from Otto Rank (1924) to Helene Deutsch (1937) – the unglamorous and non-narcissistic partner, who is capable of object-love, is the one who is really independent and can cope with the hazards of everyday life: the partner without whose help and ministration the glamorous and seemingly independent narcissistic hero would perish miserably. In real life often enough the unglamorous partner is the narcissistic hero's actual mother.

Thus we come to the conclusion that a truly narcissistic man or woman is in fact a pretence only. They are desperately dependent on their environment, and their narcissism can be preserved only on the condition that their environment is willing, or can be forced, to look after them. This is true generally from the greatest dictator to the most humble catatonic.

A good opportunity for observing changes from adult object relationship to narcissism, and then to this sort of primitive relationship and back again in fairly rapid succession, is provided for us by the analysis of alcoholics, especially of periodic drinkers. Their object relationships, though usually fairly intense, are shaky and unstable. In consequence, these people are easily thrown off their balance; the most common cause being a clash of interests between themselves and one of their important love objects. This clash easily appears to them so overwhelming that they feel utterly unable to remedy the situation; they then withdraw practically all their object libido; no one matters any more, only their narcissism; on the one hand they feel themselves to be the centre of every attention both friendly and hostile and, on the other, utterly wretched and forsaken.

Usually it is in this state that they start to drink – though of course there may be other precipitating causes. But whatever the cause, the first effect of intoxication is invariably the establishment of a feeling that everything is now well between them and their environment. In my experience the yearning for this feeling of 'harmony' is the most important cause of alcoholism or, for that matter, any form of addiction. At this point all sorts of secondary processes set in which threaten the 'harmony', and the alcoholic in his despair drinks more and more in order to maintain, or at any rate salvage, some of it.

A most important feature of this state of harmony surrounding the intoxicated drinker is that in this world there are no people or objects of love or hate, especially no demanding people or objects. The harmony can be kept up only as long as the drinker is capable of getting rid of everything and everybody who might demand anything from him; many periodic drinkers either shut themselves in and drink by themselves, or escape from their familiar world of objects and people and seek out an environment with which they have had no previous contact, which cannot demand anything, least of all lasting libidinal commitment, from them. (An impressive realization of these two worlds – the normal with lasting libidinal commitments and the drunken one with only fleeting cathexes – was enacted in Chaplin's film *City Lights*.) People in this new world can be tolerated only as long as they are sympathetic and friendly; the slightest criticism or clash of interest provokes violent reactions in the drinker because of his desperate need to maintain his harmony with the world created by alcohol.

One more group of clinical observations is pertinent to our problem. This is the analytic atmosphere apparently necessary for the treatment of certain difficult patients. The difficulty may be caused by the patient's regression, by his severe narcissism, by the nature of his illness, or by his character make-up; these people are usually characterized in analytic literature by some adjective such as 'deeply disturbed'. It was with these patients that I first recognized the existence of primitive relationships to their environment. However, it could easily be argued against me that though my descriptions corresponded to certain phenomena during treatment, these were caused not so much by the patient as by my technique. To take the wind out of my critics' sails, I would quote the descriptions of one analyst who, beyond any suspicion, uses classical technique; this is Phyllis Greenacre (1953, p. 48). She writes: 'I shall indicate the ways in which I believe this excess narcissism and anxiety may be managed during the course of analysis – the ways which must be used, in fact, in order that a "regular" analysis dealing primarily with the disturbances of libidinal development may proceed. Certainly the excess of narcissism in these cases is a presenting and terrifying problem to the analyst. But I am inclined to think that the narcissism can be educated sufficiently, if it is carefully done, to permit the patient to stand the pain of the analysis, provided that due heed is given at the same time to the blind anxiety which is the cornerstone of his insecure character structure.' When this passage is compared with my description of the needs of a schizophrenic patient in his regressed state, it will become evident that both of us are talking about the same clinical experience.

When discussing patients who come in a panic to analysis, Greenacre says: 'It is extremely important in these early stages to have the understanding cooperation of the people who are close to the patient during most of the other twenty-three hours of the day, whether this be in a hospital or at home; much of the gain of the therapeutic hour may be lost by hostile, solicitous, or too active friends or relatives' (op. cit., pp. 54–55). Of course, I could not have said it differently.

Somewhat further (op. cit., pp. 57–60), Greenacre apparently equates what she calls 'the education of narcissism' with the strengthening of the ego. I have no quarrel with this description but wish to point out that the method advocated by Greenacre prescribes that to begin with the analyst must as nearly as possible be 'in tune' with his patient and then gradually and cautiously try to turn into a normal object, that is, one who may make demands. Of course, being 'in tune' does not necessarily mean that from now on the analyst must satisfy automatically the patient's wishes, desires, and needs, but it means definitely that the analyst must honestly endeavour to see that he and his patient should approximate as far as possible in their relationship to what I call the 'harmonious mix-up', discussed in more detail in Chapter 12.

I wish to add here an important rider. Greenacre's description of the clinically observable phenomena as well as the therapeutic recommendations could be used as they are, that is, without changing anything in them, as illustrations of events belonging to the area of the basic fault, described in Part I. There is the exclusively two-person

57

relationship, the absolute demand that one partner – the analyst – must be 'in tune' with the other – the patient – all the time, the absence of conflict, the relative unimportance of the customary forms of interpretation, etc., etc. I expect that the study of the clinical picture of narcissistic disorders, their metapsychology, and above all, their therapy, would make considerable progress if they were approached in the light of the theory of the basic fault. An attempt of this sort will be made in the subsequent Parts III and V.

How important this new approach might be is well shown by a recent, otherwise excellent, paper by W. G. Joffe and Joseph Sandler (1965), 'Disorders of Narcissism', which ignores all criticism against the theory of primary narcissism. Their main concern is to show that for the understanding of narcissism and its disorders, in addition to the gratification (in German *Befriedigung* – literally 'pacification') of the drives, 'deviations from an ideal state of well-being . . . in its affective and ideational aspects' must also be taken into account. This 'ideal state of well-being' is, as will be discussed in Chapter 12, the ultimate aim of primary love, in fact of all human striving, and any serious disturbance in its early phases leads to the establishment of a specific basic fault. By omitting to examine the dynamic structure of this 'ideal state of well-being', the authors fail to recognize its object-related nature and can equate it, without any further proof, with primary narcissism. Otherwise, although they do not state it explicitly, their discussion relates only to phenomena belonging to the field of secondary narcissism; therefore, I need only say that I agree with practically all their conclusions.

The gist of what has been found in this section is that schizo-phrenics – contrary to theoretical expectations – are capable, even in their most regressed states, of responding to their environment and are, thus, accessible to attempts at analytical therapy. The response is, however, tenuous and precarious because of their compelling need for 'harmonious' relationship. This suggests that their narcissistic withdrawal is secondary, subsequent to frustration. The other states reviewed briefly in this section – alcoholics and 'deeply disturbed' or 'narcissistic' patients – present the same picture; everywhere the same primitive need for harmony, frustration because of the exacting demands from the partner in general and from the analyst in particular, and withdrawal into secondary narcissism.

Chapter 11

Ante-natal and early post-natal states

After having surveyed the clinical facts used by Freud to support the introduction of narcissism, we are left with the conclusion that, apart from two, all of them were clear-cut cases of secondary narcissism. We found only two phenomena that could not be explained purely on the basis of secondary narcissism: the regressive states in schizophrenia and deep dreamless sleep; yet even in these two instances it appeared that the fixation point towards which the regression tended was not necessarily primary narcissism, but a very primitive form of relationship in which a probably undifferentiated environment was very intensely cathected.

We must not forget, however, that this difficulty was correctly forecast by Freud, the clinician, who had stated already in 1914: 'the primary narcissism of children which we have assumed and which forms one of the postulates of our theories of the libido, is less easy to grasp by direct observation than to confirm *by inferences from elsewhere*' (Standard Edition, XIV, p. 90. Italics are mine). A convincing picture of Freud's state of mind: the theoretician is optimistic and goes on with his constructions, while the clinician, to say the least, is cautious, if not sceptical.

Furthermore, in this passage Freud talks about *the primary narcissism of children*, while the prevailing psychoanalytic theory forces us to consider *the primary narcissism in the ante-natal state*. This tendency to ante-date is fairly general in analytic theory: if an assumption proves to be incompatible with clinical observation, instead of rejecting it as untenable or, at any rate, re-examining it, it is ante-dated to refer to still earlier phases of development, so early as to be beyond the reach of any clinical observation.

In order to simplify matters, I shall discuss chiefly Phyllis Greenacre's ideas relating to this topic. This is justifiable as she is a recognized authority in this field and dealt with our topic extensively in her book *Trauma. Growth and Personality* (1953). Although not all

59

the ideas to be discussed in this section have originated with her, I shall quote as many of them as possible in her words. For the sake of simplification I shall discuss these ideas in three groups: (1) those relating to foetal life proper; (2) those relating to the changes caused by birth; and (3) those relating to the earliest phase of extra-uterine life.

Greenacre says quite categorically: 'From a biological viewpoint narcissism may be defined as the libidinal component of growth' (op. cit., p. 20). Following Freud she then states: 'Narcissism is coincidental with life throughout, . . . narcissistic libido is in fact to be found wherever there is a spark of life' or, more specifically, 'In the foetus the narcissism is reduced to the simplest terms, being almost or entirely devoid of psychic content' (op. cit., p. 45).

My problem here is that while Greenacre's statements are plausible and make sense as a whole, they rest only on assumptions which cannot be proved or disproved by observation. She – and a great number of analysts with her – think that statements of this kind are justifiable extrapolations from various clinical and biological observations, though she would doubtless agree that we have only views and vague ideas but no hard facts about the distribution of libido in intrauterine life, about 'the libidinal component of growth', or about 'narcissism entirely devoid of psychic content'. I know that it is somewhat unfair to an author to isolate phrases out of their context, but I submit that the use of phrases of this kind, without stating unequivocally that they do not claim to describe clinical findings but are merely speculations, is unfair to the reader.

In her book Greenacre gives an excellent description of the imagery which people use to express their feelings about, or possibly 'memories' of, birth, which may be felt, for instance, as: 'a bridge from one mode of existence to another', 'a chiasma', 'a hiatus', 'a kind of blackout very closely resembling death', and so on (op. cit., pp. 20–21).

Greenacre then concludes that the experience of birth comprises possibly all this imagery as over-determining factors, but perhaps its most fundamental characteristic is a precipitate but successfully achieved change from one mode of life to another. She writes: 'I can only think that the disturbance of the gross economy of foetal narcissistic libido which occurs at birth is just this: some transition from the almost complete dependence of intrauterine life to the very beginnings of individuation, at least to the quasi-dependence outside the mother's body instead of the complete dependence inside' (op. cit., p. 45).

She repeats Freud's dictum that experiences during birth seem to organize the individual's anxiety pattern, and adds then 'While the establishment of anxiety pattern is a protection against danger, the organization of the narcissism forms an instrument of positive attack, a propulsive aggressive drive' (op. cit., p. 19).

All these descriptions can be interpreted – with some difficulty – as possible pointers to a state of primary narcissism, and this is how Greenacre uses them. In my opinion, however, they can be interpreted – and without straining a point – as rather strong arguments for the assumption of an early, intensive interaction between the foetus-baby and his environment. Birth means a sudden interruption of a hitherto gratifying relationship with an environment in which, it is true, there are as yet no objects, which is a kind of unstructured 'ocean'. We shall have to revert to this train of thought presently.

Returning to Greenacre's book, I shall have to omit the many interesting clinical observations about the connection of the birth trauma – assumed or real – with the symptomatology developed in adult life, as this would be quite outside my scope. On the other hand, I would point out that all the clinical descriptions given by Greenacre referring to the effects of post-natal events, can be taken as arguments for the secondary nature of narcissism, as subsequent to frustration by the environment. To demonstrate this I will quote one passage from her paper 'Pre-genital Patterning' (1952): 'Returning to the question of increased primary narcissism due to early repeated over-stimulation of the infant, such increase implies a prolongation and greater intensity of the tendency to primary identification as noted, and impairment of the developing sense of reality in combination with the increased capacity of body responsiveness and registration of stimulus' (p. 414).

Early infancy is often described as an undifferentiated state in which there is still no boundary between individual and environment – an acceptable idea which will be further discussed in Chapter 12. An alternative – or parallel – description states that early infancy is the phase of primary narcissism and primary identification, which latter is often defined as the functional aspect of primary narcissism. I would like to point out that – provided 'identification' retains its

61

normal meaning – there is a logical contradiction in accepting the co-existence of these two states. As mentioned above, Freud was fully aware of this fact and discussed it in Chapter 3 of *The Ego and the Id*. Any identification – in the usual sense – means a change in the ego under the influence of some external object, or some part of the environment, which was previously intensely cathected. Even the most primary identification is with something outside the individual, and in order to bring about a change in the ego according to any external pattern, this pattern must mean a good deal to the individual. Thus my contention is that there cannot be any *primary* identification. All identifications must be *per definitionem* secondary to some object or environment cathexis. It follows then that primary narcissism and primary identification cannot exist at the same time – if they exist at all.

Another, often used, argument for primary narcissism is that the infant in his very early days cannot be aware of the external world. As there is no external world for him to cathect, he must be thought of as living in primary narcissism. Should this argument appear in conflict with observed facts it is often attenuated; the contented infant either falls asleep and is thus 'away' from the influence of the world or, if awake, it must be assumed – as for instance by W. Hoffer (1959) – 'that the environment-mother has come to the aid of the child's primary narcissism and so there is no ego yet, no idea of danger, anxiety, or defence . . .' (p. 8). Thus 'what is needed is a hold to maintain the state of primary narcissism, an equivalent for the holding qualities of the pre-natal mother' (p. 9).

In the same paper Hoffer raises the point that Freud might have been influenced in his theories about early states by the form of infant care prevalent in his days, namely, swaddling. The swaddling clothes, according to Hoffer, 'act as a narcissistic rind for the developing ego' (p. 10), i.e. the infants are protected from external stimulation and in consequence their object relationships are possibly retarded. 'With the removal of the swaddling clothes the infant's primary narcissism has been endangered as well: not really, of course, but only for the observer who started to see object relatedness which overlaid primary narcissism', and he adds: 'I wonder . . . whether we do not claim as progress in the science of psychoanalysis what in effect amounts to an adaptation of our theories to conditions (that is in nursing habits) prevailing in the present' (p. 11).

All these arguments are hardly more than begging the question. First it is decreed that a state of primary narcissism exists, and in order to keep this decree inviolate, it is further decreed (a) that the environment-mother must 'hold' the infant to protect the state of primary narcissism, (b) that the child must not become aware of any change in this 'holding', and (c) that any *observed relationship* with the environment, and any *observed response* to a change in the 'holding' (e.g. absence of swaddling), must be disregarded as false – otherwise the whole theoretical structure will collapse.

I think that it would be much simpler to accept the idea that relationship with the environment exists in a primitive form right from the start, and that the infant may become aware of, and respond to, any considerable change in it. This would however mean, using Hoffer's argument, that the theory of primary narcissism has been based chiefly on experiences with infants who were treated insensitively, e.g. with stiff swaddling, rigid nursing routine, etc. and who in consequence were forced to develop at a much too early phase secondary narcissism largely as a response to disturbed relationship with their environment.

Chapter 12

Primary love

The assumption of primary narcissism – though offering us a neat, tidy, and logical theory – has landed us into insoluble contradictions and uncertainties. In our theoretical considerations we can easily indicate the source of libido, namely the id, but it has proved impossible to define topologically either 'the great reservoir of the libido' or the anchorage point of primary narcissism. The various descriptions given by Freud himself are contradictory and inconsistent, and the new propositions of Hartmann, Kris, and Loewenstein on the one hand, and by James Strachey on the other, while solving some problems, have created new ones. The other insoluble contradiction is about dating: primary object relationship, primary auto-erotism, primary narcissism, were each described by Freud in turn equally categorically as the earliest, most primitive form of the individual's relationship with his environment.

In this predicament, analytic theory resorted to a well-proved escape route: antedating. Whereas Freud spoke of 'the primary narcissism of children', modern theory has found it necessary to attribute primary narcissism to the foetus. In the previous chapter I tried to show that what is acquired by this attempt is a 'suitcase theory'; you can find in it only what you have put in.

During all the fifty years since the introduction of the psychoanalytic concept of narcissism, no new clinical observations have been described to prove the existence or acceptability of primary narcissism, a highly suggestive historical fact. Whereas the literature on primary narcissism is scanty and hardly goes beyond repeating the various statements and suggestions made by Freud, the literature on secondary narcissism is very rich and is based on excellent clinical observations.

A good theory must possess at least some of the following qualities: (1) It must be free from inherent contradictions; as we have seen, the theory of primary narcissism was faulty in this respect from its inception and repeated attempts to remedy the fault failed. (2) It must present an aesthetic structure that allows integration of disjointed observations so that we may understand each of them better, more truly; the theory of primary narcissism pretends but, as the previous chapters show, fails to do so. (3) On the basis of a theory one should be able to make predictions, draw conclusions or inferences that are capable of verification or refutation; to my knowledge the theory of primary narcissism led only to further theoretical speculations – some of them were discussed above – which were either beyond possible verification or, in one instance – inaccessibility of schizophrenics to analytic treatment – proved false and had to be withdrawn.

What is the alternative? My proposition is in two parts. First, I should like to submit that the theory of primary narcissism has proved self-contradicting and unproductive. It created more problems than it helped to solve; more than fifty years of hard thinking and critical observations have not been able to resolve the internal contradictions inherent in it. In consequence I cannot see any point in clinging to it. My second proposition is that clinical experiences with patients should be employed to construct a new theory that could replace primary narcissism and that might be more suitable for verification or refutation by direct observation. Those who know my writings will anticipate that my proposition is a theory of primary relationship to the environment: briefly, primary love.

To avoid any possible misunderstanding, I wish to point out that calling my theory 'primary love' does not mean that I think that sadism or hate have no, or only a negligible, place in human life. On the other hand, I do think that they are secondary phenomena, consequences of inevitable frustrations. The aim of all human striving is to establish – or, probably, re-establish – an all-embracing harmony with one's environment, to be able to love in peace. While sadism and hate seem to be incompatible with this desire, aggressiveness – and perhaps even violence – may be used, and even enjoyed, well into the stages immediately preceding the desired harmony, but not during the state of harmony itself. These are the main reasons that led me to call my theory 'primary love', *a fortiori fiat denominatio*.

Although this theory has taken many years of clinical experience to reach its present form – I reported my first tentative formulations in 1932 – I shall present it here, for the sake of brevity, in a somewhat apodictic form, the more so as it was discussed at some length in my book *Thrills and Regressions* (1959).

According to the theory of primary narcissism the individual is born having hardly any or no relationship with his environment. In this world only one object exists as yet: the self, the ego, or the id – as the case may be – and all libido is concentrated in one, or in all three of them. To start with biological facts, we know that the foetus's dependence on its environment is extreme, certainly more intense than an infant's or an adult's. In consequence it is essential for its well-being and orderly development that the environment should be all the time very near to what the foetus needs. Great discrepancies between need and supply will be followed by severe repercussions and may even endanger life.

If we may make this biological situation a model for the distribution of libido in foetal life, that is a psychological condition, we reach the assumption that the cathexis of the environment by the foetus must be very intense – more intense than a child's or adult's. This environment, however, is probably undifferentiated; on the one hand, there are as yet no objects in it; on the other hand, it has hardly any structure, in particular no sharp boundaries towards the individual; environment and individual penetrate into each other, they exist together in a 'harmonious mix-up'. An important example of this *harmonious interpenetrating mix-up* is the fish in the sea (one of the most archaic and most widely occurring symbols). It is an idle question to ask whether the water in the gills or in the mouth is part of the sea or of the fish; exactly the same holds true about the foetus. Foetus, amniotic fluid, and placenta are such a complicated interpenetrating mix-up of foetus and environment-mother, that its histology and physiology are among the most dreaded questions in medical examinations.

Lastly, it is worth remembering that our relationship to the air surrounding us has exactly the same pattern. We use the air, in fact we cannot live without it; we inhale it in order to take parts out of it and use them as we want; then, after putting substances into it that we want to get rid of, we exhale it – without paying the slightest attention to it. In fact, the air must be there for us, and as long as it is there in sufficient supply and quality, we do not take any notice of it. This kind of environment must simply be there, and as long as it is there – for instance, if we get enough air – we take its existence for granted, we do not consider it as an object, that is, separate from us; we just use it. The situation changes abruptly if the environment is altered – if, for instance, in the adult's case the supply of air is interfered with – then the seemingly uncathected environment assumes immense importance, that is, its latent true cathexis becomes apparent.

As was the case for the relationship of fish and water, so in our relationship to the air there are no sharp boundaries. It is an idle question to enquire whether the air in our lungs, or in our bowels, is us or not us, or where the exact boundary between us and this air is; we still live with the air in an almost harmonious interpenetrating mix-up. The importance of states reminiscent of this kind of relationship for analytic technique will be discussed in Parts III, IV, and V.

According to my theory, the individual is born in a state of intense relatedness to his environment, both biologically and libidinally. Prior to birth, self and environment are harmoniously 'mixed up', in fact, they interpenetrate each other. In this world, as has been mentioned, there are as yet no objects, only limitless substances or expanses.

Birth is a trauma that upsets this equilibrium by changing the environment radically and enforces – under a real threat of death – a new form of adaptation. This starts off or, at any rate considerably accelerates, the separation between individual and environment. Objects, including the ego, begin to emerge from the mix-up of substances and from the breaking up of the harmony of the limitless expanses. The objects have – in contrast to the friendlier substances – firm contours and sharp boundaries which henceforth must be recognized and respected. Libido is no longer in a homogeneous flux from the id to the environment; under the influence of the emerging objects, concentrations and rarefactions appear in its flow.

Wherever the developing relationship to a part of the environment or to an object is in painful contrast to the earlier undisturbed harmony, libido may be withdrawn to the ego, which starts or accelerates developing – perhaps as a consequence of the enforced new adaptation – in an attempt to regain the previous feeling of 'oneness' of the first stages. This part of the libido would be definitely narcissistic, but secondary to the original environment cathexis. Accordingly the libidinal cathexes observed in early infancy would be of four sorts: (a) remnants of the original environment cathexis

67

transferred to the emerging objects, (b) other remnants of the original environment cathexis withdrawn to the ego as secondary comforters against frustration, i.e. narcissistic and auto-erotic cathexes, and (c) re-cathexes emanating from the secondary narcissism of the ego. In addition to these three fairly well-studied forms of cathexis, there is a fourth which results in the development of the ocnophilic and the philobatic structures of the world (Balint 1959). In the ocnophilic world the primary cathexis, though mixed with a great deal of anxiety, seems to adhere to the emerging objects; these are felt to be safe and comforting while the spaces between them are threatening and horrid. In the philobatic world the objectless expanses retain the original primary cathexis and are experienced as safe and friendly, while the objects are felt as treacherous hazards.

The ocnophil's reaction to the emergence of objects is to cling to them, to introject them, since he feels lost and insecure without them; apparently he chooses to *over-cathect his object relationships*. The other type, the philobat, *over-cathects his own ego-functions* and develops skills in this way, in order to be able to maintain himself alone with very little, or even no, help from his objects. Ocnophilia and philobatism are probably instances of the basic fault, certainly not the only ones. It is upon this foundation that, on the one hand, the Oedipus complex is built and on the other, possibly the area of the creation (see Chapter 5). This latter may entail as a first step a regressive *withdrawal from objects* found too harsh and frustrating, to the harmonious mix-up of earlier states, which is then followed by *an attempt to create something better,* kinder, more understandable, more beautiful, and above all, more consistent and more harmonious than the real objects proved to be. Unfortunately this attempt does not succeed each time; much too often the creation is no better – even worse – than the bitter reality.

At first most of the objects are possibly indifferent or even frustrating, but some of them prove to be sources of gratification; provided the infant care is not too deficient or insensitive, parts of the environment may retain some of its original *primary cathexis,* they become what I called *primary objects,* and one's relationship to them and to their derivatives in later life will always be different, that is, more primitive than the relationship to anything else in the world. Such primary objects are, first of all, one's mother and, remarkably, for many people most of the four 'elements' which are archaic mother

68

symbols: water, earth, air, and, less frequently, fire. May I anticipate here that during certain phases of a satisfactory analytic treatment the analyst assumes, in fact must assume, the qualities of a primary object. I shall return to this topic in Chapter 13 and again Parts IV and V.

Before going further, I wish to refer here to some clinical and linguistic observations of T. Doi (1962). According to him, there exists in Japanese a very simple, everyday word, *amaeru*, an intransitive verb, denoting 'to wish or to expect to be loved' in the sense of primary love. *Amae* is the noun derived from it, while the adjective *amai* means 'sweet'. These words are so common that 'indeed the Japanese find it hard to believed that there is no word for *amaeru* in the European languages'. Moreover, in Japanese there is a rich vocabulary describing the various attitudes and moods that develop if the wish to *amaeru* is frustrated or must be repressed. All these attitudes are known in the West, but they cannot be expressed by simple words, only by complicated phrases like 'sulking or pouting because he feels he is not allowed to show his wish to *amaeru* as much as he wants to, thus harbouring in himself mental pain, possibly of masochistic nature', etc., etc. Doi adds that according to his information, the Korean and the Aimu languages have equivalent words, as possibly has the Chinese.

Returning now to our main topic, it is very likely that in the early stages of post-natal life the maintenance of a primitive form of an exclusively two-person relationship is about the limit of the developing infant's capacity. As discussed in Chapter 10, this is probably the point of regression in schizophrenia. For many years I thought that there was only one type of this primitive two-person relationship, the type that I now call ocnophilia. In this relationship, as just described, the object is felt as a vitally important support. Any threat of being separated from it creates intense anxiety and the most frequently used defence against it is clinging. On the other hand, the object inherits so much cathexis from the primary substances that it becomes so important that no concern or consideration can be given to it, it must have no separate interests from the individual's, it must simply be there and, in fact, it is taken for granted. The consequences of this kind of object relationship are (a) an over-valuation of the object – which is thus not necessarily due to an over-cathexis by narcissistic libido, and (b) a comparative inhibition

69

against developing personal skills which might make the individual independent from his objects.

During the past fifteen years or so I have discovered a second type of primitive relationship to objects or, perhaps more correctly, to the environment. I proposed for it the term 'philobatism'. In this objects are considered as indifferent, or even as deceitful and untrustworthy hazards, better to be avoided. To achieve this, the individual must develop some personal skills – that is his ego – in order to retain, or regain, the freedom of movement in, and harmony, with, the objectless expanses, such as mountains, deserts, sea, air, etc., all of which belong to the class of potentially primary objects – or more correctly, primary substances – but *pari passu* his object relationships may become thwarted.

A common feature of all these primitive forms of object relationship is that in it the object is taken for granted; the idea that an indifferent object exists and that it should be changed into a cooperative partner by the 'work of conquest' has not yet arisen. In this harmonious two-person relationship only one partner may have wishes, interests, and demands on his own; without any further need for testing, it is taken for granted that the other partner, the object, or the friendly expanse, will automatically have the same wishes, interests, and expectations. This explains why this is so often called the state of omnipotence. This description is somewhat out of tune; there is no feeling of power, in fact, no need for either power or effort, as all things *are* in harmony.

If any hitch or disharmony between subject and object occurs, the reaction to it will consist of loud and vehement symptoms suggesting processes either of a highly aggressive and destructive, or profoundly disintegrated, nature, i.e. either as if the whole world, including the self, would have been smashed up, or as if the subject would have been flooded with pure and unmitigated aggressive-destructive impulses. On the other hand, if the harmony is allowed to persist without much disturbance from outside, the reaction amounts to a feeling of tranquil, quiet well-being which is rather inconspicuous and difficult to observe.

This difference expressed in adult language would run somewhat like this: 'I must be loved and looked after in every respect by everyone and everything important to me, without anyone demanding any effort or claiming any return for this. It is only my own wishes,

interests, and needs that matter; none of the people who are important to me must have any interests, wishes, needs different from mine,
and if they have any at all, they must subordinate theirs to mine
without any resentment or strain; in fact, it must be their pleasure and
their enjoyment to fit in with my wishes. If this happens I shall be
good, pleased, and happy, but that is all. If this does not happen, it
will be horrifying both for the world and for me.'

If we bear in mind that the ongoing harmonious relationship in
this phase between subject and object or expanse is as important as
the ongoing supply of air, we understand that loud, vehement, and
aggressive symptoms appear when the harmony between the subject
and its primary object or substance is disturbed. This primary
relationship is so important to the subject that he cannot tolerate
any interference with it from outside, and if anything contrary to
his needs or wishes happens, he simply must resort to desperate
methods.

How does hatred enter into this relationship? Hatred is the per-
petuation of the unconditional dependence on primary love, with the
one difference that its sign has been changed into negative. As I
pointed out in my paper 'On Love and Hate' (1951), to liberate the
individual from the fixation to his hate, the cooperation of his
environment is indispensable, internal changes only are hardly ever
sufficient. In rare cases external events may by chance provide the
required changes in the environment, but conditions for this are so
exacting that the probability is very small indeed. The only situation
in which the environment can be expected to comply intentionally
and systematically with these exacting requirements is the analytic
situation, especially during the phase of 'new beginning'. If the
analyst succeeds in responding in the right way to the primitive,
unrealistic wishes, the patient may be helped to reduce the oppressive
inequality between himself and his object. With the waning of this
inequality, the patient's dependence on his primary object, which
was re-enacted in the new beginning phase of the analytic process,
may decrease considerably, or even disappear altogether. When the
inequality, and with it the dependence, has been reduced, there will
be no more need for any defence against them; hatred can then be
largely given up, and with it the intensity of the aggressive, destructive urges.

If my theory is correct, then we must expect to come across all

71

these three types of object relationships – *the most primitive harmonious interpenetrating mix-up, the ocnophilic clinging to objects, and the philobatic preference for objectless expanses* – in every analytic treatment that is allowed to regress beyond a certain point. In fact, I arrived at my theory the other way round, through observing in my analytic practice these three types of relationship to me and to the environment in general, and then building up my theory from these observations.

Where is the place of narcissism in this theory? In my opinion *all narcissism is secondary* to the most primitive of these relationships, that of the harmonious interpenetrating mix-up; its immediate cause is always a disturbance between the individual and his environment; this leads to frustration as a consequence of which the individual comes to differentiate what was until then the harmonious fusion of self and environment, withdraws part of his cathexis from the environment, and invests it in his developing ego.

Chapter 13

Adult love

In 'On Narcissism' Freud wrote: '. . . the aim and the satisfaction in a narcissistic object-choice is to be loved' (Standard Edition, XIV, 98.) Of course this is another impeccable clinical observation but somewhat of a theoretical *non sequitur*. Narcissistic object-choice means that the subject takes himself, or somebody representing or deriving from himself, as a love-object, but it does not follow necessarily from the theory of narcissism that he should desire to be loved by others. On the contrary, as he has withdrawn his libido from the external world – or alternatively has not yet cathected it – and thus only himself or somebody representing him can matter at all, one would expect that the rest of his environment would be more or less indifferent to him. Evidently this is another of the internal contradictions inherent in the theory of primary narcissism.

All the clinical literature on narcissism – that is, secondary narcissism – shows this same picture of excellent, easily verifiable observations which fit uncomfortably into the Procrustean bed of primary narcissism. Annie Reich (1953), for instance, says that objects at the pre-genital sexual level are 'selfishly' used for one's own gratification; their interest cannot yet be considered, and 'whether we define such behaviour as fixated on pre-genital levels, or as object relationship, or as narcissistic, is a question of terminology'. She adds: 'At these early levels passive attitudes are more frequently found than an active reaching out for an object' (pp. 22–24).

I think it is rather doubtful whether any logical connections are to be found between the wish to be loved passively, the use of objects 'selfishly', inability to be concerned with their interests, the prevalence of passive expectant attitudes over actively reaching out for satisfactions, and the theory of primary narcissism, which states that all the libido is concentrated either in the ego or in the id – or in the self.

Equally, we do not understand why it does not matter for our

73

theory whether we describe these clinical observations as fixations to pre-genital levels, as object relationship, or as narcissism, and why all this should be merely a question of terminology. Instead of the last phrase I would repeat that all this is a natural consequence of using a 'suitcase theory', such as the theory of primary narcissism. Before setting out on a journey one has to decide what will be needed on it and pack the cases accordingly. Should it turn out that one needs something else, one must buy it *en route* – there is no other solution.

All these observations fit well into the theory of primary love; in fact they can be predicted from it and thus may be considered as confirmatory evidence. 'Passive attitudes' and the need to be loved are an integral part of a relationship to a primary object, as are the 'selfish' form of love and the inability to be concerned about the object's interests or well-being. As I have pointed out several times, in all three forms of primitive relationship – the harmonious inter-penetrating mix-up, ocnophilia, and philobatism – one demands to be allowed to take one's objects, or environment, for granted; they simply cannot have any interest of their own; their only concern must be the preservation of the harmony – whatever the cost to them.

The ultimate aim of all libidinal striving is thus the preservation or restoration of the original harmony. May I again quote Annie Reich, who describes the feeling of ecstasy accompanying the orgasm in these words: 'In this state it was as though the woman's indivi-duality had ceased to exist, she felt herself thrown together with the man' (op. cit., p. 27). She compares this *unio mystica* with what Freud called the oceanic feeling – 'the flowing together of self and world of self and primary object, it has to do with a temporary relinquish-ment of the separating boundaries' (op. cit., p. 27). May I repeat that this clinical observation too had to be packed separately into the suitcase theory of primary narcissism but is a natural consequence of the theory of primary love.

This *unio mystica*, the re-establishment of the harmonious inter-penetrating mix-up, between the individual and the most important parts of his environment, his love objects, is the desire of all humanity. To achieve it, an indifferent or possibly hostile object must be changed into a cooperative partner by, what I have called, the work of conquest (1948). This induces the object, now turned into a

74

partner, to tolerate being taken for granted for a brief period, that is, to have only identical interests. Individuals vary greatly in the skills required for this 'conquest' and, in consequence, not every one is capable of achieving periodically an orgasm or, for that matter, a harmonious partnership. Still this is the most common way to re-establish the primary harmonious mix-up.

In adult life there are a few more possibilities for achieving this ultimate aim, all of them requiring considerable skills and talents. These comprise religious ecstasy, the sublime moments of artistic creation, and lastly, though perhaps more for patients, certain regressive periods during analytic treatment. Although in all these states the individual is on his own, creating the impression of narcissistic withdrawal, all of them have in common the fundamental characteristic that for these very brief moments the individual may truly and really experience that every disharmony has been dispelled, he and his whole world are now united in undisturbed understanding, in completely harmonious interpenetrating mix-up.

SUMMARY

1. Freud proposed, equally categorically, three theories about the individual's most primitive relationship with his environment. These are primary object relationship, primary auto-erotism, primary narcissism. Although these three theories contradict each other, Freud never discussed this fact in print.
2. He attempted instead a synthesis of these three theories in favour of primary narcissism. Auto-erotism was described as the satisfaction characteristic of the phase of primary narcissism, while any type of object relationship, no matter whether of the anaclitic or narcissistic type, was considered as secondary. This theoretical construction contains several inherent contradictions, none of them recognized by Freud. In recent years they were pointed out in particular by Hartmann, Kris, and Loewenstein, who also proposed a new terminology which, though solving some of the old problems, seems to create new ones.
3. Re-examining the arguments used by Freud, and after him by the analytical literature, to make the existence of primary narcissism acceptable, it is found that they prove only the existence of secondary narcissism. The only two exceptions that could not be explained

purely on the basis of secondary narcissism were the regressive states in schizophrenia and during sleep; but even in these two cases it appeared that the regression is to a primitive form of relationship rather than to primary narcissism.

4. Since clinical observations seemed unable to provide a safe enough basis for the acceptance of the theory of primary narcissism, analytic theory resorted to antedating it to the period of foetal life. A close scrutiny of the available data suggested that the theory of primary narcissism, although compatible with, does not follow necessarily from, these observations. A theory of primary love is proposed which seems to accord better with the observed facts.

5. Using this theory, a number of clinical observations can be better understood and integrated with each other to form a suggestive argument for its validity. These observations include: experience with schizophrenics, with alcoholics, with 'narcissistic' patients, and the various modifications of technique proposed by several authors to enable the patient to establish a therapeutically effective relationship in the analytic situation.

6. Last, the examination of man's erotic life provides some further support for the theory of primary love.

PART III

The gulf and the analyst's responses to it

Chapter 14

Regression and the child in the patient

Analysts, as a rule, tolerate communications in the therapeutic situation in addition to those expressed in words. This 'tolerant' policy leads to certain consequences. Perhaps the most important of them is that it opens the door to acting-out, which is tantamount to regression, for words are always a more adult form of communication than action or even gesture.

In a way, the process of maturation and civilization amounts to moving less and less physical mass, i.e. using less and less muscular energy, for the expression of the same idea, effect, or message. That means that as fewer and fewer muscles are involved, the movements become finer and subtler. Of all the skeletal muscles perhaps the speech muscles have the smallest mass and are the subtlest and finest; consequently, moving them uses less energy than moving any other. The maturation process, however, does not stop here. The child, or the primitive, first substitutes shouting or screaming in place of acting, then he learns to shout and scream less, i.e. to express the same intensity of emotion by using smaller amounts of physical mass and muscular energy. The reward for this restraint and discipline is an ever increasing subtlety and richness of expression involving the conscious and preconscious mental life. It is thinkable that it may extend beyond it into the unconscious; this would be another instance of what Freud called the education of the instincts.

It is in the nature of the analytical situation to reverse, to some extent, these processes of maturation and civilization. Instead of subtly adumbrating or implying, the patient learns to state explicitly and often with primitive intensity what he thinks and feels; soon he realizes that detached factual descriptions are not sufficient, their concomitant emotions will have to be expressed as well. He then proceeds to vary the intensity and pitch of his voice, to use gestures or movements; he may even be carried away by his emotions, and so he comes to act-out in the transference, or in the analytical situation.

All this inevitably amounts to giving way to a regressive trend involving both the patient and his analyst. What will happen now depends on the analyst's responses. Of course, every analyst will try to understand what the patient tries to convey to him by the acting-out; but in order to influence the acting-out the analyst must communicate – i.e. express – his understanding of it in some way. However, his individual way of expressing his understanding or, as I like to call it, his habitual responses to the patient's 'acting-out', 'behaving', or 'repeating', may vary greatly, and all such variations, whether used consistently or not, will influence considerably the 'atmosphere' in the analyst's consulting room.

The first analyst who described the atmosphere created by his consistent 'responses' was, of course, Freud, who likened it to the reflection by a well-polished mirror. This means – if taken literally – that the analyst does not bring any alien material into the analytic work, he only *reflects* without distortion what originates from the patient. This can happen only – though this has never been explicitly stated – if the material produced by the patient consists almost exclusively of words and, *a fortiori*, the analyst's contributions to the developing situation also consist exclusively of words. All these words coming from the patient as well as from his analyst are used and mutually understood in the conventional adult way. In fact, in the case histories published by Freud, I could not find an interpretation of any non-verbal material produced by a patient, though as early as in the *Studies on Hysteria* (1895) he recorded observations of non-verbal phenomena. Knowing how mercilessly accurate Freud's reports about his clinical work are, this self-imposed restriction appears self-evident. A mirror reflects an image but does not change its nature; words, therefore, may be reflected by words, but the translation of non-verbal material into words would go beyond the function of mirror-like analytic work.

Gradually we have learned to understand and to use not only the verbal material produced by our patients, but also what I call the 'atmosphere', created partly by words, partly by the patient's manner of using them, and partly by all that is called 'acting-out', 'behaving', or 'repetition' in the analytic situation. This latter group, as I have just pointed out, always has an aspect of regression.

Clinically this means that phenomena suggesting regression will be observed from time to time during any analytic treatment. There are, however, widely differing views among analysts about the frequency, the meaning, and the importance of these phenomena. Views vary also about the extent to which these phenomena are caused by the patient, that is, by his personality, by the nature and severity of his illness, or by the analyst's individual technique. In my opinion, both analyst and patient have their share in it but it is not easy to disentangle how much is due to whom. Any description singling out exclusively one partner's share will probably be faulty from the start. But even if one is aware of this pitfall, it must be expected that every description will be coloured by the personal bias of its author, in particular by his ordinary experiences which, at any rate partly, are determined by his individual technique. My description will be no exception to this rule.

Of course, the contributions of neither partner are fully verbalized during the treatment – or, for that matter, in scientific discussions – though the scales are definitely weighted. On the whole, it is the patient who is gradually made to express his non-verbal contributions – among them his regressive propensities – in words, thus 'changing his repetition into recollection'; whereas the analyst is, as a rule, under no such pressure. His professional behaviour, i.e. the details of his technique, are felt to be so well standardized that they appear to him 'natural', sensible and scientifically justified, so much so that in 'normal', smoothly proceeding, cases he will not feel any need to change his 'repetition into recollection' by expressing his habitual behaviour in the therapeutic situation in words, so that it may be subjected to a searching scrutiny. In many respects this policy is sensible and realistic – if for no other reasons than those of mental economy. The analyst can further reassure himself that his behaviour had passed a searching scrutiny of this kind in the past, during his training. It is in this way that analysts arrive at the idea of 'classical' or 'proper' technique – as the case may be.

Let us follow, though only for a short while, this example and start with the patients' contributions. Patients differ considerably as regards regression. On the whole, one may differentiate two extreme types among them, of course with a number of intermediate grades. With one extreme type quite satisfactory therapeutic results can be achieved without much regression beyond the Oedipal level. With the other, for quite a while, hardly any real, stable, results can be obtained, merely what is called short-lived transference improvements;

81

real therapeutic results occur only after a period of regression, which may be short or long but is always more primitive in nature than the well-known phenomena belonging to the Oedipal level.[1]

Let us turn now to the analyst's responses which, as just discussed, are an important part of his contribution to the developing 'atmosphere'. Good examples of possible variations are the analyst's responses to a patient's request to prolong the analytic session. The

[1] One possible theoretical explanation of these differences uses the idea of trauma. According to it the individual had developed more or less normally up to the point when he was struck by a trauma. From that point on his further development has been fundamentally influenced by the method he developed at the time for coping with the effects of that particular trauma – his basic fault. The trauma itself, of course, is not necessarily a single event; on the contrary, usually it amounts to a situation of some duration caused by a painful misunderstanding – lack of 'fit' – between the individual and his environment. As a rule, the individual is a child and his environment consists of the world of his adults.

True, despite the general lack of 'fit', in some cases some adult, or even adults, may be on the child's side, but much more often than not the immature and weak individual has to cope on his own with the traumatic situation; either no help is available to him, or only help of a kind that is hardly more than a continuation of the misunderstanding, and is thus useless to him.

Thus it comes about that the individual is made to adopt his own method for coping with the trauma, a method hit upon in his despair or thrown at him by some un-understanding adult who may be a well-wisher, or just indifferent, negligent, or even careless or hostile. As I have just said, the individual's further development will then be either prescribed or, at any rate limited, by this method which, though helpful in certain respects, is invariably costly and, above all, alien. Still, it will be incorporated in his ego structure – as his basic fault – and anything beyond or contrary to these methods will strike him as a frightening and more or less impossible proposition.

The task of analytic treatment consists then in dealing with the fears obstructing the way to re-adaptation – called 'fixations' – and of enabling the patient to broaden his potentialities and develop new methods for coping with his difficulties. The result of this undertaking, of course, depends also at what point the trauma struck the individual and how far the method chosen at the time is compatible with the development of any form of 'genital love'. In some cases of treatment it is apparently necessary to go back to the pre-traumatic period, to enable the patient to relive the trauma itself in order that he may mobilize his 'fixated' libido and find new possibilities for dealing with the problems involved. If the trauma happened at a comparatively late stage of his development, the point to which the treatment has to go back will already be in the area of the Oedipal level, and thus no regression beyond this will be needed, and possibly still less observable in the analytic situation. On the other hand, if the trauma struck the patient at a point beyond the Oedipal area, it is likely that considerable regression must take place and will be observed.

traditional length is fifty minutes[1] and as a rule the analyst has five to ten minutes free before subsequent sessions. In principle, shall one, or shall one not, agree to a patient's request to be allowed to stay occasionally five or ten minutes longer? Or shall one compensate him if he arrived five to ten minutes late? Disregarding the fact that the analyst's flexibility is also limited by external circumstances (the next patient may already be waiting; on the other hand, the analyst may happen to have a free session following his patient's and the patient for some reason or other has, or has not, got a knowledge of this fact, etc.), should he agree to an extension of the session at all and, if so, what criteria should he use to determine whether an extension is advisable or not?

A still more difficult form of the same problem arises when the request is for an extra session during the week-end, after a day's work, or even during the analyst's holiday. I think it is irrefutable that, in whatever way he responds, it will be not only the patient but also the analyst who contributed to creating an 'atmosphere' in the analytic treatment. Anna Freud's often-quoted patient who was allowed to ring up the analyst any time during the day or even the week-end is a convincing proof that acceptance and gratification of some regressive tendencies, or of acting-out, is not altogether incompatible with 'classical' technique; in other words, is not an irreversible parameter.

The instances just described are rather gross samples of the analyst's responses to a patient's regressed acting out; I chose them since, because of their simple structure, they could be easily discussed. Although it is more difficult to demonstrate, it is certain that there are innumerable ways in which the analyst may respond to his patient's subtle forms of regression. His response may amount to indifference, disapproval, or perhaps only to some slight sign of annoyance; he may tolerate the acting out, but follow it immediately with a correct and timely interpretation which, in turn, will take the patient some steps further towards learning the analyst's language and will inhibit further acting-out; he may sympathetically permit it as a kind of safety valve; or he may take it in his stride, as a matter of course, feeling no more, or for that matter no less, need for interpretation, i.e. for interfering with the acting out, than with any other

[1] When I started practising psychoanalysis, in the early twenties, it used to be fifty-five minutes.

form of communication, say, verbal associations. Evidently it is only in this last case that acting-out and verbal associations are equally accepted as communications addressed to the therapist.

The analyst may accept his patient's needs to regress only as understandable communications, as fantasies, which in all other respects are completely unrealistic; consequently the analyst's response – explicit or implicit – will mean that any gratification of such needs would be incompatible with the analytic situation. A somewhat different way would be to accept them as justifiable within the analytic situation. And lastly, it is also possible not only to accept some of these needs as fully justified, but also to gratify them – as far as the gratification is compatible with the analytic situation. It was exactly this that happened in Anna Freud's case, quoted above.

Of course, all these responses contribute – each in its way – to the developing 'atmosphere' of the treatment. Some responses open widely the door to regression, others offer only a narrow opening, and still others try to prevent it. Thus regression during analytic treatment depends not only on the patient but also on his analyst. In Chapters 16–18 we shall return to examine some of the 'standardized' responses and their consequences in detail. But before doing so I will describe the inevitable consequences of regression which is allowed to go beyond the Oedipal level.

As we have just observed, under the influence of the psychoanalytic setting all patients without exception regress to a point; that is, they become childish and experience intense primitive emotions in relation to the analyst; all this, of course, is a constant part of what is generally called transference.

The impact of these highly charged emotions brings about a curious inequality in the relationship between analyst and patient. The analyst is felt as a powerful, vitally important person, but only so far as he is able or willing to gratify, or to frustrate, his patient's expectations, hopes, desires, and needs; beyond this sphere the analyst, as an everyday, real person, hardly exists. Of course, the patient has all sorts of fantasies about his analyst but these, as a rule, have more to do with the patient's inner world than with the analyst's real life and real personality. Although in comparison with the analyst the patient usually experiences himself as weak and far less important, it is only he (the patient) who matters, and matters enormously; it is exclusively his wishes, urges, and needs that must be attended to, and it is his interests that must be the focus of attention all the time.

This pattern is general; though there are no exceptions to it, its intensity and duration vary with individual patients. Some patients do not go beyond a certain point; the therapeutic processes initiated in this way are effective enough to bring about sufficient readjustment; and after a time the patient spontaneously emerges from this primitive two-person relationship and is cured. With other patients, however, additional processes take place over and above those just described.

In Part I, I surveyed at some length these processes as they may be observed by the therapist. Here I shall enumerate only the most important of these observations: words lose their reliability as agreed means of communication between patient and analyst; interpretations, in particular, tend to be experienced by the patient either as signs of hostility and aggressiveness, or of affection. Patients begin to know too much about their analysts; it is fairly common that they are more aware of their analyst's moods than of their own; in parallel their interest becomes apparently more and more detached from their own problems and sufferings, which originally prompted them to seek analytic help, and gets centred more and more on divining the analyst's 'real motives' for saying this, for behaving that way, or having a particular 'mood'. All this absorbs a considerable amount of libido and this is perhaps the reason why patients in this state apparently lose a good deal of their drive to get better, of their wish, and even their ability, to change. Parallel with this, their expectations from the analyst grow out of proportion to anything realistic, both in a positive sense, in the form of sympathy, understanding, attention, small gifts, and other signs of affection, and in a negative sense, in the form of fierce attacks, merciless retaliation, ice-cold indifference, and extreme cruelty. To condense this situation into one sentence, one might say that the importance of the past is well-nigh lost for the patient; only the analytic present matters.

In customary analytic terms all this would be described as an exacerbation of the transference neurosis or transference love which has taken full command of the therapeutic situation and, in fact, has become so intense that it is now impervious to ordinary interpretations. Some analysts think that this development is caused by the patient's paranoid, persecutory fantasies invading the transference. In my opinion all these descriptions are too weak, and so miss the real issue (1958).

It is well known that even the most skilled and experienced analysts among us at times have difficulties with some of our patients, and even occasional failures. However unpleasant, it must be accepted that there are no exceptions to this rule. My contention is that the great majority of difficulties and failures arise in the treatment of patients who exhibit the signs just described. These patients are usually characterized as 'deeply disturbed', 'profoundly split', 'seriously schizoid or paranoid', 'suffering from a deep narcissistic wound', 'having a much too weak or immature ego', and so on; all these descriptions imply that with these patients the root of their trouble goes further or deeper than the Oedipus complex, our usual concern with the average patient.

In order to get a better understanding of some of the difficulties encountered in our therapeutic work with this class of patient, I proposed in Part I to consider the human mind – or perhaps only that part of it which is called the ego – as consisting of three areas, that of the Oedipus complex, that of the basic fault and that of creation. Each area is characterized by a specific form of the mental force operating in it, and lastly, by a specific level of the mental processes. To recapitulate briefly:

In the area of the Oedipus complex the characteristic structure is a triangular relationship, consisting of the subject and two objects; the characteristic force is that originating from a conflict, and the level of mental processes is that which corresponds to, and can adequately be expressed by, conventional, adult language.

In the area of the basic fault the prevalent structure is an exclusively two-person relationship, more primitive than those obtaining between adults. The form of mental force is not that of a conflict; what the form is will be discussed later in Parts IV and V. However, already here I can mention that under certain conditions the force operating at this level creates addiction-like states, and is then habitually described in our literature as greed. The level of mental processes, in particular as they appear in the therapeutic situation, is denoted by such terms as 'pre-Oedipal', 'pre-genital', 'pre-verbal', etc. In Chapter 4, I discussed in detail the reasons why I believe these terms to be misleading and why I proposed to call it the level of the basic fault.

86

And lastly we have the the area of creation, characterized by the absence of any outside object. As our analytical method is based on transference, i.e. inseparably linked to the presence of at least one outside object in addition to the subject, we have no direct access to the study either of the level of mental processes in this area or of the form of forces operating in it. Nevertheless, processes happening in this area are of great technical importance to us, as instanced – among many other examples – by the problems created by a silent patient.

Thus one may expect to encounter three different sets of therapeutic processes in the mind, and possibly expect also that analysts may need three different sets of technical measures, each directed so that it should influence the corresponding area of the mind. Moreover, as the analytic situation is an essentially two-person relationship, with many qualities that are definitely more primitive than those belonging to the Oedipal level, one would also expect that our theoretical knowledge relating to the area of the basic fault, and our technical methods for dealing with the problems encountered in it, would be in a far better developed and far more securely founded state than anything pertaining to the two other areas.

Of course, exactly the opposite is the case. Almost the whole of our theory pertains to mental structures and processes belonging to the Oedipal level, and what is called the 'classical' analytic technique – doubtless the best founded variety of all analytic techniques – deals almost exclusively with problems that have a dynamic structure activated by some conflict, or conflicts, and can be expressed without much difficulty in conventional language, i.e. with problems belonging to the Oedipal area.

To demonstrate the nature of the difference between technical problems arising from the Oedipal area and those arising from the area of the basic fault, let us review the phenomena of regression from yet another angle. It is one of the earliest clinical observations that at some point or other during analytic treatment patients cease to be willing to cooperate. This may take the form of a refusal to move, to change, of an apparently complete inability to accept any adverse external condition or to bear any increase of tension. If the period of non-cooperativeness is limited, it is said to be due to a passing resistance or to 'splitting', but if it is lasting, to prevalence of schizoid-paranoid mechanisms. Another class of interpretation

87

attributes these states to an insoluble resentment against the mother, and her later representatives, for not giving the patient the affection, sympathy, and understanding that he should have had.

Though it has always been accepted that there is an uncooperative part in every patient, there has been little discussion on what decides how much or how little of a particular patient cooperates in a particular analytic situation at a given period. In severe cases of regression the patient seems to be unable to apprehend what is expected from him, e.g. compliance with our 'fundamental rule'; at such times it is practically useless to try to remind him of his original complaints that prompted him to seek analytic help since he has become exclusively preoccupied with his relationship to his analyst, the gratifications and frustrations that he may expect from it; all sense for continuing with the analytic work seems to have been lost. When it is realized that this kind of transference, absorbing nearly all the libido of the patient, has the structure of an exclusively two-person relationship – in contrast to the 'normal' Oedipal trans-ference, which is definitely triangular – one recognizes it as yet another diagnostic sign that the patient has reached the area of the basic fault.

This leads us directly to our main topic, namely, how to enable an uncooperative part of an individual to cooperate, that is, to receive analytic help. What I mean here is something different from resolving resistances, i.e. conflicts, at the Oedipal level, or from undoing a 'split' – it is something more akin to stimulating, or perhaps even to creating, a new willingness in the patient to accept reality and to live in it, a kind of reduction of his resentment, lifelessness, etc., which appear in his transference neurosis as obstinacy, awkwardness, stupidity, hypercriticism, touchiness, greed, extreme dependence, and so on.

It was in order to explain this utterly different clinical impression that I assumed that there was something to be called the basic fault, which is not a complex, nor a conflict, nor a split, but is a fault in the basic structure of the personality, something akin to a defect or a scar. Most patients, of course, cannot tell us what causes their resentment, lifelessness, dependence, i.e. what the fault or defect in them is. Some, however, are capable of expressing it by its opposite, i.e. by fantasies about a perfect partner, or of perfect harmony with their whole environment, perfect untroubled happiness, perfect

88

contentment with themselves and with their world, and so on. In the most frequent form, however, the patient repeats over and over again that he has been let down, that nothing in the world can ever be worth while unless something that was taken away or withheld from him – usually something unattainable in the present – is restored to him, and in severe cases even says that life is not worth living without his loss being made fully good, and he behaves as if this were really true.

I wish to illustrate this kind of atmosphere by two dreams experienced by a patient during the same night.[1] (1) She was walking in a wood; suddenly a large flesh-coloured bird swooped down, hit her violently, and made a gash in her forehead. Patient was stunned and fell to the ground unconscious. The terrible thing was that the bird never looked back; it was quite unconcerned about what it had done. (2) Patient was then in a room with a number of friends who were playing games which she used to share with them. Nobody took any notice of her. The terrible thing was that she was alone for ever because she would never be able to get over the thought that the bird did not look round. It should be added that many dreams of this pattern were brought during a particular period.

In another pattern the patient repeats endlessly that he knows he ought to cooperate, but he must get better or even quite well before he can do anything about it. At the same time he is fully aware of the reality situation, namely, that improvement is impossible without his cooperation; this insight, however, only exacerbates the despair in him. This vicious circle – in the patient's sincere conviction – can be broken only if either something that has gone wrong is replaced in him, or if he can get hold of something in him which he had had at one time but has since lost.

Sophisticated patients – and analysts – may express this something irretrievably lost or gone wrong as the penis or the breast, usually felt to possess magical qualities, and speak of penis or breast envy, of castration fear; Jones's (1927) concept of aphanisis belongs here, as do Melanie Klein's (1957) ideas about inborn jealousy and envy; however, in nearly all cases all this is coupled with an unquenchable and incontestable feeling that, if the loss cannot be made good, the patient himself will remain no good and had better go mad or even die.

[1] I am indebted to my wife for this clinical material.

89

The gulf and the analyst's responses to it

All the phenomena of regression, as observed in the analytical situation, strike one irresistibly as primitive, reminiscent of early childish behaviour; a strong argument for the thesis that any neurosis or psychosis possesses necessarily some infantile features and that any psychotherapist must always be aware that he will have to deal — in one way or another — with 'the child in his patient'.

We know that there are fairly great difficulties when 'the child in our patient' is of the age of the Oedipus conflict. But the gulf separating us adults from 'the child in our patient' of the age of the basic fault — the 'infant' in the true sense of the word, i.e. one who cannot speak, at any rate, the language of adults — is considerably deeper and wider than anything encountered at the Oedipal level where, after all, everyone is using agreed conventional language. In spite of this increased difficulty, the gulf separating patient and analyst must be bridged if the therapeutic work is to continue. It must be realized, however, that the patient — that is, 'the child in the patient' of the age of the basic fault — is unable to bridge the gulf on his own. The great technical question is, how to bridge this gulf? Which part of this task should be undertaken by the analyst and which should be left to the patient?

To avoid a possible misunderstanding, I wish to emphasize that in what follows I shall discuss the technical problems encountered with patients regressed to the level of the basic fault. It is probable that this is only one type of the so-called 'deep' regressions. I think that a closer analytic study of truly schizophrenic patients — but not that of 'schizoid characters' — may possibly reveal characteristics which will differentiate 'schizophrenic' regression from the form with which we are concerned here.

Analysts, of course, have long recognized these two technical problems — the task of bridging the gulf separating us adults from 'the child in the patient' and overcoming the patient's inability to accept reality and to cooperate in the therapeutic work — and have developed various methods for coping with them. What is not emphasized sufficiently in the literature on this topic is that there are several hazards that threaten a therapist who is trying to bridge the gulf separating him from a regressed patient, especially when the regression has reached the area of the basic fault; and that all the hazards are caused by his responses to phenomena belonging to this area.

90

My plan is to discuss in Chapter 15 the general influence of language on the analytical situation and then to devote Chapters 16–18 to a description of some of the 'standardized' responses to a regressed patient, and their consequences. This will be followed, in Parts IV and V, by a discussion of my clinical experiences with regressed patients and of the techniques that I have found useful in these situations.

Chapter 15

The problem of language in upbringing and in psychoanalytic treatment

The most general, but not always fully recognized, difficulty is caused by the analyst's continued use of his customary language as a vehicle for his responses to a regressed patient. This, of course, is only a special case of the problem of language in the analytic situation. There is no question but that any Englishman or any American will analyse an English-speaking patient in English and that patient and analyst will understand each other. Admittedly, the analyst will use with each patient a somewhat different set of words, phrases, and clichés; on the whole, however, most of these 'dialects' will be mutually intelligible. On the other hand, they certainly will *not* be intelligible to a Frenchman or a German; they must be translated first.

Obviously, this does not mean that English, or for that matter German or French, are superior, but it means that they are *different* languages. The reason for this difference is historical: Englishmen, Frenchmen, and Germans in their early formative stages learnt different languages from *their parents*.

On the whole, most things, objects, relationships, emotions, and so on, can be expressed equally well in the various languages. I would emphasize that most of them can, because I want to add that some of them can *not*. This is particularly true of emotionally highly-charged communications. Good examples of this kind are lyric poetry or words sung to music; to translate any of these is an almost impossible task; as is well known, operas are preferably sung in their original language. My favourite explanation of this difficulty uses the idea of the 'cluster of associations' that surrounds each word and is different in every language, different even in varying human relationships using the same language. Obvious examples are the almost secret languages of the various trades or professions; slang used by people who were together at the same school, in the same unit of the Army, in a certain prison, or by those trained in the same Analytical Institute. Another convincing example is the difficulty of finding an exact definition, especially in psychology. An exact definition aims at stripping the words used of all their undesirable or unwanted associations, a task which only very seldom succeeds.

As experience shows, potentially every child, every patient – or every candidate – can learn any language; which language he actually *will* learn depends on his parents, his therapist – or on his training analyst. It is not his choice; *in fact, he has no choice whatever*; he must learn the language of his environment.

This is a fact of paramount importance for our analytic practice and theory; patients (and candidates) must learn, and in fact do learn, the language of their analysts. True, all the time the analyst also learns from every one of his patients, but this learning, though highly important, is very limited indeed by comparison with what an accommodating parent may learn from his child. Although this learning may amount to a good deal, the fact is that if the parent is English, the resulting language will inevitably be English, and never, say, Hungarian or Chinese. This means that the child will be able to express with ease only such feelings, thoughts, experiences as are commonly experienced by his parents, and to the expression of which the English language lends itself; but never those which, though absent in English, might be easily expressed by a Hungarian or a Chinese child in his mother tongue – and vice versa.

This simple fact has been, I would say, systematically repressed in our theoretical considerations. As a rule, the patients' associations are paraded as proofs for the correctness of their analysts' ideas. Once and for all we have to recognize the fact that the first wish of a patient is to be understood, and so he must speak a language understandable to his analyst, which means one of the dialects of the analyst's individual language. Moreover, in the same way as an English parent will never question the wisdom of speaking English to his child, so every analyst will automatically use his individual – or group – language with his patients; nothing can be more natural to him than this.

Thus every analyst develops an analytic language that remains in its essential structure the same, although it changes and grows in order to become richer, more exact, more expressive, more efficient, and more easily intelligible – to everyone who has learnt it. On the other hand, it always strikes anyone else as strange and irritating. What we must never forget, however, is that the mere fact that people speak and understand it does not raise it to the rank of a universal language, however much those using it would like this to happen.

If we accept this as inevitable, what is there that we can do about it? For our theory the answer is a laborious programme; first, we have to compile for every one of the analytic languages a dictionary and a grammar, i.e. a collection, as complete as possible, of words and of the various possible connections among the words; when we then compare these various dictionaries and grammars, we will find that in every language there are numerous untranslatable words, phrases, and grammatical structures characteristic of that particular language; third, we can then compare the various languages in order to see which language is more suitable as a mode of expression for what. This, the most important piece of research, can be tackled only after the previous two tasks have reached a certain stage.

Moreover, all words have their own cluster of associations, some diffuse, some more concentrated, some vague, extended, and fluid, others rather condensed, almost solid, but all of them highly individual. It is hardly possible to find two absolutely identical words in two different languages. There are many examples of this lack of correspondence, so may I mention a few awkward technical terms of our own science to illustrate what I mean. The German *Besetzung* may mean in English 'occupation', 'charge', 'cathexis'; the German *Lust* and *Unlust* are simply untranslatable; the English 'pleasure' means something utterly different, while 'unpleasure' is a clumsy neologism; and the same is true of 'pleasurable' and 'unpleasurable'; German *Angst* may mean 'fear', 'anxiety', and even 'panic'. All these English words have their own clusters of associations largely different from their German counterpart. Conversely the English 'sentiment' has no equivalent whatever in German, and the English 'depressed' certainly means something quite different from its German linguistic equivalent *deprimiert*. The English 'skill' and 'thrill' have no real equivalents in any other European language known to me. Last, not least, the Germans have no 'mind', but the English feel uncomfortable if anyone, except a priest, reminds them that they have a 'soul'. In English we speak of the 'diseases of the mind'; the German equivalent, *Geisteskrankheiten* means 'diseases of the spirit'.

Selbstgefühl and *Selbstbewusst*, though quite simple concepts in German, have no equivalent in English because of their widely different clusters of associations in the two languages. *Selbstbewusst* denotes one who is aware of his personal qualities, is realistically confident of his own ability; the English linguistic equivalent, 'self-conscious', means exactly the opposite. *Selbstgefühl*, literally 'the feeling of oneself', means – thanks to the ameliorating effect of its cluster – 'pride', 'manliness', 'dignity', 'confidence'. Analytic theory translated it by 'self-esteem' and thereby shifted its meaning considerably under the influence of the cluster surrounding the word 'esteem', which is quite different from that surrounding *Gefühl*, that is, 'feeling'.

I have to add that all my examples were taken from the correspondence between English and German; of course, any pair of languages will show similar problems – and the same is true about the languages of any two analytic schools.

Unfortunately – or fortunately – in free association not only the word matters but also, and in a highly important way, the whole of its cluster. Good examples of this are the technical terms mentioned above. Freud could never have developed his theory of *Besetzung* in English as there was no word available to express what he meant. As is well known, 'cathexis' was made to measure to fill the gap, but it is improbable that it will ever be a living word. The same is true, still more, about *Lust* and *Unlust*. On the other hand, our modern theory of 'depression' could develop only in English, in which this word covers a vague and widely extended field – in the same way as *Besetzung* or *Abwehr* does in German. The German *deprimiert* with its narrow and almost solid cluster of associations would have discouraged any such use right from the start.

Thus we shall need not only a vocabulary and a grammar for each of the analytic tongues, but also a collection of the clusters of associations surrounding each word. This will perhaps be the most difficult task; even in linguistics, the corresponding branch, semantics, is still in its early stages, hardly beyond the phase of collecting curiosities. Still, this work has to be done.

In the meanwhile, I am afraid, all analytical languages must be accepted as peers; although obviously some of them are better developed, while others are as yet in a primitive and deficient state, and will perhaps never grow out of it. However, each of them expresses important details of analytic experience, and as long as we cannot translate confidently and reliably the communications expressed in one language into any of the others, we have to tolerate all of them.

At this point an argument usually arises. It states that Freud gave us a fairly good and efficient language, easily understood by every analyst; let us accept it as the standard 'classical' language of psychoanalysis, and demand that henceforth any reformer compiles a dictionary and a grammar showing up clearly at what point and in which way his language diverges from that of Freud. This proposition sounds highly reasonable, but I am afraid it is unacceptable. As I tried to show in Chapters 1–3, Freud's classical investigations did not go much beyond the nuclear complex, whereas all the 'modern' idioms try to describe findings related to the area of the basic fault. Consequently the various descriptions of clinical findings in the 'modern' analytical languages cannot be compared with Freud's 'classical' descriptions; we have no 'primus', only 'pares'. However unpleasant, this fact must be mutually accepted.

For our practice the consequences are equally important. True, the existence of different, mutually not always intelligible, analytical languages may be disregarded as long as the therapeutic work remains at the Oedipal level. Although – as just exemplified by the untranslatable words: *Angst*, *Besetzung*, *Lust*, 'depressed' – we may encounter some difficulties, they do not represent real technical problems. These emerge, however, immediately when our work with the patient goes beyond the area of the adult conventional language into the area of the basic fault. In this area the patient's non-verbal communications are just as important as his verbal associations, no matter whether we call them 'behaviour', 'acting-out', 'repetition', or 'creating an atmosphere', etc. As all these 'communications' are non-verbal, it is we analysts who must act as *interpreters* between the patient's conscious adult self and his unconscious urges. In other words, it is we who have to *translate*[1] for him his primitive behaviour into conventional adult language and thus enable him to appreciate

[1] In what follows I give a short recapitulation of some ideas developed in my book *Thrills and Regressions*, chiefly in Chapters 8 and 11 (Balint, M., 1959).

its significance. Moreover, as a rule we must act not only as interpreters, but also as *informers*. Even at the Oedipal level the patient
is not always aware, or at any rate hardly ever fully aware, of
what he has been doing in the analytic situation and, in particular,
of whether his behaviour was or was not 'acting-out' or 'repetition'.
At the level of the basic fault the patient's awareness is still more
unreliable and hazy.

In this situation our role is similar to that of a traveller visiting a
primitive tribe, the language of which has not yet been studied,
whose customs have not yet been witnessed, still less reported in
objective terms. It is the informer's job to call attention to the
relevant parts of the particular behaviour and to describe them
according to their importance in an intelligible language. This double
task – informer and interpreter – is inevitable, no matter whether
we intend to contribute to the advancement of science or merely to
help our patients.

The task of translating the meaning of the observed phenomena
into adult language – whether for scientific or for therapeutic
purposes – is based on the presence of an adult vocabulary and an
adult grammar that exist only at the Oedipal level. As far as we know,
the unconscious has no vocabulary in our sense; although words
exist in it, they are neither more nor less than any other object repre-
sentation, they do not yet possess the over-riding symbolic function
that they will acquire in adult language. They are mainly pictures,
images, sounds, which may without much ado change their meaning
or merge into each other – as they do, in fact, in dreams. It seems
that, in the unconscious, words have the same vagueness of contour
and colour as the images seen in a dream, a kind of grey in grey;
though cathected with a great deal of fleeting emotion and affect,
they are not suitable for use in a clearly defined, concise way, as will
be the case with them in adult language.

Our next question is to ask what is being done in practice with
these patients? On the whole, analysts behave like the mothers
described above. They seem to have no compunction whatsoever
about which language to choose; they speak their own tongue which,
in fact, is equivalent to their mother tongue, since it was that which
they learnt in their analytic childhood. In addition to being informers
and interpreters, they assume also the role of *teachers*, and, in consequence, their patients inevitably learn one of the various dialects of

their analyst's language. As mentioned already, there are several such languages, each psychoanalytic school having developed its own.

In what follows I shall describe some of these languages. My main concern will be to study in which way they help the analyst to respond to a regressed patient, and in turn impose limitations on his choice of responses. Lastly, I will try to show the hazards inherent in each kind of response.

Chapter 16

The classical technique and its limitations

Some analysts use the 'classical' language which goes back to Freud and which was based, in the first instance, on experiences belonging to the Oedipal level; these experiences were then expressed in a slightly modified common adult language. 'Pre-genital' experiences are by no means neglected or disregarded by these analysts but they are expressed in the same adult language, that is, they are raised to the Oedipal level.

Expressed in another way, these analysts may try to restrict their responses to the regression – foremost among them their interpretations – to those found so reliable when dealing with conflicts at the Oedipal level, hoping that by this cautious technique the patient will be pulled out of his regression and attracted again by the remnants of his interests that he had previously had, in triangular relationships of real life, in the various oral, anal, genital forms of sexuality, and so forth. What is overlooked by these cautious analysts is that, using this technique, they may force the patient either to remain at the Oedipal level during the whole of the treatment, or to return there speedily after very brief regressions into the other areas of the mind. In this technique most of the phenomena belonging to the area of the basic fault are possibly interpreted as symptoms of castration complex or penis envy. These interpretations will be correct to the extent to which they bring to light one of the over-determining factors but, since they neglect all those originating from the basic fault itself, in some cases they must prove therapeutically unhelpful. True, these therapists can achieve commendable results, but only with patients who have been carefully selected.

An excellent description of the possible variations inherent in the 'classical' psychoanalytical technique was given by R. Loewenstein at the 20th International Psycho-Analytic Congress in Paris (1958). A loyal adherent to the cause of 'classical technique', he skilfully demonstrated its great flexibility and its ability to adapt itself to widely varying therapeutic situations.

Like most of his close associates, he did not say much about its limitations, nor did he discuss what should be done with patients whose illness – wholly or partly – lies beyond the reach of classical technique. He quoted approvingly two important papers dealing with this problem. One by Edward Bibring (1954), who admitted that the needs of certain patients went in fact beyond what was compatible with the 'classical technique'; in their cases these needs might be met – perhaps even successfully – by some sort of psychotherapy, but this must *not* be called psychoanalysis. This is fair enough. The other paper is by K. Eissler (1953), who showed that 'classical technique', in fact any psychotherapeutic technique, can be thought of as determined by a number of 'parameters', such as: frequency of sessions, duration of each session, the condition that Freud called 'abstinence', the physical therapeutic situation: patient in the supine position and the analyst sitting out of his sight, the analyst's overall behaviour likened by Freud to a 'well-polished mirror', etc., etc. Eissler – correctly – pointed out that any of these parameters may be changed, unwittingly or intentionally, by the analyst, but he warned us, and Loewenstein concurred with him, that some changes were irreversible, i.e. once a change has been allowed to take place, the 'classical' psychoanalytic situation may not be retrieved.

If I understood Loewenstein correctly, he considered as his task to map out in his address the permissible, or perhaps merely the safe, changes beyond which it is inadvisable for an analyst to probe. I propose to turn the tables now and ask what are the consequences of this therapeutic attitude advocated by Loewenstein, Bibring, Eissler, and others. This is an immense problem, so I shall mention only three topics pertaining to it.

The first is, of course, selection, which is the operative clause of any limitation of therapeutic technique. If this latter is limited, certain patients must be rejected as incapable of benefiting from it. Loewenstein and all his associates – wisely – omit consistently to mention this unpleasant fact and so escape the task of inquiring into the criteria on the basis of which this painful selection is to be performed.

It may be taken for granted that, when selecting a patient, even analysts are led not only by conscious, explicitly stated, ideas and criteria, but also by some unconscious expectations. Thus it is perhaps not quite unfair to say that the foremost questions asked are concerned less with the patient's 'curability' than with his 'analysability'. To put it in different words, will this analysis be rewarding or unrewarding? With some malice one could even say that one of the questions asked is whether the patient is likely to bring satisfaction to his analyst. If in no other field, it seems very likely that something of this kind happens when candidates are selected for training. I have to add that this seems to happen in every school of thought, not only in that of 'classical' technique.

All this, of course, does not mean that selection is inherently wrong; almost certainly the opposite is true. What I wanted to emphasize is that any kind of technique and the criteria for selection are interdependent; they mutually determine each other. The neglect of this fundamental issue explains the relative futility of the recurring symposia on 'Analysability', especially in America (1960, 1963). Another possible cause for these repeated symposia may be the need felt by some analysts to justify their reluctance to accept patients with risky prognoses. It should be repeated that – provided the selection has been carefully done – the results achieved by using the classical analytic language are excellent.

Intimately connected with this problem is the question whose task it should be to devise the 'other', non-classical and yet dynamic, psychotherapies that might then be used in the case of patients declared unsuitable for 'classical analysis'. Should this task be surrendered to 'wild' analysts, to eclectics, to general psychiatrists – or perhaps to faith healers? It is well worth remembering that on one occasion in our past we did not hesitate at all to extend our scope well beyond the confines of 'classical' technique. This was the case of child analysis, for which new techniques had to be developed to meet a new therapeutic situation. Some parameters of child analysis differ fundamentally from those of 'classical techniques'. To mention one striking instance: during the treatment of a child of 3–4 years old, no analyst can avoid being called upon to help the child with his excretory function, an almost unthinkable situation with an adult patient, and surely, according to Eissler, one of the irreversible parameters. Despite such fundamental differences we did not surrender child analysis to, say, the educational psychologists, but shouldered the problem ourselves – with great benefit to the science of education, to

101

child psychology, to child psychiatry and, above all, to psychoanalysis itself. Since then child analysis has been a specialized study, but none the less an integral part of the body of psychoanalysis.

It will be an intriguing historical – and psychological – study to find out what prompted psychoanalytic opinion to adopt exactly the opposite attitude in the case of group therapy. Although Freud himself adumbrated some alloying of the pure gold of psychoanalysis in order to make it suitable for the psychotherapy of the broad masses, and although almost all of the pioneers of group therapy were trained psychoanalysts, we, as a body, refused to accept responsibility for its further development – in my opinion, to the detriment of everyone concerned, above all of our own science. It is others who are now gathering a rich harvest in this important field and we lost perhaps an irretrievable opportunity to obtain first-hand clinical observations in the psychodynamics of collectivities.

Let me ask now, why it is that a great number of analysts with rich and varied experience, like Loewenstein and his associates, think that going beyond the area so clearly and convincingly mapped out by him is inadvisable, even dangerous? I think my ideas give one answer – though evidently not the only one – to this question. The classical technique with all its permissible variations presupposes a relationship between patient and analyst that may be characterized as one belonging to the Oedipal level. Any variation is safe so long as it compels the relationship to remain at this level. Any technical measure going beyond Loewenstein's safe variants permits, or even provokes, another kind – or very likely other kinds – of therapeutic relationship to develop that has not yet been properly studied and thus involves both patient and analyst in some risks. On the other hand, we know for certain that relationships, other than that of the Oedipal level, do exist, and it is clear that some of them, under certain conditions, may be used for therapeutic purposes. To avoid misunderstanding, I wish to add that the relationships observed and studied during child analysis do not, in general, belong to those I have in mind; they are simplified variants of what I call the Oedipal relationship. Later we shall have to return to this statement.

Admittedly these, non-Oedipal, relationships may involve both patient and analyst in some risks. We even know something, not enough by far, about them. May I add that when Freud abandoned the cathartic-hypnotic technique and embarked on a technique out

102

of which psychoanalysis developed, he was taking risks – as we now know, very serious ones – the nature and extent of which were almost totally unknown to him. Surely it would have been safer for him not to start on this road; but would it have been wiser?

I know that one success does not justify undertaking further hazardous ventures. Moreover, by the law of probability it is not likely that another Freud could be found in our ranks. Still, shall we surrender this, admittedly hazardous, task to some other group of workers? Despite many well-founded warnings, my opinion is that we must not.

For what is this task? To study as many primitive, non-Oedipal relationships as possible in order to find out the factors that permit or stimulate their development; to define the conditions that must be adhered to if the analyst is to control them so that they may not develop into hazards; and, last but not least, to use them as vehicles for therapeutic interventions. I think that by the virtue of our training we analysts are the only group of research workers who can undertake this task, and certainly we would be the poorer if we were to shirk it.

Some people will say that if you venture into these uncharted lands, you may not find anything, and even if you do, it is doubtful whether it is worth risking our psychoanalysis for it. I am not so pessimistic. Pure gold has the remarkable quality of withstanding any fire and even of being purified by it. I do not see any reason why we should be afraid for the essential parts of our science; and should any of its minor frills burn away, being not of pure gold, the better for future generations.

Chapter 17

The hazards inherent in consistent interpretation

Other analysts, influenced by the ideas of Melanie Klein, have approached this problem with a totally different theoretical attitude. Although they were fully aware of the immense gulf separating the *child* in the patient from the *adult*, they felt that this difference did not go beyond the reach of conventional language. True, the difference between the psychology of the adult and that of a child is fundamental, but their scientific attitude implies that by judicious use of existing notions, and by creating some new ones, our adult language is capable of dealing even with the most primitive processes in the child's mind. Two further suppositions of this school are: (a) that in the early stages of mental development the importance of urges deriving from the hypothetical death instinct is immensely greater than in adult life, and (b) that practically all the phenomena observed in adults should be assumed to be present in some form in very early childhood, possibly in the first weeks of life. This, they claim, can be validated by direct observation of infants.

This school developed a most elaborate theory, and with it a language, as well as a technique of interpretation of its own. This new language is rather different from the commonly-used adult language. However, it must not be forgotten that Freud's original language was in many respects also different from the commonly used one; but by now most of his innovations have become accepted parts of educated speech, and this may happen also with this new language. Then there is a further important difference between Freud's language and that of this new school. While Freud's language was mainly concerned with experiences at the Oedipal level, this school has set itself the conscious task of devising standardized expressions for the description of experiences that are more primitive than those belonging to the Oedipal level.

Although these analysts assume that the regressed patient has given up relationship to real whole objects, and is capable only of relating to part objects, they use for the purpose of communicating with such patients conventional language, but mix it freely with nouns like breast, milk, contents or inside of the body, part-objects, etc., and verbs like stand for, split off, take in, incorporate, project, persecute, damage, etc. By the way, breast, milk, inside of the body, etc. started their careers as normal words, having an agreed conventional meaning, but in the course of time they have undergone a curious change, and their meaning has become at the same time extended and comprehensive – in my opinion, in consequence of their being applied to the description of phenomena belonging to the area of the basic fault.

By this constant stretching of semantics, these analysts offer, and often succeed in giving, names to things and experiences that did not have names before, and for that reason could not be expressed in words. For instance, it may have been breast or milk that the infant wanted, but he would not have known these words at that time and his emotional experiences could never have been as definite as implied by the adult conventional meaning of the words breast and milk, or damage.

Using their words in this manner, these analysts have developed a very characteristic, though somewhat peculiar, 'mad' language, which is described by many of their own patients in exactly these terms. In their publications we find patients being quoted as saying something like this: 'The analyst tries to force mad thoughts into the patient; the patient had never had such disturbing and mad ideas before coming to analysis'; or after a 'deep' interpretation by the analyst, the patient may reply: 'The interpretation made the analyst appear to be mad and the analysis dangerous, because now the patient feels that the analyst was forcing his own mad thoughts into the patient in the same way as, according to the analyst's reconstruction, the patient's mother had forced her bad milk coming from her destroyed breast into him.'

These descriptions in isolation may appear exaggerated and unfair, but they occur time and again in the form quoted above in the printed publications. It must be added, however, that the attitude described here is reminiscent of the attitude of some children who find the conversation of adults 'mad' because it is unintelligible to

105

them, and at the same time feel any firm attempt at teaching them this language as forcing into them ideas against which they had better defend themselves.

If, however, the analyst – and the adults – stand firm and use their language with absolute consistency, patients – and children – eventually give in, learn what they are taught, and adopt the language of their elders and betters. As a result of this interaction between a consistent analyst and his conforming patient, an 'atmosphere' is created in which certain events will inevitably happen. Through this learning process the patients definitely become more mature, and they will be able to cope better with certain situations that have caused difficulties till then.

However, the patient, prompted by his overwhelming need to be understood, not only learns to speak his analyst's habitual language to the extent of expressing his associations in it, but will also come to accept tacitly that analysis can deal properly only with such experiences as can be verbalized without great difficulty, the intensity of which does not rise beyond a certain, critical, level. The rest, which is beyond the realm of words, gets a very faint and inexact rendering, or cannot be expressed by the patient at all. (The fact that high-intensity experiences cannot be satisfactorily rendered in words may be one reason why we know so little about the finer processes of orgasm.)

Is the result now a proof that the particular teaching method was the best possible or that the adult's language, which at one time appeared 'mad', is universal? Putting the question in this way amounts to an answer. The method is not absolutely correct, merely efficient, and the language is not universal, only a locally useful method for communication. Moreover, the fact that children and patients behave similarly while learning suggests that this kind of learning is based, to a very large extent, on introjection and identification. One may even be excused expressing the suspicion that in both cases the introjection and identification may be somewhat uncritical. In any case, this is the impression that an outsider gets while watching candidates during and after the learning process.

This impression is then reinforced by a curious but fairly uniform behaviour of the adherents to this school, all of whom seem to be confident that they possess not only a language on the whole adequate for the description of the 'pre-Oedipal' or even 'pre-verbal' phenomena, but in addition reliable criteria on how to use this language;

that is, when, what, and how, to interpret. Their interpretations – as reported at our scientific meetings and in the literature – create the impression of originating from a confident, knowledgeable, and perhaps even overwhelming analyst, an impression apparently shared by their patients. If true, this attitude of the analyst might be one of the reasons why, on the one hand, so much aggressiveness, envy, and hatred emerges in their patients' association-material and, on the other hand, why they seem to be concerned so much with intro-jection and idealization. These are the two most frequently used defence mechanisms in any partnership in which an oppressed, weak partner has to cope with an overwhelmingly powerful one.

A further puzzling feature is their relative reluctance to admit therapeutic failure. Although evidently the adherents of this school must have about as many difficult cases and failures as anyone else, in the literature originating from them any mention of this fact is conspicuously absent. On the contrary, they give the impression of saying or implying that since in their new language they have got the key for the understanding of pre-Oedipal processes, a good many of the difficulties and failures would simply disappear if all analysts would learn their technique and their language.

The full implications of the particular patient-therapist relationship characteristic of this school can be discussed only later in Part V. Here I can only point out that the peculiar inequality between the confident, knowledgeable, perhaps even overwhelming analyst, using his language and his interpretations with absolute consistency, and the patient whose only choice is between learning his analyst's apparently 'mad' language and giving up his hopes for help, is a significant sign that the analytical work has reached the area of the basic fault. This technique accepts the reality of the basic fault but attributes it, as it were, to the patient's *own fault*, in terms of what he has done in his fantasy to his internalized objects.

The hazard inherent in the kind of interpretation just discussed can perhaps be best described as 'super-ego-intropression', a term coined by Ferenczi (1932, p. 279). The analyst using this technique consistently presents himself to his patient as a knowledgeable and unshakably firm figure. In consequence the patient seems to be kept incessantly under the impression that the analyst not only under-stands everything, but also has at his command the infallible and only correct means for expressing everything: experiences, fantasies, effects, emotions, etc. After overcoming the immense hatred and ambivalence – in my opinion, aroused to a large extent by the consistent use of this technique – the patient learns the analyst's language, and *pari passu* introjects the analyst's idealized image. In successful cases the result seems to be the acquisition of a fairly – though far from absolutely – uniform mental structure, no doubt highly efficient, though remaining, perhaps for ever, somewhat alien and artificial.

There is a further hazard inherent in any type of consistent interpretation. If the patient's complaints, recriminations, and accusations remain vague and cannot be pinned down to something specific, it is nearly always possible to 'analyse' the complaining – whatever it is really about – even to analyse it away for a time; in due course, however, the patient invariably returns with the same kind of complaints. This kind of technique must impress the patient regressed to the level of the basic fault, as if the analyst tried to wave his accusations and recriminations on one side as irrelevant, or to dissolve them efficiently by clever and profound interpretations.

Good illustrations of the unintended side-effects of this policy were encountered time and again in our research work with general practitioners, and recently also with specialists (Balint, M., 1957, 1961). Most of them seem to have an irresistible urge to 'organize' their patient's complaints into an 'illness', with a name and a rank, and both doctor and patient seem to be lost, even bewildered, if this cannot be done speedily; alternatively, if the complaints cannot be 'organized' into a treatable 'illness', the patient is told that there is 'nothing wrong with him', which leads then to endless friction and irritation between a patient who feels ill and a well-meaning doctor who cannot find anything around which he can 'organize' the patient's complaint into an honest illness. Under the impact of present medical thinking, doctors cannot appreciate the importance of the fact that the patient *is able to complain* (irrespective of what the complaint is about), nor the immense and unique therapeutic potentialities in the doctor-patient relationship which enables the patient to complain at all.

I think nearly the same irresistible urge to 'organize' operates in most analysts. It compels us to make sense of our patients' complaints at all costs in order to stop them complaining. True, we have given up – more or less – the idea of 'illnesses', but we seem to be driven by a similar urge to 'organize' the complaints and symptoms into a 'conflict' or a 'position' with a definite name and a rank, as 'early' or 'deep' in our chronological hierarchy as possible. True, we do not give our patients – as doctors do – sedatives, tranquillizers, anti-depressants, and other drugs, but perhaps this makes it the more difficult for us to bear unrelieved complaints. In order to be able to do something about them, to give something to stop them, we resort to giving interpretations, and if these do not stop the complaining, we try to fix the blame somewhere: on ourselves for our bad technique; on the patient for his incurable illness, for his destructiveness, for his deep regression, for the split in his ego, and so on; or on his environment, and in particular on his parents for their lack of understanding, their unsympathetic ways of upbringing, and so on; recently an old scapegoat seems to have been resuscitated for this purpose: heredity.

In this way an endless spiral may develop; the patient complains, the analyst interprets in the way he found useful when working at the Oedipal or 'pre-Oedipal' level; however, no real change follows and feelings of guilt and failure increase in intensity in analyst and patient alike, which then lead to further complaints and further frantic interpretations, ever more clever and more profound than the previous ones.

Chapter 18

The hazards inherent in managing the regression

A third group of analysts, by no means so well organized as the previous two, and spread all over the analytic world, also start from the gulf separating us normal adults from the child in the patient, but think – in many ways similarly to myself – that it is due to mismanagement of the child during his early formative period by the adults, above all by his mother. The mismanagement, the lack of 'fit' between mother and her child, may create lasting structural alterations in the child's mind. For instance, according to Winnicott, one of the most frequently-met results is a kind of split in the ego; in response to the mismanagement – probably by introjecting the indifferent, overwhelming, or inadequate environment – a false ego or self is brought into being in order to cope with the unsympathetic world. This false ego may be highly efficient, and even successful in many fields of life, but it bars the access to the true or real self which thus remains immature, out of touch with reality. The result is a lifelong feeling of futility, emptiness and unhappiness.

This school, as I have just mentioned, lays the chief emphasis on a proper 'fit' – between the individual, who feels weak, and his environment, which he feels to be over-powerful. The true ego is usually so immature, so unaccustomed to dealing with problems of real life, that means must for some time be found both for protecting it from the onslaught of the demands of the world and for mediating between these demands and the individual's actual possibilities. Any lack of 'fit' in this respect may reinstate the efficiently functioning false ego in its 'caretaker' function, to the detriment of the true self. This very delicate piece of work, consisting of nursing, protecting, mediating, looking after, etc., is usually called 'management', which is an additional, or perhaps even more fundamental, task of analy-

110

tical therapy at this level than those better known, such as sympathetic listening, understanding, and interpreting.

It seems that only if patients are allowed to 'regress' – that is, to give up the security gained by relying on the 'caretaker' services of their false ego – which means that only if their analyst can take over the 'caretaking' by 'managing the regression', can an atmosphere be created in which interpretations can reach, and then become intelligible and acceptable to the real ego. It must be emphasized that the obverse of 'management' by the analyst is, evidently, regression by the patient; it is only the regressed patient – one who has temporarily given up the protection of his adult, and perhaps false, self – who needs management.

However, it is a well-known clinical experience that regressed patients are wont to develop exacting demands, often amounting to addiction-like states: we shall have to return to this topic in Chapters 20–22. Management of a regressed patient, therefore, is always a delicate and precarious task, difficult to perform satisfactorily.

One aspect of it may be described as being seduced by the unending suffering of the regressed patient into accepting responsibility for creating conditions in which, at long last, no more unnecessary suffering will be inflicted on him. Although this appears to be a highly commendable rationale, experience shows that in practice it rarely works.

There are many reasons for this disappointing outcome. This sort of response to the regression inevitably impresses the patient as an acceptance that his basic fault was caused by a 'bad' environment and that his analyst is willing and able to structure the world so that the effect of malicious and harmful influences may be greatly reduced. As we have here to deal with experiences belonging to the area of the basic fault, it does not make any difference whether the analyst has stated this in so many words or has only tacitly allowed the patient to interpret his behaviour as implying it, the resulting expectations will be the same. This is part of the explanation why it is so immensely difficult to prevent the development of a tragic misunderstanding, of a true confusion of tongues, once the regression has reached the area of the basic fault.

Once this atmosphere is allowed to develop, the patient will inevitably expect the return of the harmonious world in which he lived before the 'trauma' that established his basic fault. In that world, which I called primary love (see Chapter 12), there must not, and cannot, be any clash of interests between subject and environment. This, evidently, is possible only as long as the instinctual needs of the subject and his primary objects are satisfied by one and the same event, as is the case for the mother and her child: with feeding and being fed, with cuddling and being cuddled: what happens is one and the same event, only the words that we use for describing it are different.

To a limited extent this may also hold true for patient and analyst; during certain highly intense periods of the treatment, being analysed and analysing may be almost the same event, and up to a point it can gratify both partners of the therapeutic relationship. But it is rather doubtful whether this mutuality can be extended beyond a certain limit, whether the analyst can function as, or indeed actually be, a primary object, enabling the regressed patient to repeat his early pre-traumatic experiences in the therapeutic relationship, and maintain this atmosphere long enough for the patient to discover new ways of development which will avoid the repetition of the original trauma and lead to a healing-off of the basic fault. Apparently this is easier to plan than to achieve; possibly it is because the instinctual needs of any adult, no matter how far regressed, are to an extent more complex than an infant's, that it is as a rule beyond the possibilities of even a most sensitive and sympathetic analyst to achieve a faultless indentification with all of them. On the level of the basic fault any difference of this kind is felt by the patient as a major tragedy, reviving all the bitter disappointments that established his basic fault.

I was privileged to witness, fairly closely, an experiment of this kind on a really grand scale – perhaps the first of its kind in analytic history. It was carried out by Ferenczi who, in his last years of analytic work, agreed with one of his patients to fulfil this role as far as it was in his power. For example, the patient got as much time from him as she asked for, several sessions per day and, if necessary, also during the night. As breaks were considered undesirable, she was seen during the week-ends and was allowed to accompany her analyst on his holidays. These details are only a modest sample of what really happened. The experiment went on for some years. The results were still inconclusive when Ferenczi, owing to his illness, had to give up analytical work a few weeks only before he died. The patient, a talented but profoundly disturbed woman, improved considerably by that time but could not be considered as cured. I still remember, when we discussed his experiments – the case mentioned was the grandest, but by no means the only one – Ferenczi accepted that, in a way, he failed, but added that he himself learned an immense amount, and perhaps even others might benefit from his failure if they realized that this task, in the way he tried to solve it, was insoluble.

Since then I have myself experimented with this task and have witnessed the efforts of others. On the whole it seems to me that some types of analyst cannot resist this kind of temptation especially if it emanates from a 'worth-while' patient. There are few more constant characteristics of the analyst and his 'worth-while' patient, and above all of their mutual relationship during and after the experiment (Main, 1957); I shall come back to a few of them presently in Part IV. Here I want only to state that in no case in which the atmosphere of a 'grand experiment' was allowed to develop have I seen a real success. In some cases the result was disaster, and at best it amounted only to what Ferenczi achieved: the patient improved considerably but could not be considered as cured.

The idea governing the 'grand experiment' grows something like this: the analyst realizes that his traditional behaviour of sympathetic but passive objectivity is felt by certain patients as unwarranted and unbearable frustration, and that treating the sufferings caused by it just as another symptom of the developing transference neurosis does not seem to bring about any change. Perhaps he has already had some doubts about the wisdom of objective sympathetic passivity at all costs; in any case the unrelieved sufferings and privations of his patient prove too much for him and so he decides – either for himself or in agreement with his patient – that a new regime must be established by doing something more, over and above the traditional passivity.

This something more amounts always to gratifying some of his patient's regressive urges, to responding positively to the patient's acting-out. As a rule, this change brings some immediate improvement. If the new regime is decided upon towards the end of the treatment of a patient with a not too serious basic fault, the improvement may just tilt the scales and the treatment may be successfully terminated. One or two such successful experiments encourage the analyst to try this policy out with a 'worth-while' but seriously ill patient, and not towards the end of the treatment but right from the start. Whether it is decided right at the start to satisfy as many of the patient's needs as compatible with a very elastic conception of the analytic situation, or whether such decision is arrived at gradually under the pressure of the emerging clinical material, does not make much difference; the 'grand experiment' is on.

Several analysts have tried to describe what happens during such an experiment – in the analyst, with his patient, and in their relationship. To read such reports is always a stimulating and moving experience but also a melancholy one. Great vistas open up; one is allowed to penetrate to unexpected depths of the human mind and into unexpected potentialities of human relationship; and yet, something in the end slips through our fingers and we remain intrigued but disappointed. Of all the descriptions, I find most revealing Ferenczi's in his *Notes and Fragments* (1930–32), a kind of scientific diary written during his 'grand experiment'. The notes were intended only for his own use and thus escaped all secondary elaboration. They tell the tale of hopeful developments, of unexpectedly emerging complications, give a penetrating and vivid description of many unsuspected overdeterminants shaping the therapeutic processes and, over and above, show us a talented therapist at work, his sudden surprises, his hopes, his immediate asides, and his wrestling with difficult problems. Anybody considering experimenting in this field is urgently recommended to study these before starting off.

Of course, every research worker who has studied this field has his pet ideas and, consequently, must describe his experiences under their bias, resulting in another example of the confusion of analytic tongues. A conscientious reader, someone utterly different from me, will get a fertile field here; contrasting the various analytic languages, he might lay the foundations of comparative psychoanalytic semantics. Some of these descriptions try to hide, or explain away, the disappointing results; others attribute them to this or that accidental cause, and so on. My pet idea is that the results are directly determined by the developing therapeutic situation. This latter is, of course, an entirely two-person relationship, peculiar and primitive, and thus offers us a good opportunity to study processes belonging to the area of the basic fault.

114

As I have mentioned, the patient is always a 'worth-while' person, someone who badly needs – and deserves – help – a clear diagnostic sign of positive counter-transference. The analyst, instead of evaluating his positive counter-transference, his 'emotional involvement', as a symptom of his patient's illness (cf. Chapter 4), accepts it as reality and decides to act upon it. The decision has a background of some preconceived ideas: the patient's inability to tolerate the frustrations and limitations inherent in the 'normal' analytic situation is interpreted as repetition, a sign of strong fixation to some traumatic situation. Two endeavours originate from this assumption; one is to reconstruct from the patient's association material and the symptoms of his transference neurosis, i.e. his repetition, the hypothetical traumatic situation; the other is to create for the patient an atmosphere – by changing some reversible parameters – which will *not* then act as a stimulus provoking the eternal repetitions.

Some analysts, I for one, prefer to discuss these trains of thought with a patient so that they may be reassured of his cooperation. Unfortunately this does not make much difference. The reason simply is that this discussion is, of necessity, conducted in the normal conventional adult language, that is, at the level of the Oedipus conflict, whereas the repetition happens in a primitive two-person relationship belonging to the area of the basic fault. At the Oedipal level the patient acknowledges gratefully his analyst's exceptional efforts and promises his full cooperation; at the level of the basic fault he cannot help expecting full gratification of all his compelling needs irrespective of any gratitude or any interest apart from his own. Any frustration provokes at this level vehement symptoms which, however, immediately subside if the particular need is gratified. Unfortunately the particular gratification, if it is readily and safely available, loses any special value and the patient's 'greed' is attracted by another demand, apparently determined as convincingly by the patient's past as was the previous one.

In this way a vicious circle may establish itself; to use K. Eissler's ideas, certain parameters of the analytic situation may be changed reversibly by themselves, but if one change is reinforced by that of a second, third, or further parameter, the result may not be reversible any more. True, both members of the therapeutic partnership behave and act in a sensible and justifiable way; *what is wrong is with the two-person relationship developing between them.* Remarkably this leads

115

to a great amount of hatred, felt both in the transference and, as some sincere analysts admit (Winnicott, 1949), also in the counter-transference. One consequence of the exalted sincerity which is an important ingredient of these experiments, is a curious attitude of the analyst which – as reported at our scientific meetings and in the literature – strikes one as apologetic, continuously confessing to mistakes and blunders, failures and shortcomings. Although this is almost diametrically opposite to the atmosphere created by the way of interpretation used by the second school of analysts, one gets the impression that by the 'managing' technique about the same amount of hatred and aggressiveness is evoked in the patient, but perhaps less of introjection of, and identification with, the idealized analyst.

A similar difference exists between the two schools with regard to their 'languages'. True, the 'managing' school can hardly be called a school because, in contrast to the two previous ones, it lacks any organization or cohesion and, in consequence, has not developed a proper language of its own, although there are signs that this may happen under the influence of Winnicott's ideas.

Of course, the crucial question is the therapeutic efficiency of these three different techniques described in Chapters 16–18. Answering this is a most difficult task, both objectively and subjectively. Anyone belonging to any of these three schools is obviously biased, but so inevitably is an outsider like myself. Further, no outsider has the possibility of assessing another analyst's therapeutic work because the outsider simply does not know the facts. The basis of assessment is thus reduced to subjective impressions created partly by papers delivered and printed, partly by contributions to scientific discussions and, last but not least, by the quality of new analysts produced by each school. There exist unquestionably great differences in these respects, but as yet I have not got enough courage to discuss them in public, and still less in print.

Instead of this critical discussion, I shall discuss in the next Part my own clinical experiences with regression as it can be observed in private analytic practice, and in the final Part the techniques that I found useful in these situations.

PART IV

The benign and the malignant forms of regression

Chapter 19

Freud and the idea of regression

It can easily be proved that the idea of regression is as old as, if not older than, psychoanalysis. This might surprise some people who know that 'regression' appeared in print for the first time in the last, theoretical, chapter of *The Interpretation of Dreams* (1900).

This was a modest first appearance. Freud needed it to explain the hallucinatory nature of dreams, which differentiates them from remembering. He assumed a normal or 'progressive' direction of processes in the adult mind, starting with the perception of a stimulus and going first towards thought and then to action, which then aims at reducing the tension caused by the stimulus. If action is impossible, or proves inadequate, a backward, retrogressive or 'regressive' movement may take place which, in normal waking life, goes only as far as the memory traces. A regression beyond this point towards reviving the perceptual elements of experience, i.e. towards hallucination, is one of the psychological characteristics of dreaming.

This, as I have said, was a modest first appearance. It introduced regression as a minor mechanism of defence, much less important than repression. To illustrate this difference, regression is discussed only once, towards the end of *The Interpretation of Dreams*, and its role does not amount to more than a temporary measure against a repressed urge or wish, that is, to a minor contribution to the dream work. However, the idea of regression at that time already had a past, and was to have a future. To anticipate something of the latter, I would like to mention that Anna Freud (1936) ranked regression first in her enumeration of the defence mechanisms, while repression came only second.

As regards its past, it is difficult to give an exact date for its inception, but it seems probable that it was stimulated by Freud's contact with Brücke or Breuer. Breuer, in the theoretical chapter of *Studies on Hysteria* (1895, p. 189) used the adjective *rückläufig* (retrogressive) to describe the psychological processes during hallucination,

119

in exactly the same sense as Freud was to use it five years later in *The Interpretation of Dreams*. On the other hand, both in his published paper 'The Neuro-Psychoses of Defence' (1894), and in his post-humously published 'Manuscript H' (January 1895), Freud described hallucinations as methods of defence against incompatible ideas. Thus there can be no doubt that the idea of regression as a mechanism of defence is very early, but it cannot be stated with certainty when exactly it emerged, nor whether it was discovered by Breuer or by Freud.

The related but more general idea of regression as an important factor in the pathogenesis of neuroses, psychoses, perversions, etc. is entirely Freud's, and was developed later than the previous one, although the first allusions to it occur in Freud's embryological work, published in 1877 and 1878; in Lecture XXII of his *Introductory Lectures* (1916–17) he used these embryological findings to illustrate the pathogenic function of regression. But in the intervening years the word 'regression' does not occur in Freud's early writings, or in the Dora analysis (1905), Gradiva (1907), or in Little Hans (1909). The first tentative allusions to the psychological idea may be discerned in some passages of the first edition of the Three Essays (1905) but it was only in the third edition (1915) that Freud explicitly stated that regression was an important pathogenic factor. The actual date of this change seems to be 1909 to 1910, marked by his Five Lectures (1909) and the papers on the Rat Man (1909), Leonardo da Vinci (1910), and Schreber (1911) which was the time when Freud was struggling with the problem of narcissism. The connection between these two ideas, narcissism on the one hand and regression as a factor in pathogenesis on the other, would be a most interesting topic for an historical study.

Freud summed up the theoretical side of these two functions of regression – as a mechanism of defence and as a pathogenic factor – in 1914 in the third edition of *The Interpretation of Dreams* (p. 548). In it he distinguishes three aspects of regression: the topographical, the temporal, and the formal. The 'backward' movement of mental processes, 'transforming thoughts into images' (p. 544), does not take place only in space, that is, between the various instances of the mental apparatus, but also in time, from the present towards earlier experiences. And lastly, perhaps the most important characteristic is the clinical observation, that during regression the mental experiences apparently disintegrate into their past components, and simpler forms of experience re-emerge into the mental apparatus.

This distinction of the three forms or aspects of regression seems to be clear, convincing, and final. But we get the first warning that things are perhaps not quite so simple as they appear, when we discover that in his paper written a year later, 'A Metapsychological Supplement to the Theory of Dreams' (1917, p. 227), Freud distinguishes only two forms of regression, the topographical and the temporal,[1] and leaves out altogether the formal aspect, which nowadays, without any doubt, would be considered the most important.

The question now is: shall we consider this discrepancy as an event of no importance or treat it – following Freud's own example – as an instance of forgetting, indicating a dislike of the formal kind of regression? It is possible that this dislike played its part in the slow development of the whole idea. Regression as a mechanism of defence needed at least five years to see the light of day; regression as a factor in pathogenesis another ten to fifteen years.

Moreover, there is yet another function of regression, also with a long previous history, to which Freud returned time and again during the next period (c. 1912–20) and that is the function of regression as part of the transference, especially in the service of resistance. Freud's attitude towards this complex phenomenon, described by the overlapping terms of transference, acting-out, repetition compulsion, and regression, could be characterized as extremely cautious.

This attitude is already fully present in the technical chapter of *Studies on Hysteria* (1895, pp. 301–304). Although the word 'regression' is not used, Freud described vividly the regressed form of transference as an 'obstacle'. Whenever, in the years under review, Freud returned to the problem of transference, he never failed to emphasize that the regressed form of transference was the most potent type of resistance. True, transference was an ally of analytic treatment, but only in its adult, affectionate, and aim-inhibited form.[2] On the other hand, transference could become a most serious danger to analytic treatment unless the analyst could detach from it by his

---

[1] I am indebted to James Strachey for calling my attention to this particular discrepancy, as well as to several details related to the early development of the idea of regression.

[2] This idea was expanded later by E. Bibring into the 'therapeutic alliance' (Congress paper, 1936).

interpretations: (a) the negative transference, and (b) the positive transference of repressed erotic impulses, due to a revival of relationships to early imagos, that is to regressive elements ('The Dynamics of Transference', 1912).

In his classical paper, 'Remembering, Repeating and Working-Through' (1914), Freud fully recognized that certain patients could not remember some parts of their emotional past but must act them out in their relationship to the analyst, that is, that transference must be understood also as a repetition of the patient's forgotten past, which had become inaccessible to any other means; and he admitted that this repeating was partly induced by the analytical treatment itself, being one of the consequences of the 'new' technique of free association. Nevertheless, the cautious advice was repeated that the analyst should not respond to these phenomena, except by interpreting them. First, this advice was couched in the term of 'abstinence' – e.g. in his paper 'On Transference-Love' (1915, p. 165) and then a few years later in his Budapest Congress paper (1918, p. 162) in the stronger term of 'privation'.

Abstinence and privation, to be imposed by the analyst on his patient, sound rather stern measures, but there can be no doubt that they are a fair rendering of what, in Freud's opinion, was necessary when dealing with a regressed form of transference.

However, the development of Freud's ideas did not stop at this point. The next step was to recognize the regressed form of transference as one of the symptoms of the powerful repetition compulsion, extend this idea to biology, and postulate on this basis the existence of a death instinct, the ever-constant aim of which was regression, that is, to revert from the present state to a state that had existed before it; in the last analysis, from life to death (*Beyond the Pleasure Principle*, 1920).

In this connection it is important to note that the two phenomena used as illustrations for the power of the 'compulsion to repeat' are the behaviour of children in play and of patients in the transference, especially in regressed transference.

We encounter here a dilemma: if regression in the transference is a symptom of the repetition compulsion, that is, is prompted by the force of the death instinct, will our attempts to impose abstinence and privation on our patients have any chance of success? On the other hand, are we allowed to infer from the fact that in a number

122

of cases with regressed patients the analytic treatment can be successfully terminated, that the force of the death instinct is perhaps not so overwhelming after all? These questions have never been asked, certainly not by Freud.

There is yet another function of regression, that of an ally in analytical therapy. As far as I know, Freud dealt with it only once, but on that occasion in a most emphatically positive manner. This happened – of all places – in a passage in his 'History of the Psychoanalytic Movement' (1914, pp. 10–11). As mentioned above, the term 'regression' does not occur in the Dora analysis, but ten years later in his historical essay he pointed out with admirable precision that any attempt at resolving the pathological effects of a recent trauma by direct analysis had failed, and Dora had to be allowed to make 'a long detour, leading back over her earliest childhood' before a solution of the current conflict became possible. He rounded off his discussion of the case by pointing out how fallacious it was to advocate 'the neglect of regression in analytic technique'. In spite of this statement, I do not know of a passage in Freud's writings which dealt at any length with the problems of therapeutic, not of defensive or pathogenic, regression. Moreover, Freud stated explicitly, just before the passage quoted above, that regression during treatment was observed already when the cathartic method was used by Breuer and himself: 'We discovered the mental process, characteristic of neurosis, which later I called "regression"' – and then continued, with the same breath, so to speak, with the example of the Dora analysis. Thus there can be no doubt that the observation that regression is an important therapeutic factor is as old as analysis itself, if not still older.

The situation has now become rather puzzling. Regression during treatment was recognized as an important factor of therapy in the early cathartic cases, this observation was confirmed by the Dora analysis, and certainly by others as well. Equally, we have printed evidence that the theoretical idea of regression was one of the oldest; and still it had to wait until 1900 to appear in print, and more than another ten years till its full significance as a factor in pathogenesis was fully recognized. From then on it had a spectacular career, but only in its pejorative aspects, as a redoubtable form of resistance, then as a symptom of the repetition compulsion and, lastly, as the most important clinical example of the death instinct. On the other hand, its role as a therapeutic ally was mentioned only once, very cursorily, and then apparently forgotten or overshadowed by its threatening aspects. I shall return to this apparent inconsistency in Chapters 22 and 23.

In consequence, Freud's advice on how to treat regression during analytical treatment has been absolutely consistent – perhaps with one temporary exception; and it is even debatable whether one is justi-fied in calling this exception an exception at all. His advice was that, no matter how regressed the patient was, the analyst must maintain his normal sympathetic passive objectivity and should not respond to the patient's longings or cravings in any other way than by interpreting them. Freud even stated in his paper 'Observations on Transference-Love' (1915, p. 16) that it is inadvisable to go beyond this, because the cases in which this policy fails will prove, as a rule, unsuitable for analysis. It is this policy of not responding that is described by the assertion, 'the treatment must be carried out in the state of abstin-ence, or of privation'.

Now the debatable exception. Towards the end of the first world war, shortly after his analysis with Freud, Ferenczi started his technical experiments which – in their first phase, called 'active technique' – were fully backed by Freud. The guiding principle of this phase was that at the right moment the analyst should propose that the patient should expose himself to, or even produce inten-tionally, situations which would lead to a considerable increase of tension in him. It was expected that this would produce two results: a breakthrough into consciousness of a hitherto repressed instinctual urge or drive changing an unpleasurable symptom into a pleasurable satisfaction, and getting the patient's dried-up associations flowing again. Freud, in his Budapest Congress paper (1918), mentioned above, justifiably claimed that the original idea which stimulated these technical innovations was his, and quoted his two experiments: (a) that severely agoraphobic patients should, at the proper time of their treatment, be induced to expose themselves to the dreaded situation, and (b) that in certain cases, like that of the Wolf Man, the analyst should fix a day for the termination of the treatment. He confirmed Ferenczi's findings that, if the intervention happened at the right moment and in the right way, the result was a great move forward in the treatment.

I hope it is now clear why I called this technical procedure a debatable exception to the general rule. On the one hand, it may be considered as a logical extension of the rule of abstinence or privation; the patient's longing or craving is not satisfied, instead a still greater tension is imposed on him. On the other hand, it definitely means doing more than merely interpreting the patient's regressed or not so regressed transference; it means abandoning the sympathetic passive objectivity by responding to something in the patient in a specific way. In addition, in the light of what we have learned from Ferenczi's experiments, and since, it appears rather questionable whether in fact the raising of tension in the patient achieves its intended aim of privation or something quite different.

Still, in some cases the breakthrough achieved in this way had sufficient momentum to last till the termination of the analytic treatment; in others, unfortunately in the majority, the momentum petered out and the patient relapsed. Freud foresaw this possibility, and when his experiences convinced him that success was elusive and unpredictable, he abandoned this idea, and it is not mentioned in his writings after 1918.

Ferenczi had the same experiences as Freud, but he was so impressed by the very primitive nature of his patient's reactions to his interventions that he decided to extend his study by varying his interventions while continuing with the analytic work. He discovered in this way that infantile pathogenic traumas, when re-activated by the analytic treatment, appeared to have – to use a modern phrase – a biphasic structure.

In the first phase the infant or child appears to have been subjected to a traumatic over- or under-stimulation by his environment, that is by his most important adult object or objects; when in the second phase the child tried to obtain reparation, comfort, or even mere understanding from the same adults, these – under the influence of their own conscious or unconscious guilt feelings – had to deny any participation in the preceding phase, and had to show by their words and behaviour that they really did not know what all the fuss was about – or to use our terminology: though they were most sympathetic and objective, they clearly showed that they were not involved. Ferenczi had to admit to his patients that producing the repetition of the traumatic situation by his active intervention, and then watching the events with the customary sympathetic detachment was very similar in its structure to the original trauma, and came to the further conclusion that the classical analytic technique, when inducing the patient to recollect or repeat the original trauma while the analyst maintained his objective sympathetic passivity, might in some cases create conditions similar to those produced by the active intervention ('Notes and Fragments' 4.11.1932, in *Final Contributions*, 1955).

Reaching this point, the next step seemed evident to Ferenczi. If the original trauma consisted of over- or under-stimulation by the environment, with subsequent lack of understanding and indifference by the same people, then the aim of therapy must be: (a) to help the patient to regress to the traumatic situation, (b) to watch carefully what degree of tension the patient will be able to bear in this state, and (c) to see to it that the tension will remain at about that level by responding positively to the regressed patient's longings, cravings, or needs. A by-product of this research was the first intensive study of the doctor-patient relationship and the discovery of what nowadays is called the technique of counter-transference interpretations (Ferenczi 1930, 1931, and 1932).

It was at this point that the disagreement between Freud and Ferenczi became critical. Freud predicted that it would prove impossible to satisfy unconditionally every need of a regressed patient, that any attempt of this kind would improve the patient's state only as long as the analyst was able and willing to be at the patient's beck and call and, lastly, that most of these patients, even though improved, would never become really independent.

The controversy between Freud and Ferenczi has never been settled. Ferenczi died before finishing his last experiments. The analyst's death is always a highly traumatic event for any patient, but especially so for a deeply regressed one. By this I do not want to say that his results would all have been favourable had he lived long enough; but I certainly wish to say that under these conditions any question about the value of his experiments cannot be answered by a simple yes or no, based on clinical observations relating to his last set of patients. I shall return to this topic in Chapter 23.

Chapter 20

Symptomatology and diagnosis

To sum up, we learn from Freud that, clinically, regression may have four functions: (a) as a mechanism of defence, (b) as a factor in pathogenesis, (c) as a potent form of resistance, and (d) as an essential factor in analytic therapy.

In this Part, I shall discuss only a small sector of the complex field of regression, comprising the phenomena observable during analytic treatment. This limitation practically excludes regression as a mechanism of defence, since cases of serious hallucinations are rather rare in my ambulant practice. Furthermore, this will make the study of regression as a pathogenic factor somewhat limited and one-sided. This is because during analysis regression is treated as a temporary measure only; although regression is tolerated, the patient is not supposed to settle down in it and establish it as an acceptable solution. Studied in this way, regression in its pathogenic function appears hardly as an event of the past, but rather as a dynamic process of the present; one sees it coming, taking over the situation, ruling it for some time, relinquishing its hold to some other powers, for instance reality, and then disappearing. Evidently, the two functions that an analyst can observe most frequently during treatment are regression as a form of resistance, and regression as a therapeutic ally.

I intend to discuss this field under three headings. First, the symptomatology and the diagnosis of regression. The relevant questions will be: what constitutes a regression during analysis, that is, what are its differential diagnostic criteria? Does it occur only in one form or, if in several, what are these various forms? The second group of questions relates to its dynamism. What are the essential events during a phase of regression and what is the specific significance of each of these events? And, lastly, the third group of questions will be about technique and therapy. This last group will only be touched upon in this Part, for I intend to discuss it in detail

127

in Part V. The problem is to decide what determines whether any regression will have a pathogenic or a therapeutic effect. If this issue is determined or even influenced by external events, what can the analyst do to ensure that his patient's regression should be therapeutic and any danger of a pathological regression avoided?

I propose to start with my early clinical experiences in this field. The recurring features of these were as follows: At one point of the analytic treatment, after an apparently correct interpretation, a sudden change occurred and the patient tentatively presented in the analytic situation a form of primitive satisfaction or a form of simple object relationship, hitherto impossible, distasteful, or repulsive to him. If this was interpreted in the customary manner of sympathetic objectivity, no further development was discernible. If, however, the analyst accepted and responded to it, an immediate break-through occurred with signal therapeutic developments.

This difference means that both the patient and his analyst do a bit more, in addition to – but not instead of – what happens in a 'classical' analytic treatment.

Now a concrete case: In the second half of the 1920's, I started the analytic treatment of an attractive, vivacious, and rather flirtatious girl in her late 20's. Her main complaint was an inability to achieve anything. She had finished successfully the university course for a degree quite some years before, but could not take the final examination. She was popular with men, and a number of them wanted her, either for marriage or for an affair, but she simply could not respond. Gradually, it emerged that her inability to respond was linked with a crippling fear of uncertainty whenever she had to take any risk, that is, take a decision. She had a very close tie to her forceful, rather obsessional, but most reliable father; they understood and appreciated each other; while her relationship to her somewhat intimidated mother, whom she felt to be unreliable, was openly ambivalent.

It took us about two years before these connections made sense to her. At about this time, she was given the interpretation that apparently the most important thing for her was to keep her head safely up, with both feet firmly planted on the ground. In response, she mentioned that ever since her earliest childhood she could never do a somersault; although at various periods she tried desperately to do one. I then said: 'What about it now?' – whereupon she got up from the couch and, to her great amazement, did a perfect somersault without any difficulty.

This proved to be a real breakthrough. Many changes followed, in her emotional, social, and professional life, all towards greater freedom and elasticity. Moreover, she managed to get permission to sit for, and passed, a most difficult post-graduate professional examination, became engaged, and was married.

On her marriage, as was customary at that time in analytic practice, the treatment was interrupted, but two years later she returned for another stretch of about fourteen months. The follow-up, amounting almost to thirty years, shows that she was able to keep up a normal life, in spite of the many upheavals and great external difficulties which were her share to bear – German occupation, war, siege by the Russians, Russian occupation, changeover to a Communist regime, revolution, etc. Thus the breakthrough led to acceptable results which stood up well to the test of time.

What is the correct diagnostic term to describe the somersault, the crucial event, in this case history? First, I would propose an unequivocal description which I hope will be acceptable without much argument. For a young woman of thirty to do a somersault certainly means the emergence of a primitive childish form of behaviour after more mature, more adult, forms have firmly established themselves. This is a correct, but long-winded phrase, instead of which analytic theory uses four, largely overlapping, terms: transference, acting-out, repetition, and regression. All four of them are in our case partly correct, partly incorrect.

There is no question that the somersault was a piece of acting-out, but it is not clear what actually was acted-out. Equally, it happened in the transference, if we mean by transference the whole analytic situation. If, however, we mean to use the term in its strict sense, that which is transferred from an original object to the analyst, it is not certain whether it is applicable in our case. We shall have similar troubles with repetition and regression. One can only repeat something that one has done at least once before; and perhaps equally, one can regress to something that has existed at least once before. But, as the case history shows, my patient had never been able to do a somersault. Thus it would be a logical contradiction to call the first somersault in her life a repetition or a regression. In spite of this contradiction, I shall use the term regression to denote rather loosely

129

the emergence in response to analytic treatment of primitive forms of behaving and experiencing, after more mature forms have firmly established themselves.

By the way, this lack of proper differential diagnosis, that is, the custom of loosely calling everything 'primitive' that is produced by the patient in the analytic situation, *ipso facto*, transference and/or regression, led to a number of misconceptions and bedevilled the progress of research in this field. I shall try to clarify some details here and there but am not too confident about the future of my propositions. It is much easier to start a new bad habit than to reform an old one.

In addition, there are a number of clinical states that resemble regression in many respects and, in consequence, are often mixed up with it, although their dynamic structures are fundamentally different. Perhaps the commonest among them is *withdrawal*, giving up contact with the analyst, or the environment. A specific form of this state was described by Winnicott (1958) as the ability of being alone in the presence of someone else. If a person is *absorbed almost entirely in his area of creation*, he may create the impression of being withdrawn. All these states may be short-lived or may last for quite some time; they may be pathological or absolutely normal; and lastly a small, or even a considerable, amount of regression may be present in them. Still, I think, they ought to be differentiated from regression proper.

The same is true of another very similar clinical state which could be called *disintegration* in which a higher, more complex structure is put out of action, in consequence of which more primitive forms of functioning and experiencing appear, perhaps even re-appear. A pathological form is progressive schizophrenia; an almost normal form is the passing of genitality in old age. Both of these two states show a number of true regressive features and could perhaps be quoted as instances of 'regression as a factor in pathogenesis'. But even if the regressive nature of these states of disintegration is accepted, these forms should be differentiated from the regression observed during analytic treatment.

Returning now to my case, this episode happened around 1930. Using the theory of instincts and ego psychology, the two theories then prevalent in psychoanalysis, I could claim that what I achieved in my case was: (a) I raised the tension in my patient by offering

130

her the possibility of doing a somersault there and then, that is, exposing her to the dreaded situation; by that (b) I helped her to achieve a breakthrough of an instinct, leading to an enjoyable gratification of an urge or drive which hitherto had been inhibited by repressions; and (c) parallel with, or through, this experience her ego became stronger.

At that time our theoretical conceptions, especially in Budapest, were gradually changing from the almost exclusive preoccupation with the older libido and instinct theory and the new ego psychology towards a recognition of the importance of object relationships. It is difficult to give an exact date to this change. It was first announced by Ferenczi in Chapter III of *Thalassa* (1924), 'Stages in the Development of the Erotic Sense of Reality', received further impetus from his disappointing results with his active technique, and from his intensive study of the patient-analyst relationship, but it gathered momentum only after 1928, with the publication of his two papers 'The Problem of Termination of the Analysis' and 'The Elasticity of Psycho-analytic Technique'.

Under the influence of this new orientation, I recorded also the changes in the patient's object relationships. True, the result of the breakthrough amounted to a removal of repression; an ego function which, because of its symbolic meaning had become inhibited, ego-dystonic, was now liberated and, after detaching its secondary erotic cathexis, was integrated into the ego as something enjoyable. But, it was also true that the breakthrough happened in the psycho-analytic situation, that is in an object relationship, and it opened up new ways of loving and hating for the patient. This amounted to a new discovery, and from then on the patient's relationship towards her objects of love and hate bcame freer and more realistic.

It was on this wider basis that I developed the concept of new beginning for the description of a fair number of clinical experiences of the kind reported here. I listed the following points which I thought were characteristic of a new beginning (Balint, M., 1932 and 1934). This list was a first attempt at a clinical symptomatology of beneficial regression during analytic treatment. I intend to discuss in the following chapters how this list has changed in the light of my clinical experiences during the last thirty years.

1. During the increase of tension, that is before the gratification of the urge, most impressive and noisy symptoms appear, then a

131

sudden change sets in, resulting in the feeling of a tranquil, quiet, well-being which, if not carefully watched, may escape observation.
2. Intensity of gratification of the newly-begun activities never reaches end-pleasure levels.
3. All new beginnings happen in the transference, that is, in an object relationship, and lead to a changed relationship to the patient's objects of love and hate and, in consequence, to a considerable diminution of anxiety.
4. New beginnings also lead to character changes. Nowadays the same clinical observation would be described as a change in the ego. And, lastly, the most important:
5. New beginning means: (a) going back to something 'primitive', to a point before the faulty development started, which could be described as a regression, and (b), at the same time, discovering a new, better-suited, way which amounts to a progression. In my book *Thrills and Regressions* (1959) I called the sum-total of these two basic phenomena: regression for the sake of progression.

Let us now return to my case. Accepting that the breakthrough was an important factor in the good therapeutic result, the question arises how to understand its dynamism. The good result might have been brought about by: (a) forcing the consciousness – or the ego – to lift part of the repression and accept an instinctual urge as ego-syntonic and enjoyable; (b) strengthening the ego by extending its boundaries at the expense of the id; and (c) helping the patient to a new beginning or, if preferred, to a regression.

Of course, one could argue that the decisive factor in bringing about the good therapeutic result was the analytic work that preceded the incident described, and the proper working-through that followed it. The incident itself, though impressive, was insignificant, apart perhaps from permitting some harmless relief from the strenuous work both to the patient and her analyst. It is difficult to answer this argument on the basis of a successful case. Success can be attributed to any one factor, or to any combination of factors; consequently it is well nigh impossible to use success as proof for the validity of any technical proposition. So I suggest that for the time being we suspend judgement and continue our inquiry.

Chapter 21

Gratifications and object relationships

This was about as far as I got at the time when Ferenczi died in May 1933, more than thirty years ago. The general view at that time was that Ferenczi's experiments had shown that responding to a regressed patient's cravings was a mistake; it caused endless and useless troubles both for the patient and the analyst, and was anyway condemned by Freud. For some time I tried to reopen the case by pointing out that this wholesale condemnation was both unjust and unprofitable (Balint, M., 1934, 1935, 1937, 1949, 1951, etc.). What I asked for was a critical reappraisal – not an uncritical acceptance – of what was valuable in the ideas developed in Budapest under Ferenczi's leadership. There was no response. Having failed, the only policy remaining to me was to continue with my clinical work and test the validity of these ideas by further experience. In recent years I think there have perhaps been some signs of a change in the general attitude, though I may be mistaken. So I am trying again.

Of the events in the new beginning phase described in my list at the end of Chapter 20, I thought there were three that appeared promising, that is, worth further study and research. The most conspicuous of them was the primitive gratification itself; the second the sudden changes in the intensity of the analytic atmosphere, a most passionate demand for gratification as long as the urge remained unsatisfied, and an almost complete disappearance of any passion immediately after satisfaction; and third, the absolute condition that all this had to happen in the analytic situation, that is, in an object relationship.

Let us start with the aspect of gratification. There can be no question that something must be satisfied, but it is rather difficult to identify this something as a derivative of a particular component instinct. In some cases this can be done by stretching a point, for instance, in the case of my patient who did a somersault. Another patient – also a successful treatment with a follow-up of about twenty-five years – wanted and had to hold one of my fingers for

133

quite some time during a particular period of her analysis. With a little effort one could find – or create – an instinct to cling for the explanation of the satisfaction observed in her case. Yet another patient, a man this time, had to be on sick leave for several weeks during a new beginning period. It would be difficult to say whether he was or was not ill at that time; he was not able to work, spent most of his time in bed and had to be nursed, but he came regularly to his sessions – did not miss one. At about the same time, he asked for extra sessions, especially during week-ends or, alternatively, that I should ring him up. It would be difficult to connect these satisfactions with any particular component instinct, but it is clear that all three patients needed a certain kind of simple, yielding (*gewährend*), relationship to their environment, that is, to their most important object of the time: their analyst.

Returning to the question of differential diagnosis, in each of the three reported cases, primitive forms of behaving and experiencing emerged after more mature forms had firmly established themselves, and this is what I proposed to call regression. This regression resulted in longing and craving, and in all three cases the analyst responded positively to them, that is, satisfied them. I wish to emphasize that *the satisfaction did not replace interpretation*, it was in addition to it. In some treatments interpretation preceded and in others followed satisfaction, as the situation demanded.

By the thirties I began to realize that the satisfaction demanded and received by the patient in the new beginning period, though conspicuous, was not all-important; perhaps it was only a means to an end. What really mattered was that the patient was helped to free himself of complex, rigid, and oppressive forms of relationship to his objects of love and hate – called at that time: character-traits – and to start simpler, less oppressive forms. For instance, in my first case, at the crucial moment the analyst was not felt as a stimulating, exciting, or forbidding adult object, in whose presence no proper young lady would think of doing somersaults, but as a safe object in whose presence a patient could and might indulge in childish pleasures. By the way, it would not matter much if the same difference were expressed in the language of the triangular Oedipal conflict or in any of the pre-Oedipal – oral, anal, phallic, etc. – languages. Moreover, it is fairly certain that any of these expressions will prove correct by describing one of its many over-determinations.

134

To characterize this special atmosphere of the new beginning period, I used the German adjective *arglos* which, like *Lust* or *Besetzung*, has no English equivalent. The dictionary translates it by the cluster: 'guileless, innocent, simple, harmless, inoffensive, unsophisticated, unsuspecting', none of which expresses its proper meaning. For this we would need a word describing a constellation in which an individual feels that nothing harmful in the environment is directed towards him and, at the same time, nothing harmful in him is directed towards his environment. We might get some help from our analytical terminology which could offer us adjectives like: pre-ambivalent, pre-persecutory, or pre-paranoid. The trouble with these latter is that they are too sophisticated to describe the simple, trusting, and unsuspecting atmosphere of this period. What the patient experienced in the transference was that, at long last, he was able to shed all sorts of character and defensive armours and to feel that life had become simpler and truer – a real new discovery.

All this differentiated the new beginning from what Freud called regression, which was a process entirely within the individual's mind, whereas the regression I observed during analytic treatment – the new beginning – belonged, to use a modern term, to the field of two-person psychology. As development of object relationships was not a fashionable topic of the day, hardly any notice was taken of my findings, although I reported about them repeatedly (Balint, M., from 1932 on).

First I accepted Ferenczi's theoretical idea of the 'passive object love' (1924) for the description of this primitive relationship. He thought that the real aim in erotic life was to be loved, and any other observable activity was only a detour, an indirect way towards that goal. This idea sounded promising and, in fact, was able to explain a number of primitive attitudes to one's love objects, not only of infants but also of adults. In the long run, however, it proved untenable. Closer observation of patients in the new beginning period showed the immense importance of tranquil, quiet periods of contentment as well as expectations of being loved and satisfied by one's environment, but also an active seeking-out of contact with the environment. In view of this undeniable activity the term 'passive object-love' had to be abandoned, and since then I have been using the terms of primitive or primary, object-love, or primary object relationship (Balint, M., 1937).

135

I must, however, admit that this, too, proved to be an inadequate phrase. As my powers of observation improved, and my ability to listen became sharper, I was able to learn from my patients – as I have summarized in Chapter 12 – that there is one more phase prior to the emergence of primary objects (Balint, M., 1957, 1959), which might be called the phase of the undifferentiated environment, the phase of the primary substances, or – a somewhat clumsy phrase – the phase of the harmonious interpenetrating mix-up (Balint, M., 1959). To repeat what was discussed in more detail in Chapter 12, the best illustration for this state is the relationship we have towards the air surrounding us. It is difficult to say whether the air in our lungs or in our guts is us, or not us; and it does not even matter. We inhale the air, take out of it what we need, and after putting into it what we do not want to have, we exhale it, and we do not care at all whether the air likes it or not. It has to be there for us in adequate quantity and quality; and as long as it is there, the relationship between us and it cannot be observed, or only with very great difficulty; if, however, anything interferes with our supply of air, impressive and noisy symptoms develop in the same way as with the dissatisfied infant, or with the unsatisfied patient in the first phase of the new beginning.

The air is not an object but a substance, like water or milk. As I have already mentioned, there are a few – not many – more such substances, among them the elements of the pre-Socratic philosophers: water, earth, and fire; with some others used in present-day child guidance clinics, such as sand and water or plasticine. Their chief characteristic is their indestructibility. You can build a castle out of wet sand, then destroy it, and the sand will still be there; you can stop the jet of water coming from a tap but, as soon as you take your finger away, the jet is there again, and so on.

The analyst's role in certain periods of new beginning resembles in many respects that of the primary substances or objects. He must be there; he must be pliable to a very high degree; he must not offer much resistance; he certainly must be indestructible, and he must allow his patient to live with him in a sort of harmonious interpenetrating mix-up. I know this sounds rather comical and I am prepared for a goodly number of well-aimed jokes commenting on this new technique, but may I plead that I am trying to render into words experiences that belong to a period well before – or beyond –

the discovery of words, and largely even before the emergence of objects out of the ~~undisturbed harmony of the friendly substances~~.

In my experience ~~regression during analytic treatment – the first phase of a new beginning – aims at establishing an object relationship similar in structure to the primary relationship~~. Evidently this can be done only if the analyst realizes that this is what is happening, recognizes that this is what is needed at this moment, accepts this wish as part of the therapeutic process and does not try to inhibit its unfolding either by his behaviour or by his interpretations.

This is the positive side of the situation. Unfortunately there are negative sides as well, and these will be discussed in the next chapter.

Chapter 22

The various forms of therapeutic regression

Up to this point I have reported only on patients who went through a successful therapeutic regression, which may have created the impression that in my opinion regression was all that mattered in a difficult analytic treatment, and furthermore, that Freud's repeated warning for caution when dealing with a regressed form of transference was without much clinical foundation, while Ferenczi's technical ideas were all in the right direction, and only his premature death prevented him from proving that this was so. To dispel these false impressions, let us return to clinical observations.

Some years ago (Balint, M., 1952) I dealt at some length with the problem of those patients who, though capable of regression, were not able to reach the *arglos* unsuspecting state which is an absolutely necessary pre-condition for new beginning, and whose treatment had to be terminated with a partial result. Though these results were quite acceptable, they were below those achieved after a proper new beginning. For details I must refer the reader to the original publication.

According to my experience – apart from the partial successes due to the inability of the patient-analyst unit to reach the area of the new beginning – patients fall into two groups: in some treatments only one, or at most a few, periods of regression or new beginning occurred, after which the patient spontaneously emerged from his primitive world and felt better, or was even cured – as predicted by Ferenczi; while with some others it seemed that they could never have enough; as soon as one of their primitive wishes or needs was satisfied, it was replaced by a new wish or craving, equally demanding and urgent. This in some cases led to the development of addiction-like states which were very difficult to handle, and in some cases proved – as Freud predicted – intractable.

138

I found some explanation of this important difference in the third group of events in the symptomatology of the period of new beginning – the first two were the primitive forms of gratification and the changes in the object relationship. The events to which we now turn are the sudden changes of intensity in the analytical atmosphere, or in the transference. As long as one does not go deeper, the clinical symptomatology seems fairly simple. While the tension in the patient rises, that is to say, the expected satisfaction has not yet arrived, impressive and noisy symptoms are developed and maintained; as soon as the expected satisfaction has been experienced, the noisy symptoms disappear, and only a most careful observation can detect in the patient the signs of a tranquil, quiet well-being. This was about as far as I was able to go in the mid-thirties and, of course, I drew the obvious parallel between these observations and the change from the hungry to the satisfied baby.

However, I soon realized that this parallel, though plausible, was valid only within the confines of one-person psychology. To illustrate what I have in mind, may I go back to the precursor of all analytic therapy – the treatment of Miss Anna O. by Breuer.

A few ever-recurring features of regression already clearly emerge in her case history, although neither Breuer nor Freud seems to have recognized their fundamental nature; at any rate, there is no printed evidence for it. Miss Anna O. had no access to her repressed memories in her normal state, only in a hypnotic trance, which is a more primitive (i.e. regressed) state. Then we have the famous final scene, just before the termination of her treatment, in which she arranged her room like her father's sick room used to be; today this would be called a case of acting-out.

The relationship between the patient and her therapist during this period had become more primitive than that between two normal adults. One striking characteristic of this changed relationship was that, though the therapist became all-important for the patient, she could not feel or show much concern for him – he simply had to gratify the patient's expectations – exactly as happens in a relationship to primary objects. For instance, Breuer, a very busy physician, had to pay, as a matter of course, two daily visits of considerable length, and this had to go on for quite some time.

Other aspects of the situation were the great rewards received by the therapist. Provided he was able to meet his patient's demands, he

139

was allowed to observe and understand intimate and highly revealing secrets of the human mind and feel that his help mattered enormously. Over and above this, we must not forget that Miss Anna O. gave to Breuer as a free gift the method of 'talking cure' and, almost certainly, also the discovery of transference; and it was not her fault that he did not realize the full value of what he was given.

This is a fairly common picture with this type of patient. As long as the patient's expectations and demands are met, the therapist is allowed to observe most interesting, revealing events and *pari passu* his patient will feel better, appreciative and grateful. This is one side of the coin, but there is an obverse side too. If the expectations are not or cannot be met, what follows is unending suffering or unending vituperation, or both together. Once this situation has established itself, the analyst will find it very difficult to resist its power, to extricate his patient and himself from it, and still more difficult to terminate the relationship. Often the end amounts to a tragic or heroic finale.

This tragic situation has several determinants. One is the nature of the regression which in turn is determined by the patient's character, ego structure, and illness; the other is the analyst's response to his patient, regressing or regressed, prompted by his technique, that is, his counter-transference. If, as we discussed in Chapter 16, the analyst conscientiously follows Freud's classical instructions, it is unlikely that he will be exposed to these dangerous situations; but the probable price to be paid for this will be a number of broken-off analyses of patients who perhaps might have been helped by a more elastic technique. Since not every regression ends in a tragic way, the more we restrict the range of our responses, the more we restrict our potentiality to learn from the comparison of our failed and successfully terminated cases.

A further consequence of this technique is a limitation of our theory. In the previous chapter, I pointed out that Freud and, following him, almost the entire analytic literature, treated regression as an intrapsychic event, a phenomenon belonging to the field of one-person psychology. This simplification is valid only as long as the analyst restricts his study to cases of regression in which the response by the environment is negligible or is governed by Freud's instructions. If these restrictions are not considered as absolutely binding, regression appears as a phenomenon belonging to the field of two-person psychology, determined by the interaction of subject and object, that is, patient and analyst.

Returning to clinical observations we find that, with some patients, regression leads to these precarious or tragic situations; with others the whole atmosphere is totally different. With them – as I mentioned in the beginning of this chapter – only one period of regression occurred which turned out to be a real new beginning; with some others a few such periods. With others, as in the case of Miss Anna O., this sort of experience seemed to be interminable. A kind of vicious spiral developed; as soon as some of the patient's 'cravings' had been satisfied, new cravings or 'needs' appeared, demanding to be satisfied, leading eventually to a development of addiction-like states (Balint, M., 1934, 1937, 1952). To differentiate these two clinical types, one could be called the benign, the other the malignant, form of regression.

Of course, my first idea was that the patients with the malignant form of regression were those in whom there was a serious disproportion between the strength of their instincts and the strength of their ego; either the instincts were too strong even for a normal ego, or their ego was so weak that it was not able to cope with a normal equipment of instincts. If my theory was correct – so I thought – the malignant nature of the regression would show itself in causing excessively noisy symptoms, such as one would expect from a spoilt child or a severely psychopathic adult. However, this prediction proved correct only in a limited way, so I had to look round for other diagnostic criteria.

There is yet another fundamental difference. In some types of regression – or new beginning – the patient's aim is apparently to achieve gratification. The wish for it is so intense that it overshadows everything else in the analytic situation. I think it was this form that suggested to Freud the term 'craving'. Although the form of the gratification demanded by the patient was, as a rule, pre-genital, the high intensity of the demand could not fail to give rise to suspicion; in some cases, though not in all, further analysis proved these suspicions to be more or less correct; the high intensity revealed itself as a sign of the genital-orgastic nature of these wishes. This is an important point to which we have to return at the end of this chapter.

Moreover, as I have already mentioned, these regressions happen always within the analytic situation, that is, within an object relationship. In consequence, the gratification expected or demanded by the patient is never auto-erotic, it must come from the environment, which means that it must be initiated by an event in the external world, an event in which the analyst is willy-nilly deeply involved. In fact it depends on his passive consent or active participation – that is, on his decision – whether this external event will or will not take place, whether the patient's expectations or 'needs' will be gratified or frustrated. Now, there is another type of regression, the true new beginning, which equally depends on a deep involvement of the analyst; but in this type the accent is not so much on the expected change in the external world; though the participation of the external world, of the analyst, is essential, the event that matters is in the patient himself.

To illustrate this latter type, may I quote another of my cases which has already been used elsewhere (Balint, M., 1960). 'The patient, who at that time had been under analysis for about two years, remained silent, right from the start of the session for more than thirty minutes; the analyst accepted it and, realizing what was possibly happening, waited without any attempt whatever at interfering, in fact, he did not even feel uncomfortable or under pressure to do something. I should add that in this treatment silences had occurred previously on several occasions, and patient and analyst had thus had some training in tolerating them. The silence was eventually broken by the patient starting to sob, relieved, and soon after he was able to speak. He told his analyst that at long last he was able to reach himself; ever since childhood he had never been left alone, there had always been someone telling him what to do. Some sessions later he reported that during the silence he had all sorts of associations but rejected each of them as irrelevant, as nothing but an annoying superficial nuisance.'

In order to avoid misunderstandings, I will repeat here my ideas about how our terminology relating to this complex field ought to be clarified. I expect there will be general agreement that the event reported here belongs to what we call transference, and constitutes a piece of acting-out. Equally, there will be no argument that what happened amounted to an emergence of a primitive form of behaviour after more mature forms had established themselves. Perhaps with some reluctance it will, I think, be admitted that the technique adopted helped the patient towards a better integration, by

142

removing some of his inhibitions or even repressions. But, can this episode be called a regression or a repetition? My answer is the same here as in my previous case of the somersault, namely, that logically it cannot. One can repeat something only if the something existed at least once before; and on the whole, the same holds true for regression. Instead of these two misleading terms, I suggest calling this episode a 'new beginning' or a new discovery, leading to a different, more satisfactory, relationship to an important object. In this respect, the episode resembles closely that of the somersault. The difference is the conspicuous absence of any action and, therefore, of any obvious instinctual gratification that was present in the previous case.

To express this important difference in another form: nothing happened in the external world apart from the fact that it remained quiet, left the patient in peace. This in turn enabled the patient to get on with his inner life, recognize that some of his habitual, automatic ways of experiencing the external world and relating to it were – at any rate in this particular situation – unnecessary, unfounded, and pointless. This discovery led to a new beginning. In place of the old automatic forms of relationship, he can now start something new and different which may lead to the establishment of a more satisfactory relationship to his important objects.

On the other hand, because of the absence of action, which could be understood and then interpreted, the demands on the analyst's technique were somewhat higher in this case than in that of the somersault. He had to understand, without words, what the patient expected from him and live up to these expectations, that is, accord the patient unreservedly, without using words, the form of object relationship that he needed. May I add that this case in other respects, too, is true to type. If understood and satisfied, the patient was very grateful, got better, and gave his analyst most interesting material; had he not been understood and gratified, this would have caused him further 'dull' suffering and possibly despair. Moreover, had the analyst interpreted the patient's silence as a symptom of resistance or as a piece of acting out (correct interpretations by the way), he would have been seduced to tell his patient what to do and would only have colluded with his patient in the acting-out without much chance of ever recognizing that he was doing so.

Although in many ways my two cases of benign regression or new beginning and the malignant case of Miss Anna O. are similar, there is an important difference, which I hope is well illustrated by the case material. In the one form the regression is aimed at a gratification of instinctual cravings; what the patient seeks is an external event, an action by his object. In the other form what the patient expects is not so much a gratification by an external action, but a tacit consent to use the external world in a way that would allow him to get on with his internal problems – described by my patient as 'being able to reach himself'. Although the participation of the external world, of the object, is essential, the participation is entirely different in nature; apart from not interfering with, not causing unnecessary disturbance in, the patient's internal life (two important aspects), the chief form of this expected participation is the recognition of the existence of the patient's internal life and of the patient's own unique individuality. To contrast the two types, I would propose to call the first 'regression aimed at gratification', and the second 'regression aimed at recognition'. I am sure that both phrases are inexact and somewhat clumsy, but I could not devise anything better.

These observations show an interesting parallel to the other series of observations or, perhaps more correctly, inferences, about the real primary substances or objects (cf. Chapter 12). Gratification by events in, or actions by, the external world presupposes a world consisting either of already whole objects, or of well-developed part-objects, which means that the patient's regression could not have gone much beyond the narcissistic, phallic, pre-Oedipal level. Our literature contains many excellent reports about the passionate nature of wishes, fantasies, and instinctual behaviour, of children belonging to these early periods; in particular, of children who were previously subjected to traumatic experiences which – immediately or later – led to serious neurotic disturbances, such as the immense difficulty of satisfying the cravings of children suffering from these passionate desires or 'needs', the tendency of these children to produce addiction-like states, like compulsory masturbation, their great proneness to sexual seduction and, last but not least, their disposition for developing acting-out types of hysterical states. I mentioned above that in some patients I was doubtful about the genuineness of their new beginning because of the excessively passionate nature of their demands. I wish to add here that all these patients belonged to the class just described.

The other type, the regression for the sake of recognition, pre-supposes an environment that accepts and consents to sustain and carry the patient like the earth or the water sustains and carries a man who entrusts his weight to them. In contrast to ordinary objects, especially to ordinary human objects, no action is expected from these primary objects or substances; yet they must be there and must – tacitly or explicitly – consent to be used, otherwise the patient cannot achieve any change: without water it is impossible to swim, without earth impossible to move on. The substance, the analyst, must not resist, must consent, must not give rise to too much friction, must accept and carry the patient for a while, must prove more or less indestructible, must not insist on maintaining harsh boundaries, but must allow the development of a kind of mix-up between the patient and himself.

All this means consent, participation, and involvement, but *not* necessarily action, only understanding and tolerance; what really matters is the creation and maintenance of conditions in which events can take place internally, in the patient's mind.

The symbolic expression of this primitive *arglos* relationship in the analytic situation is often some sort of physical contact with the analyst, the most frequent form of which is the holding of the analyst's hand, or one of his fingers, or touching his chair, etc. This contact is definitely libidinous, on occasion may even be highly charged, and is always vitally important for the progress of the treatment; with it the patient can get on, without it he may feel abandoned, lost, despoiled of his possible changes, incapable of moving. In spite of all this, the actual experience in the cases of 'regression for recognition' never has the qualities of despair and passion which characterize the patient's experience in the other form of regression: that for the sake of gratification, or that found in severe hysteria. I am inclined to think that the desperate forms of clinging, so often encountered in the treatment of these latter conditions, denote a regression merely to the phase of part-objects, while an intense anxiety seems to block the way towards the development of a mutually trusting *arglos* atmosphere, which is essential for a true new beginning. Relationship to part-objects is apparently akin in origin, and possibly even in nature, to persecutory anxieties; desperate passionate clinging is an expression of this relationship and, at the same time, a defence against its concomitant anxieties. This is in

145

striking contrast to the relaxed need for physical contact observed in the period of a true new beginning.

Of course, in life nothing is simple or clearly defined. In most cases of therapeutic regression what the analyst gets to see is a mixture of all these features, with, on the whole, one or some characteristics prevailing. Still, according to my experience, there seems to be a definite tendency for certain features to occur together, creating the impression of two not quite sharply defined areas of associations, two clinical syndromes of some sort which I propose to call Clusters A and B.

Most cases belonging to Cluster A, the benign form of regression, show the following clinical features:

1. not much difficulty in establishing a mutually trusting *arglos*, unsuspecting relationship, which is reminiscent of the primary relationship towards primary substances;

2. a regression, leading to a true new beginning, and ending in a real new discovery;

3. the regression is for the sake of recognition, in particular, of the patient's internal problems;

4. only moderately high intensity of the demands, expectations, or 'needs';

5. absence of signs of severe hysteria in the clinical symptomatology and of genital-orgastic elements in the regressed transference.

In contrast, most cases belonging to Cluster B, the malignant form of regression, show the following picture:

1. since the mutually trusting relationship is highly precariously balanced, the *arglos*, unsuspecting, atmosphere breaks down repeatedly, and frequently symptoms of desperate clinging develop as safeguards and reassurance against another possible breakdown;

2. a malignant form of regression, several unsuccessful attempts at reaching a new beginning, a constant threat of an unending spiral of demands or needs, and of development of addiction-like states;

3. the regression is aimed at gratification by external action;

4. suspiciously high intensity of demands, expectations, or 'needs';

5. presence of signs of severe hysteria in the clinical picture, and of genital-orgastic elements both in the normal and in the regressed form of transference.

These abstractions are based on fairly well substantiated clinical experiences, except one of them, which is not yet so firmly founded as the rest, though I think it will be proved by further experiences. It is my impression that the malignant regression, and the regression aimed at gratification by external action, are found, as a rule, in patients suffering from a fairly severe form of hysteria, or hysterical character disorder, who have contrived to derive a fair amount of secondary gain from their illness, and also from their treatment. It is not quite clear to me why it has to be so, but I think it ought to be recorded that in my clinical material this association occurred in several cases. I shall return to this problem later in Part V.

Before going further, however, I wish to sum up very briefly what we know theoretically about regression. Following Freud, we conceive regression as a process consisting of a reversion of the normal 'progressive' direction of happenings in the mental apparatus. Its cause may be anything that obstructs the normal direction; as a rule, at the Oedipal level, it is a conflict. The effect or result of regression is the emergence of something 'primitive' or 'simple'; in some cases, certainly not in all, this something belongs to the area of the basic fault. Clinically this may appear: (a) as a special form of instinctual gratification, like an hallucination or a dream; (b) as a specific form of behaviour, like regressive transference in the service of resistance; and (c) as repetition, the most important example of which is transference in general.

As we have learnt from Freud, regression may have four functions or roles: (a) as a mechanism of defence, (b) as a factor in pathogenesis, (c) as a specific form of resistance, and lastly (d) as an important ally in therapy. Remarkably, one aspect of regression was left out by Freud, and following him by almost every theoretician in psychoanalysis, and that is the role of regression in object relationship. The reason for this omission is that regression was studied only within the limits of one-person psychology. The two notable exceptions to this rule have been: (a) regression as a therapeutic ally, which was mentioned only once and very briefly by Freud, and (b) regression as a specific form of transference in the service of resistance, which was described only in its threatening aspects as a severe obstacle and a serious warning.

What I have tried to show in Parts III and IV is that regression is not only an intrapsychic phenomenon, but also an interpersonal one; for its therapeutic usefulness, its interpersonal aspects are decisive. In order to understand the full meaning of regression and to deal with it in the analytic situation, it is important to bear in mind that the form in which the regression is expressed depends only partly on the patient, his personality, and his illness, but partly also on the object; in consequence it must be considered as *one* symptom of the interaction between the patient and his analyst. This interaction has at least three aspects: the way (a) in which regression is recognized by the object, (b) in which it is accepted by the object, and (c) in which it is responded to by the object. As we have seen in Chapters 20–22, what is expected from the object, the analyst, is for him to respond in a manner reminiscent of primary substances, that is, to allow the patient to enter with him into a form of primary relationship or primary object-love. Our task in Part V will be to examine what this means in terms of psycho-analytic technique.

Chapter 23

The disagreement between Freud and Ferenczi, and its repercussions

Let us now return to the historical difference between Freud and Ferenczi where we left it at the end of Chapter 19. The technical problem of how to respond to a regressed patient who had developed an intense transference, was perhaps the major cause of this tragic disagreement. The impact of this event was so painful that the first reaction of the analytic movement to it was denial and silence, broken only in recent years, since when all sorts of fictitious statements about Freud and Ferenczi have found their way into print: Freud was described as a ruthless autocrat, a dictator (Fromm, 1963) and Ferenczi as a mean, cowardly schemer (Jones, 1957). Of course, all the monstrosities alleged are utterly untrue; what they show up is the difference between the greatness of the victims and the pettiness of their calumniators.

The clinical experiences discussed in this Part may give us some clues to the understanding of the probable build-up of the disagreement. I think that Freud in his early psychotherapeutic years encountered, almost exclusively, cases of malignant regression, and these encounters left a deep impression on him. Ferenczi, on the contrary, had some remarkable successes with a few benign cases of regression as well as some failures with malignant ones, but was so impressed that his well-known enthusiasm carried him away into an ill-founded generalization. Can these rather bold assumptions be substantiated from the literature? My contention is that there are a number of passages in both Freud's and Ferenczi's writings that point in these directions.

Freud's first experience with a malignant regression was in Breuer's treatment of Miss Anna O., at which time Breuer and Freud were already friends; we know from Freud's letters to his fiancée, quoted by Jones (1953), that Breuer discussed his worries caused

149

by his patient's serious regression with his young friend – Freud was then twenty-seven – and further, that Freud was rather critical of Breuer's approach. We know also of his later unpleasant experiences with gross sexual manifestations by patients just emerging from a hypnotic trance – mentioned in his 'Autobiographical Study' (1925, p. 27); and last, perhaps the most important, of his being led astray by his hysterical patients into accepting as a fact that in early childhood they had been victims of sexual seduction, that is, had suffered a 'passive sexual trauma'. It is perhaps worth recalling that in his paper 'The Aetiology of Hysteria' (1896) Freud stated in so many words that this theory was now based on *eighteen fully analysed cases*, evidently all of them hysterics. We know also that this spell could be broken only by his self-analysis.[1] It is understandable that he called these patients' expectations 'cravings', which strongly suggests that he recognized already at that time the danger of addiction-like states.

In Chapter 19, I discussed at some length the very slow development of the idea of regression and how with the passing years its threatening aspects became more and more prevalent in Freud's writings, resulting in his extremely cautious attitude. *Pari passu* with this development the therapeutic function of regression receded into the background, one might say, became forgotten.

It is then no wonder that when he saw Ferenczi, for whom he had so much affection and whom he held in such high esteem, slipping away into the same morass from which he (Freud) could escape only by a supreme effort, he could not help becoming alarmed, critical, and – what is very rare indeed for Freud – somewhat insensitive. He saw, clearly and correctly, the dangers that Ferenczi was courting, but could neither recognize, nor appreciate, the possibilities of a new and important development both in our technique and our theory.

---

[1] We do not know, of course, whether there were any causal connections between the two events, but the chronological connections are there. Before his self-analysis Freud firmly believed in the reality of the seduction scenes; after his self-analysis he equally firmly believed that the seduction happened only in the children's fantasy. Furthermore, we know that he started, or perhaps got really going with his self-analysis in the summer of 1897, and in September of that year, in a letter to Fliess, he gave his reasons why he would have to abandon his idea about the reality of the infantile sexual traumata – even among Freud's writings a most impressive and masterly piece of argument.

Ferenczi, whose impetuous optimism and ready enthusiasm for any new idea I have discussed on several occasions (Balint, M., 1933, 1948), made his usual mistake of disregarding all warning signals of his failures and over-valuation of his successes. He was so impressed by the results of his new technique that he came to the conclusion that if a patient was willing to come regularly to analysis, the analyst must find techniques to help him. In his sincere belief in this principle, he went to really incredible lengths to meet his patients' expectations (cf. Chapter 18). Ferenczi summed up the essence of his new experiments by calling it 'the principle of relaxation' (1930). This name was a natural association, since the new technical idea, in contrast to the active technique, aimed at avoiding any unnecessary increase of tension. Ferenczi thought that responding positively to the patient's expectations, demands, or needs, now that he had learned to understand them in their true significance, might change the lifeless situation of a long drawn-out analysis so that fruitful work might follow leading to a speedy termination. This, however, meant abandoning the principle of abstinence.

The immediate results of this technical approach were encouraging. His patients – most of them with more than a decade of treatment by other analysts behind them – came to life again, their state improved, and they presented Ferenczi with two major discoveries. One was about the immense effect of the analyst's 'customary', 'habitual', or 'classical' attitudes towards practising as an analyst on the developing transference relationship, and on the course of the analytic treatment; the other was about the technical possibilities of a counter-transference interpretation (Ferenczi, 1932, and his posthumous notes).

All this does not mean that Ferenczi did not see the problems raised by his technical innovations; that he did so is quite clear from his posthumously published papers and notes; but he honestly believed that his findings amounted to a major progress in analytic technique. What remained the most painful problem for him, to which he returned time and again, was why it was that Freud could not see the importance of these new ideas. I am certain that the feeling of not being understood by Freud hindered him – after all, Freud had been his training analyst – for quite some time in realizing that the unquestionable improvement in some of his patients would last only as long as he was able to satisfy their cravings; this

151

realization came only gradually towards the end of 1932, and the beginning of 1933, when, because of his increasing physical weakness, he had to give up his analytic practice. A number of his patients reacted to this with confused despair or bitter resentment and a deterioration in their state. Although this was a very severe blow to his scientific pride, he accepted it fully, spoke a good deal about his possible mistakes in the recent past, and said that if he ever got better he would have to start right from the beginning; but he expressed his hope that his experiments and his mistakes would be used by future generations as important signposts and warning signals.

In spite of this, I doubt very much whether he got so far as to differentiate between the various types of regression described in Chapter 22. I too arrived at this differential diagnosis only during the last fifteen years or so, but would like to record that I received the first stimulus towards it by remaining in contact with a number of Ferenczi's last group of patients, following their developments, and especially the ways in which they talked about their experiences while under treatment with him, and after.

The tragic disagreement between Freud and Ferenczi, which caused both of them so much pain, and considerably delayed the development of our analytic technique, is now, I hope, clearer. Ferenczi, because of his own uncertainty, could not make use of Freud's well-meant and well-founded criticisms; he saw in them only lack of understanding. Freud, for his part, was still under the influence of his disappointing experiences in the nineties, and found in Ferenczi's experiments nothing but confirmation for his cautiousness. The characters of the two men, although very different in their superficial appearance, had many roots common to both. As it has happened in many tragic historical friendships, these common roots acted first as a powerful attraction, served for many years as a basis for an intimate and happy friendship, but led irresistibly to a tragic end; and in the end everyone became a loser, including all of us psychoanalysts.

The historic event of the disagreement between Freud and Ferenczi acted as a trauma on the psychoanalytic world. Whether one assumed that a consummate master of psychoanalytic technique like Ferenczi, the author of a great number of classical papers in psychoanalysis, had been blinded to such an extent that even Freud's repeated warnings could not make him recognize his mistakes; or that Freud and Ferenczi, the two most prominent psychoanalysts, were not able to understand and properly evaluate each other's clinical findings, observations, and theoretical ideas, the shock was highly disturbing and extremely painful. The first reaction to it was a frightened withdrawal. By tacit consent, regression during analytic treatment was declared a dangerous symptom and its value as a therapeutic ally completely, or almost completely, repressed. This is particularly true for the attitude of what may be called the 'classical' massive centre of psychoanalysis.

For most analysts belonging to this group regression retained only its threatening, pejorative aspects that were discussed in Chapter 19: it was a mechanism of defence difficult to tackle, it was an important factor in pathogenesis, and it was a formidable form of resistance. Its function as an ally of therapy has practically disappeared from their considerations. In consequence, if phenomena of a regressive nature appeared during treatment, they were considered either as undesirable symptoms caused by a questionable technique, or as indications of such a deep disturbance in the patient as to make the prognosis doubtful. It seems as if the most frequently adopted measure in such cases was to get the patient out of his regression as quickly as possible and then to terminate the treatment with an acceptable part result. At any rate, this is the picture that emerges from the Panel Discussion on 'Technical Aspects of Regression during Psychoanalysis' at the mid-winter meeting of the American Psychoanalytical Association in 1957. Incidentally, parallel with the Panel on Regression, another panel was held on 'Technical Aspects of Transference'. Comparing the lists of the discussants in the two panels, it is easy to ascertain which analysts belong to the massive 'classical' centre and which belong merely to the fringe.

The only new, and very fruitful, idea that originated from this group is that of Ernst Kris who, during his investigation of artistic creativity, came to distinguish between two forms of regression. In the one form 'the ego is overwhelmed by regression'; in the other 'the regression is in the service of the ego'. This latter form, according to Kris, is only a special case of the more general capacity of a well-integrated ego to regulate and control some of the primary processes. This idea was first formulated in 1935, but Kris returned to it in several of his later papers. Unquestionably, this differentiation has much in common with my two clusters; the malignant regression

153

and the regression for the sake of gratification are very near to the regression that overwhelms the ego; equally, with some effort, one can see some similarity between the regression in the service of the ego and the regression for the sake of recognition. The chief reason for this difficulty will be what I called (Balint, M., 1949) our different bias. Kris was interested in artistic creativity, that is sublimation, which belongs to the field of one-person-psychology. This difference was admirably expressed by Peter Knapp in the panel discussion on 'Criteria for Analysability'. After pointing out that 'regression in the service of the ego' is capable of explaining what happens in an individual during artistic creation, but is incapable of describing and explaining what happens during analytic treatment, he continued: 'For a psychoanalysis to be possible, an additional capacity must supplement "regression in the service of the ego", namely, "regression at the behest of an object"' (Knapp, 1959).

This must have been a revolutionary remark and was, very likely, subjected to repression. In any case, as far as I could discover, it has not elicited any echo in the literature. Even such an original thinker as Bertram Lewin could not free himself completely from the limitations of Kris's ideas in his Freud lecture on 'Dreams and the Uses of Regression' (1958). Neither were two such unorthodox therapists as Gill and Brenman able to do so (Gill and Brenman, 1959).

The other protagonists belonging to this group do not venture even that far; instead they go on faithfully and monotonously repeating the eternal connections between fixation and regression, already described by Freud in his *Introductory Lectures*. To prove my point, may I quote, among many others, Phyllis Greenacre: 'Regression and Fixation' (1960), Jacob Arlow: 'Conflict, Regression and Symptom Formation' (1963), and Jeanne Lampl-de Groot: 'Symptom Formation and Character Formation' (1963).

The general impression, thus, is that of bleakness and stagnation. Still, in recent years there have been a few analysts, admittedly very few, who were interested in the problem of therapeutic regression. One of them was Alexander (1956), who proposed to differentiate between two types of regression: that to the trauma and that to the pre-traumatic satisfactory situation. It is very likely that there will be many parallels between his two types and mine. Then there is the interesting research carried out in Chestnut Lodge with severely regressed patients, the most important results of which were published by Searles (e.g. 1961, 1963). And lastly, in London, we have Winnicott, who has studied regression in the analytic setting for many years; his widely scattered original papers have been collected in two volumes (1958 and 1965). Under his influence several analysts, among them Little (1957) and Khan (1960, 1962), have become interested in the same field.

That is about all. All these analysts, including myself, belong – not to the 'classical' massive centre – but to the fringe. We are known, tolerated, perhaps even read, but certainly not quoted. A good illustration of this statement is the book by Gill and Brenman (1959). Although one of the main topics of the book is the therapeutic use of regression, and it has an extensive bibliography, not one of us is mentioned. There are signs, however, that this period is ending. The tragic event occurred in the early thirties, more than thirty years ago. This means that since then a new generation of analysts has grown up, and one may hope that they will be able to – or are already about to – re-examine certain tenets and beliefs, which for many years were taboo for a proper analyst. One of these promising signs is the recent paper by W. Loch (1963–64) entitled 'Regression'.

In the same year Anna Freud published a paper: 'Regression as a Principle in Mental Development' (1963), in which she stressed – instead of the customary threatening aspects of regression – its benign aspects as well. This was quickly followed by yet another Panel of the American Psychoanalytic Association at its Fall Meeting in December 1965 on 'Severe Regressive States during Analysis'. The situation has changed considerably since the last panel in 1957. Although a number of the discussants were the same as in 1957, they were this time evenly balanced by members of the 'classical' centre. There were still some unmistakable signs of the old apprehension, but the atmosphere was utterly different. Several impressive case histories were reported in detail, demonstrating not only that severely regressive states can be tolerated in the analytic situation, but also that some of them can be used to further the process of analytic treatment. There were hardly any signs of prejudice or preconceived ideas in the excellent discussion; each discussant was sincerely interested and keen to contribute his share to the clarification of a puzzling problem.

One comment must, however, be made. Although a few speakers – among them the Chairman, John Frosch, and Martin Cang – tried on several occasions to direct the discussion to the analyst's share both in promoting or even provoking regression and to his technical responses to it, they could not succeed. The discussion remained confined within the limits of one-person psychology: the ego over-whelmed by regression, the nature of the patient's ego in whose treatment this can happen, the forces in the mind that lead to regression, the changes that may bring the patient out of it, etc.

What was almost entirely avoided was to consider regression – in its structure, its causation, and its significance for the treatment – as an interaction between the particular patient and the particular analyst, that is, a phenomenon belonging to the field of two-person psychology, in particular to that area of the mind that I described as the area of the basic fault.

PART V

The regressed patient and his analyst

Chapter 24

Therapeutic regression, primary love, and the basic fault

In the previous Part we have found that regression, as observed in the analytic situation, may have at least two aims: gratification of an instinct or drive and recognition by an object; in other words, it is both an intrapsychic and an interpersonal phenomenon. We also found strong indications that for the analytic therapy of regressed states its interpersonal aspects were more important.

The problem at which we have arrived here may be termed 'the healing power of relationship'. Although, as a rule, it is not stated quite so explicitly, we are compelled to recognize that the two most important factors in psychoanalytic therapy are interpretations and object relationship. It should be borne in mind, however, that with the latter we are on comparatively unsafe grounds because psychoanalytic theory knows much less about it.

We have some systematic knowledge about the instincts or drives and their vicissitudes, about the structure of the mind and the various defensive mechanisms working in it, and also about the role of conflict in psychopathology. It was on these three pillars – the theory of the instincts, of the structure of the mind, and of the pathogenic effects of conflicts – that Freud based his technical recommendations. The aim of his technique was to make the unconscious conscious – or in a later version: where id was, ego shall be – and the tool for achieving this aim was almost exclusively interpretation. Although as early as 1912 and 1915 in his two papers on Transference, he stated in so many words that transference, that is an object relationship, may have considerable healing powers, he evidently mistrusted them, and never considered them worthy of a proper study. In consequence, interpretation became accepted as far the most important technical measure.

As I tried to show in Part IV, putting all the emphasis on the

159

analyst's interpretative work amounted, perhaps, to an over-simplification. This worked as long as we were able to select from all the people, who asked for analytic help, those who without much difficulty could adapt themselves to the analytic setting created by us according to Freud's early papers on technique (1911–15). As long as this setting was accepted as obligatory for all of us, the analyst's work could be considered as consisting almost solely of interpretations.

However, if we recognize that the setting recommended by Freud represents only one of the many possible settings – that is, it is a sort of *primus inter pares* – a new task emerges for us which is to find other settings in which analytical work with less strictly selected patients can profitably be carried out. This task has a special importance for patients in regression.

To repeat what we have found in the previous chapters, in certain periods of the treatment, creating and maintaining a workable relationship, particularly with a patient in regression, is perhaps a more important therapeutic task than giving correct interpretations. Possibly something like this was in Freud's mind when he wrote about the therapeutic effects of transference. However, as just mentioned, his interest was centred chiefly on the intrapsychic processes that may have therapeutic effects, and he did not pay much attention to the interpersonal phenomena and their possible effects on therapy.

But, whatever the case may be, interpretations are, of necessity, always verbal. Although one of their principal aims is to help the patient to have feelings, emotions, and experiences that he was incapable of having before, they demand intellectual understanding, thinking, or a new 'insight'. All of these descriptions have close connections either with 'seeing' or 'standing', that is with philobatic activities, which can be performed alone. In contrast, object relationship is always an interaction between at least two people and, more often than not, is created and maintained also by non-verbal means. It is difficult to find words to describe what it is that is created. We talk about behaviour, climate, atmosphere, etc., all of which are vague and hazy words, referring to something with no firm boundaries and thus reminiscent of those describing primary substances. In spite of the fact that the various forms of object relationship cannot be described by concise and unequivocal words, that is, the translation of the various object relationships into words must always be

160

subjective, arbitrary, and inexact, the 'atmosphere', the 'climate', is there, it is felt to be there, and more often than not there is even no need to express it in words – although words may be an important contributory factor both to its creation and its maintenance. In contrast to 'insight', which is the result of a correct interpretation, the creation of a proper relationship results in a 'feeling'; while 'insight' correlates with seeing, 'feeling' correlates with touching, that is, either primary relationship or ocnophilia.

Returning now to our main topic, regression, it was its intra-psychic aspects that remained in the focus of Freud's interest throughout his life. One reason, perhaps, for this comparative neglect might be that at the time when he described the regressive forms of transference, his instinct theory was practically finished; the third edition of his *Three Essays on Sexuality* appeared in 1915, that is the same year in which he published his paper 'On Transference-Love'. On the other hand, a developmental theory of object relationship was at that time in its earliest beginnings.

It was on his instinct theory that Freud based his often-quoted therapeutic recommendations that the analyst should not respond positively to a regressed patient's 'cravings', in particular, should not satisfy them. The analytic therapy must be carried out in the state of 'abstinence', 'frustration', or 'privation'. In many ways this recommendation is correct. If the analyst does not do anything else apart from gratifying his regressed patient's cravings, his action cannot but produce temporary results. Since the source of the cravings has not even been touched, after a while new cravings will appear demanding, equally strongly, new gratifications. If then the analyst, influenced by the blissful peace immediately following his action, is induced to experiment with further gratifications, a never-ending vicious spiral may develop which is not uncommon in regressed states.

Thus, responding positively to a regressed patient's longings and cravings by gratifying them, will be very likely to prove a technical error. On the other hand, responding to a patient's needs for a particular form of object relationship, more primitive than that obtaining between adults, may be a legitimate technical measure which possibly has nothing to do with the rule of 'frustration' or 'privation'.

But, if we accept this idea, we leave the boundaries of instinct or drive theory, which belongs to the sphere of one-person psychology, and enter the realm of two-person psychology. Whereas, on the basis of the former, we could maintain that both the form and the depth of regression are determined solely by the patient, his childhood, his character, the severity of his illness, etc., etc., in the latter we must consider them as the result of an interaction between the particular patient and his particular analyst. Concentrating for a moment on the analyst's contributions, that is, on his technique, we may say that the clinical appearance of a regression will depend also on the way the regression is recognized, is accepted, and is responded to by the analyst.

Perhaps the most important form of the analyst's response is interpretation; it may have a crucial influence on the treatment, whether the analyst interprets any particular phenomenon as a demand for gratification or as a need for a particular form of object relationship.

Supposing the analyst is prepared to consider regression as a request, demand, or need, for a particular form of object relationship, the next question will be how far should he go or, in other words, what sort of object relationship he should consider offering to, or accepting from, his regressed patient. This is an important technical problem and, as with almost every problem in psychoanalytic technique, it has several aspects.

The first aspect belongs to the borderland between one-person and two-person psychologies; it may be described as a problem of differential diagnosis. The analyst must be able to recognize which forms of object relationship will be adequate, or even therapeutic at this moment for his regressed patient. In order to do so, he must not only accept that these relationships exist and may have therapeutic effects but must also know enough of them to be able to choose the one with the best therapeutic possibilities.

With this we enter a controversial field. Some analysts firmly believe that only those forms of object relationship are compatible with a proper running of analytic therapy that allow the analyst to retain his role of passive, sympathetic objectivity described by Freud. I have the impression that they still feel that this is an absolute parameter, and if the analyst, for any reason whatsoever, abandons it, the treatment should no longer be called psychoanalysis. If this impression is correct, it follows that these analysts will probably maintain that this differential diagnosis is unnecessary, or even conducive to faulty, harmful technique. In Part III, in particular in Chapters 14 and 16, I discussed some of the consequences of this general policy.

In order to avoid a possible misunderstanding, it is important to realize that interpreting to the patient that he has always tried to establish a particular genital, or even pre-genital, relationship, is something utterly different from accepting, and working with, the fact that the patient at this particular stage needs a certain form of object relationship, and allowing him to create and maintain it in the analytic situation. However, in the cases of the better-known, later, object relationships, interpretations, as a rule, have enough power to start and to maintain a therapeutic readjustment to reality; in some cases there may come to be some 'acting-out' but this, too, can be dealt with by interpretations. Most of this class belong to what I called the Oedipal area, and thus the events occurring during them can be expressed fairly adequately in conventional adult language. The most important of them are – in reverse chronological order: the phallic-narcissistic form with its many variants, such as egotistic-self-assertive, aggressive-castrating, submissive, masochistic, etc.; the many anal-sadistic forms with all the over-compensations and reaction-formations belonging to them, and so on.

For the sake of completeness I must mention here the various oral forms of object relationship, summed up nowadays as 'oral dependence' which many analysts would include here as a matter of course. Since, in my opinion, 'oral dependence' is a misleading concept, may I sum up briefly my arguments against it.

The relationship that 'oral dependence' tries to describe is *not* a one-sided dependence, but an 'inter-dependence'; libidinally, the mother is almost to the same extent dependent on her baby as the baby is on her; neither of them may have this particular form of relationship and the particular satisfaction independently from the other. Though oral aspects constitute an important part of the whole phenomenon, there are various other factors present, and it is difficult to assess with certainty which is the most important. Furthermore, the mother's breast, the counterpart of the child's mouth, is about as often as not excluded by present-day nursing fashion – in most cases without seriously interfering with the mutual interdependence which, in my opinion, is the decisive factor in this relationship.

The interdependence should remind us that any attempt at describing this relationship using terms of one-person psychology will

163

necessarily be misleading. Although this is true up to a point for all relationships, the effect of interdependence diminishes at the same rate as the importance of the partner's cooperation. An instructive example is anal domination, the theory of which is perhaps the best developed in psychoanalysis. Here the cooperation of the partner is minimal, in consequence the relationship can be described adequately by terms belonging to one-person psychology. On the other hand, in genital love it is essential that an indifferent object whom we love should be changed by us into a cooperative partner. The relationship between an individual and his indifferent object can be described fairly well with our terminology, whereas the relationship between cooperating partners needs a new terminology belonging to two-person psychology.

A further important difficulty is that all primitive relationships belong, as a rule, to the pre-verbal period of development. As we have seen in Part I, phenomena belonging to this area do not lend themselves easily to verbal description. In what follows we have to bear these two difficulties constantly in our minds: the one caused by the intense interdependence of two individuals, and the second caused by the primitive nature of the developing relationship which is hard to render in adult conventional words.[1]

After removing this obstacle, and the confusion created by it, we may return to our main problem: what sort of primitive, possibly preverbal, object relationships should the analyst consider accepting from, or even offering to, his regressed patient?

In the preceding chapters, in particular in 4, 12, 15, and 22, I

[1] 'Oral dependence' is a relatively new concept. I could not discover any reference to it in Freud's writings, so it seems to be a post-Freudian, and most probably American, creation. I think it would be an interesting study to find out the exact history of its development. Here are a few data for it. 'Dependence' without the adjective 'oral' occurs a few times in Fenichel's textbook (1945). The first use of 'oral dependence' that I found was by F. Alexander in 1950. To my surprise I could not find it in Melanie Klein's writings; the first reference to it by her school seems to occur in *New Directions in Psycho-Analysis* (1955), a collection of papers written for Melanie Klein on the occasion of her seventieth birthday in 1952. Here too the adjective 'oral' was missing but the term 'dependence' referred to what today would be called oral dependence, the dependence of the child on his mother; the two authors using it were Paula Heimann and Joan Rivière. From about 1952, dependence, and even oral dependence, occurs with ever-increasing frequency in Winnicott's papers, but apparently not before that date.

described in detail the characteristics of the three chief forms observed in my analytic practice. These were: (a) the most primitive, which I called *primary love*, or primary relationship, a sort of harmonious interpenetrating mix-up between the developing individual and his primary substances or his primary object; (b) and (c) *ocnophilia* and *philobatism* which form a kind of counterpart with one another; they already presuppose the discovery of fairly stable part and/or whole objects. For the predominantly ocnophilic individual, life is safe only in close proximity to objects, while the intervening periods or spaces between objects are felt as horrid and dangerous. These phenomena have been known for some considerable time; recently under the influence of ethology they are referred to as 'attachment behaviour' (e.g. Bowlby, 1958). In contrast, the predominantly philobatic individual experiences the objects as unreliable and hazardous, is inclined to dispense with them, and seeks out the friendly expanses separating the treacherous objects in time and space.

The next question is, of course, what can a patient gain from regression? Why is it so important to him? As I have mentioned several times, not all patients go necessarily through a regressive period. That means that some patients can do without it, perhaps they do not even need it. However, it is difficult to get any indication about the distribution of those people who do, and those who do not, need a regressive period. The reason for this is that patients who go through an analytic treatment do not constitute a representative sample, because they have been selected according to their analyst's ideas about analysability. Still, there is perhaps some truth in the impression that in our present patient material the number of those who need regression is greater than in the past and is perhaps still increasing.

The answer to our question lies in the idea of the basic fault and in the observations that led me to the discovery of the 'new beginning'. My train of thought runs as follows: all of us have certain character traits or, expressed in modern terminology, compulsive patterns of object relationship. Some of these are the outcome of a conflict or complex in us; if the analyst with his interpretations can help his patient to solve these conflicts and complexes, the compulsive nature of these patterns will be reduced to a level flexible enough to permit adaptation to reality. In a number of cases in which, according to my ideas, the patterns originate in a reaction to the basic fault, interpretations will have incomparably less power, since there is no conflict or complex in the strict sense to solve and in the area of the basic fault, words are not quite reliable tools anyhow.

In some cases in which words, that is associations followed by interpretations, do not seem to be able to induce or maintain the necessary changes, additional therapeutic agents should be considered. In my opinion, the most important of these is to help the patient to develop a primitive relationship in the analytic situation corresponding to his compulsive pattern and maintain it in undisturbed peace till he can discover the possibility of new forms of object relationship, experience them, and experiment with them. Since the basic fault, as long as it is active, determines the forms of object relationship available to any individual, a necessary task of the treatment is to inactivate the basic fault by creating conditions in which it can heal off. To achieve this, the patient must be allowed to regress either to the setting, that is, to the particular form of object relationship which caused the original deficiency state, or even to some stage before it. This is a precondition which must be fulfilled before the patient can give up, very tentatively at first, his compulsive pattern. Only after that can the patient 'begin anew', that is develop new patterns of object relationship to replace those given up. These new patterns will be less defensive and thus more flexible, offering him more possibility to adapt himself to reality under less tension and friction than hitherto.

The next and last question in this chapter will be: what can the analyst do to foster this process? The greater part of the answer will follow in the next chapter; here I would like to stress only three highly important *negative* aspects, that is, what the analyst must try to avoid doing. Our present fashion in technique – which recommends that, if at all possible, everything should be interpreted first as transference – tempts us to turn into mighty and knowledgeable objects for our patients, thus helping – or forcing – them to regress into an ocnophilic world. In this world there are ample opportunities for dependence but very meagre ones for making independent discoveries. I hope it will be generally agreed that the latter is at least as important therapeutically as the former. Conversely, this means that the analyst must not stick rigidly to one form of object relationship that he found useful in other cases or during the preceding phases of this treatment but must all the time be prepared to alternate with his patient between the ocnophilic and the philobatic primitive worlds, and even go beyond them towards primary relationship. This can be done only if the analyst is capable of the differential diagnosis described above.

The other important negative aspect is that at times the analyst must do everything in his power not to become, or to behave as, a separate, sharply-contoured object. In other words, he must allow his patients to relate to, or exist with, him as if he were one of the primary substances. This means that he should be willing to carry the patient, not actively but like water carries the swimmer or the earth carries the walker, that is, to be there for the patient, to be used without too much resistance against being used. True, some resistance is not only permissible but essential. However, the analyst must be careful that his resistance should create only as much friction as is needed for progress but definitely not much more, otherwise progress may become too difficult owing to the resistance of the medium. Over and above all this, he must be there, must always be there, and must be indestructible – as are water and earth. We discussed some of these aspects in Chapter 22, and we shall continue with them in those following.

A corollary to the previous negative aspect is our last one, also negative, that the analyst must avoid becoming, or even appearing in the eyes of his patient, 'omnipotent'. This is one of the most difficult tasks in this period of the treatment. The regressed patient expects his analyst to know more, and to be more powerful; if nothing else, the analyst is expected to promise, either explicitly or by his behaviour, that he will help his patient out of the regression, or see the patient through it. Any such promise, even the slightest appearance of a tacit agreement towards it, will create very great difficulties, almost insurmountable obstacles, for the analytic work. Here too, the only thing that the analyst can do is to accept the role of a true primary substance, which is there, which cannot be destroyed, which *eo ipso* is there to carry the patient, which feels the patient's importance and weight but still carries him, which is unconcerned about keeping up proper boundaries between the patient and itself, etc., but which is not an object in the true sense, is not concerned about its independent existence.

Several other authors tried to describe this sort of object

167

relationship or, more correctly, environment-patient relationship, using other terms. Anna Freud (war years) used 'the need-satisfying object'; Hartmann (1939) 'the average expectable environment'; Bion in a paper to the British Psycho-Analytical Society (1966) contrasted the 'container' with the 'contained'. The most versatile inventor of such terms seems to be Winnicott, who used (1941) the 'good enough environment', then talked about the 'medium' in which the patient can revolve like an engine in oil, then (1949) came his 'ordinary devoted mother', in 1956 the 'primary maternal preoccupation', then (1960) the 'holding function' of the mother, while in 1963 he borrowed the term 'facilitating environment' from the American literature and used it as part of the title of his last book (1967). Margaret Little called it the 'basic unit' (1961), while M. Khan proposed (1963) the 'protective shield' and R. Spitz 'mediator of the environment' (1965), while M. Mahler preferred (1952) 'extra-uterine matrix'. Any one of these terms is correct. Each describes one or the other aspect of this non-omnipotent relationship that I have in mind. Of course I am biased in favour of my term, among many others, for the one reason that mine is more general and can accommodate all the others as its particular aspects.

If we accept these ideas, then the problem of whether or not to gratify a regressed patient's cravings appears in a different light, so different that doubt arises whether we have not been struggling with a false problem which can never be solved because it is wrongly formulated. The real problem is not about gratifying or frustrating the regressed patient but about how the analyst's response to the regression will influence the patient-analyst relationship and by it the further course of the treatment. If the analyst's response, e.g. satisfying the patient's expectations, creates an impression in the patient that his analyst is knowledgeable and capable, bordering on being omniscient and omnipotent, this response should be considered as risky and inadvisable; it is likely to increase the inequality between patient and analyst, which may lead to the creation of addiction-like states by exacerbating the patient's basic fault.

On the other hand, if the satisfaction can be done in a fashion that does not increase the inequality but creates an object relationship according to the pattern of what I call primary love, then it should be seriously considered as a method of choice.

At this point I propose to digress briefly to discuss what I call *the ocnophilic bias of our modern technique* and its consequences. Psycho-analytic technique – and theory – were so impressed by the intensity of ocnophilic phenomena met in the analytic situation that they concentrated their interest on them, neglecting almost entirely the equally important primary and philobatic relationships. Thus developed the theory of object-seeking, clinging, 'attachment beha-viour', and ambivalent dependence. As I pointed out in *Thrills and Regressions* (1959), especially in Chapter 12, our modern technical procedure recommends that everything that happens or is produced by the patient in the analytic situation should be understood and interpreted first and foremost as a phenomenon of transference. Conversely this means that the principal frame of reference used for formulating practically every interpretation is a relationship between a highly important, omnipresent object, the analyst, and an unequal subject who at present apparently cannot feel, think, or experience anything unrelated to his analyst.

It is easy to see that this modern technique of interpreting trans-ference first must lead to a picture of the world consisting of a rather insignificant subject confronted with mighty, knowledgeable, and omnipresent objects who have the power of expressing everything correctly in words, an impressive example of whom is the analyst. If one accepts this picture as a true and representative sample of the early stages of human development, one gets easily to the theory of 'oral dependence'. The dependence is obvious, and the adjective 'oral' is speedily added to it under the influence of our theory of instincts, which has only this one word for the description of any-thing primitive or early. The fact that during the treatment conducted in this way nearly all transactions between patient and analyst happen through the medium of words, reinforces the 'oral' aspects, and analysts, patients, and our theory associate to it that interpre-tations – that is, words – may stand for 'milk' and the analyst for 'the breast'.

A circular argument develops in this way; everything that happens in the analytic situation is understood and interpreted in this fashion, which in turn 'teaches' the patient – as described in Chapter 15 – to express, and to some extent even to feel, all his pre-verbal experiences according to this language, thus convincing the analyst that both his theory and his interpretations were absolutely right. This is another instance of an event that has happened on many occasions in practically every science, and especially in our psycho-analysis, that parts of the truth have been used to repress the whole truth. In our present instance the parts are: that 'oral' and 'dependent' phenomena occur in every primitive human relationship. What is repressed is that they are far from being able to explain the whole picture; the only thing that happened was that by our present technique their importance has been magnified out of proportion.

A very good proof for this view is Freud's example. As the study of his case histories proves, he paid due attention to transference but did not interpret it before anything else. In consequence, although he was a very important object to his patients, his technique did not force them to build up a picture of the world according to the oppressive inequality between an ocnophilic subject and his all-important object described above. As I have just mentioned, in the indexes of the twenty-three volumes of the Standard Edition the catchword 'dependence' occurs very rarely, while 'oral dependence' does not occur at all.

To illustrate a number of problems raised in this chapter, may I quote an episode from a long treatment. After an unsatisfactory session on a Friday in which the patient accepted, rather reluctantly, that no real contact could be established between himself and his analyst because during the whole session the patient had to make his analyst useless, he had great difficulties in leaving the room. Just before the door was opened he said that he felt awful and asked for an extra session, any time during the week-end, to help him to recover.

The problem of course, is how to respond to this request which, undoubtedly, is a request for gratification. I would add that this patient occasionally got extra sessions during the week-end; these always brought him very great satisfaction and, true to type, eased the tension in him considerably each time; however, it was only very rarely that in these extra sessions real analytical work was possible.

Let us suppose that the request is interpreted as another 'craving' of his, and refused on this account; even if the patient accepts this interpretation, he will feel still more wretched for having unneces-sarily pestered his kind and patient analyst, and his misery will get worse. If the patient disagrees with the interpretation, he will experi-ence the analyst as unkind and cruel, increasing thereby the tension in the therapy; it is doubtful whether the situation will be made more tolerable if the analyst interprets it as a resistance or as a transference of some aggressiveness and hatred from childhood.

On the other hand if he satisfies the request for an extra session, no matter whether he interprets it as a repetition of some early frustration prompted by, or leading to, greediness or envy, he turns himself into an omnipotent object and forces his patient into an ocnophilic relationship.

What I tried to do in this case was first to recognize and accept his distress so that he should feel that I was with him, and then to admit that I did not feel that an extra session granted by me would be powerful enough to give him what he expected and perhaps even needed at this moment; in addition this would make him small and weak while his analyst would become great and powerful, which was not desirable. For all these reasons the request was not agreed to. The patient then departed dissatisfied.

I had two aims in mind when choosing my response. On the one hand, I tried to prevent the development of undesirable relationships, such as that between someone let down or frustrated by a harsh or superior person in authority who knows better what is right, or that between someone weak and in need of kind support, and a benign and generous authority – all leading to a reinforcement of the inequality between the subject and his mighty object. On the other hand, I tried to establish a relationship in which neither of us would be all-powerful, in which both of us admitted our limitations in the hope that in this way a fruitful collaboration could be established between two people who were not fundamentally different in importance, weight, and power.

I have to add here that it was a very rare event indeed that my patient rang me up, perhaps not even as much as once per year in an emergency. This time he telephoned me the same evening after 8 p.m. He could hardly speak on the telephone, dithered to and fro for a long time, but at the end he was able to say that he had to ring me up . . . to tell me that he was very near crying . . . nothing else . . . he did not want anything from me, no extra session, . . . but he had to ring me up, to let me know how he felt.

This episode shows how the analyst's response turned a process that started in the direction of a 'craving' for satisfaction – i.e. a possibly malignant form – into a benign one – i.e. a regression for

171

recognition. It was done by the analyst avoiding even a semblance of being omniscient and over-powerful; on the other hand he demonstrated his willingness to accept the role of a primary object whose chief function is recognizing, and being with, his patient.

The immediate effect of this incident was a considerable lessening of the tension, the patient had a comparatively good week-end, and for quite some time afterwards he was capable of contact and cooperation. I would even say that it initiated – or reinforced – a change for a better atmosphere in the analytic situation, in which it was possible to make some considerable progress.

Chapter 25

The unobtrusive analyst

We finished Chapter 22 with the two forms of regression but left undiscussed the technical problems as to what the analyst can do to avoid, as far as humanly possible, any risk of a malignant regression and assure the development of a benign form. The discussion in the preceding chapter gave us some general directives on how this could be done. The more the analyst's technique and behaviour are suggestive of omniscience and omnipotence, the greater is the danger of a malignant form of regression. On the other hand, the more the analyst can reduce the inequality between his patient and himself, and the more unobtrusive and ordinary he can remain in his patient's eyes, the better are the chances of a benign form of regression.

Thus we have arrived at one of the most important problems of modern analytic technique, which is how much of the two therapeutic agents – interpretation and object relationship – should be used in any one case; when, in what proportion, and in what succession should they be used? This problem is important in every case, but is especially acute in the treatment of a regressed patient when the work has reached the area of the basic fault. Since, as we have found, words have only a limited and uncertain usefulness in these areas, it seems to follow that object relationship is the more important and more reliable therapeutic factor during these periods, while in the states after the patient has emerged from his regression, interpretations will regain their importance.

The question now arises as to what sort of technique the analyst can use to create the object relationship which, in his opinion, is the most suitable for that particular patient; or, in other words, will probably have the best therapeutic effect. The first analyst who experimented with these effects fairly systematically was Ferenczi. Viewed from this angle his 'active technique' and his 'principle of relaxation' were deliberate attempts at creating object relationships which, in his opinion, were better suited to the needs of some patients than the atmosphere of an analytic setting created according to Freud's classical recommendations. Ferenczi recognized fairly soon that, whatever he tried to do, the result was that his patients became more dependent on him, that is, he became more and more important for them; on the other hand he could not recognize the reasons why this had to happen. Today we may add that his technique, instead of reducing, increased the inequality between the patients and himself, whom they felt to be really omniscient and all-important.

It was fairly early in my career that I realized that keeping to the parameters of classical technique meant accepting strict selection of patients. In my beginner's enthusiasm this was unacceptable, and under Ferenczi's influence I experimented with non-verbal communications; starting with 1932 I reported on my experiments and results in several papers; most of them reprinted in *Primary Love* (Balint, M., 1952). Of course, my techniques and my ways of thinking have undergone considerable change during the years, and though I am fully aware that my present ideas are anything but final, they have again reached a stage at which I can 'organize' them, that is, express them in sufficiently concrete form so that they can be discussed and, above all, criticized.

In my endeavour to overcome the difficulties just mentioned, for some years now I have experimented with a technique that allows the patient to experience a two-person relationship which cannot, need not, and perhaps even must not, be expressed in words, but at times merely by, what is customarily called, 'acting-out' in the analytic situation. I hasten to add that all these non-verbal communications, the acting-out, will of course be worked through after the patient has emerged from this level and reached the Oedipal level again – but not till then.

May I recapitulate here the several trains of thought that led me to these experiments. On many occasions I have found to my annoyance and despair that words cease to be reliable means of communication when the analytic work reaches the areas beyond the Oedipal level. The analyst may try, as hard as he can, to make his interpretations clear and unequivocal; the patient, somehow, always manages to experience them as something utterly different from that which the analyst intended them to be. At this level explanations, arguments,

174

improved or amended versions, if tried, prove of no avail; the analyst cannot but accept the bitter fact that his words in these areas, instead of clarifying the situation, are often misunderstood, misinterpreted, and tend to increase the confusion of tongues between his patient and himself. Words become, in fact, unreliable and unpredictable.

This clinical observation is so important to my train of thought that I will show it from yet another angle. Words – at these periods – cease to be vehicles for free association; they have become lifeless, repetitious, and stereotyped; they strike one as an old worn-out gramophone record, with the needle running endlessly in the same groove. By the way, this is often equally true about the analyst's interpretations; during these periods they, too, seem to be running endlessly in the same groove. The analyst then discovers to his despair and dismay that, in these periods, there is no point whatever in going on interpreting the patient's verbal communications. At the Oedipal – and even at some of the so-called 'pre-Oedipal' – levels a proper interpretation, which makes a repressed conflict conscious and thereby resolves a resistance or undoes a split, gets the patient's free associations going again; at the level of the basic fault this does not necessarily happen. The interpretation is either experienced as interference, cruelty, unwarranted demand or unfair impingement, as a hostile act, or a sign of affection, or is felt so lifeless, in fact dead, that it has no effect at all.

Another train of thought started with the discovery of the ocnophilic bias of our technique discussed already in the previous chapters (and in 1959, Chapter XII). Nowadays analysts are enjoined to interpret everything that happens in the analytic situation also, or even foremost, in terms of transference, i.e. of object relationship. This otherwise sensible and efficient technique means that we offer ourselves to our patients incessantly as objects to cling to, and interpret anything contrary to clinging as resistance, aggressiveness, narcissism, touchiness, paranoid anxiety, castration fear, and so on. A highly ambivalent and strained atmosphere is created in this way, the patient struggling, prompted by his desire for independence, but finding his way barred at every point by ocnophilic 'transference' interpretations.

The third train of thought originated from my study of 'the silent patient'. Silence, as is more and more recognized, may have many

175

meanings, each of them requiring different technical handling. Silence may be an arid and frightening emptiness, inimical to life and growth, in which case the patient ought to be got out of it as soon as possible; it may be a friendly exciting expanse, inviting the patient to undertake adventurous journeys into the uncharted lands of his fantasy life, in which case any ocnophilic transference interpretation may be utterly out of place, in fact disturbing; silence may also mean an attempt at re-establishing the harmonious mix-up of primary love that existed between the individual and his environment before the emergence of objects, in which case any interference either by interpretation or in any other way is strictly contra-indicated as it may destroy the harmony by making demands on the patient.

The last train of thought is connected with my ideas about the area of creation, an area of the mind in which there is no external organized object, and any intrusion of such an object by attention-seeking interpretations inevitably destroys for the patient the possibility of creating something out of himself.

It was discussed in Chapter 5 that objects in this area are as yet unorganized, and the process of creation leading to their organization needs, above all, time. This time may be short or very long; but whatever its length, it cannot be influenced from outside. Almost certainly the same will be true about our patients' creations out of their unconscious. This may be one of the reasons why the analyst's usual interpretations are felt by patients regressed to this area as inadmissible; interpretations are indeed whole, 'organized', thoughts or objects whose interactions with the hazy, dreamlike, as yet 'unorganized' contents of the area of creation might cause either havoc or an unnatural, premature, organization.

The outward appearance of all these, widely different, states is a silent patient, seemingly withdrawn from normal analytic work, 'acting-out' instead of associating, or possibly even repeating something instead of recollecting it; and, last but not least, he may also be described as regressing towards some primitive behaviour instead of progressing towards complying with our fundamental rule. All these descriptions – withdrawal, acting-out, repetition instead of remembering, regression – are correct but incomplete and thus may lead to mistaken technical measures.

Thus the technique that I found usually profitable with patients who regressed to the level of the basic fault or of creation, was to bear with their regression for the time being, without any forceful attempt at intervening with an interpretation. This time may amount only to some minutes, but equally to a more or less long stretch of sessions. As I have mentioned several times, words at these periods have anyhow ceased to be reliable means of communication; the patient's words are no longer vehicles for free associations, they have become lifeless, repetitive, and stereotyped, they do not mean what they seem to say. The standard technical advice is correct in this case too; the analyst's task is to understand what lies behind the patient's words; the problem is only how to communicate this understanding to a regressed patient. My answer is in accepting unreservedly the fact that words have become unreliable and by sincerely giving up, for the time being, any attempt at forcing the patient back to the verbal level. This means abandoning any attempt at 'organizing' the material produced by the patient – it is not the 'right' material anyway – and tolerating it so that it may remain incoherent, nonsensical, unorganized, till the patient – after returning to the Oedipal level of conventional language – will be able to give the analyst the key to understand it.

In other words, the analyst must accept the regression. This means that he must create an environment, a climate, in which he and his patient can tolerate the regression in a mutual experience. This is essential because in these states any outside pressure reinforces the anyhow strong tendency in the patient to develop relationships of inequality between himself and his objects, perpetuating thereby his proneness to regression.

I wish to illustrate what I have just said by repeating from Chapter 21 an episode from an analysis which, at that time, had been going on for about two years. The patient remained silent right from the start of the session for more than thirty minutes; the analyst accepted this and, realizing what possibly was happening, waited without any attempt whatever at interference; in fact, he did not even feel uncomfortable or under pressure to do something. I should add that in this treatment silences had occurred previously on several occasions, and patient and analyst had thus had some training in tolerating them. The silence was eventually broken by the patient starting to sob, relieved, and soon after he was able to speak. He told his analyst that at long last he was able to reach himself; ever

177

since childhood he had never been left alone, there had always been someone telling him what to do. Some sessions later he reported that during the silence he had all sorts of associations, but rejected each of them as irrelevant, as nothing but an annoying superficial nuisance.

Of course, the silence could easily have been interpreted as resistance, withdrawal, a sign of persecutory fear, inability to cope with depressive anxieties, a symptom of a repetition compulsion, etc.; moreover since the analyst knew his patient fairly well, he could even have interpreted or guessed one or the other topic emerging in the associations and also some of the reasons why the patient felt that particular idea irrelevant and was rejecting it. All these might have been correct interpretations in every respect – except in one: they would have destroyed the silence and the patient would not have been able to 'reach himself', at any rate, not on that occasion. There is one more unintended side-effect of any, however correct, interpretation: it would inevitably reinforce the patient's strong repetition-compulsion, there would again be someone there, telling him what to feel, to think, in fact what to do.

Furthermore, all this happened in an exclusively two-person relationship; the dynamic problem to be dealt with did not have the structure of a conflict for which a 'solution' had to be found. The situation demanded somewhat more skill from the analyst than, say, the understanding of verbal association; by finding a correct answer to the silence, the analyst was running the risk of raising expectations in his patient that this would possibly happen time and again and trigger in this way the development of addiction-like states; another risk was to impress the patient that he has got an analyst so wise and so powerful that he can read his patient's unspoken thoughts and respond to them correctly, the risk of becoming 'omnipotent'; and lastly, words would have been unreliable in this situation, more likely than not they would have forced the patient prematurely into the Oedipal area and created further obstacles to the therapeutic work instead of removing some. Of course, all these are characteristic signs that the analytic work has reached the area of the basic fault.

The right technique, as long as the patient is regressed to this level, is to accept 'acting-out' in the analytic situation as valid means of communication without any attempt at speedily 'organizing' it by interpretations. Emphatically, this does not mean that in these periods the analyst's role becomes negligible or is restricted to sympathetic passivity; on the contrary, his presence is most important, not only in that he must be felt to be present but must be all the time at the right distance – neither so far that the patient might feel lost or abandoned, nor so close that the patient might feel encumbered and unfree – in fact, at a distance that corresponds to the patient's actual need; in general the analyst must know what are his patient's needs, why they are as they are, and why they fluctuate and change.

From another angle, the technical problem is how to offer 'something' to the patient which might function as a primary object, or at any rate as a suitable substitute for it, or still in other words, on to which he can project his primary love.

Should this 'something' be (a) the analyst himself (the analyst who undertakes to treat a regression), or (b) the therapeutic situation? The question is which of these two is the more likely to achieve sufficient harmony with the patient so that there may be only minimal clash of interest between the patient and one available object in the present. On the whole, it is safer if the patient can use the therapeutic situation as a substitute, if for no other reason, because it diminishes the risk of the analyst becoming a most important, omniscient, and omnipotent object.

This offering to the patient a 'primary object', of course, is not tantamount to giving primary love; in any case mothers do not *give* it either. What they do is to behave truly as primary objects, that is, to offer themselves as primary objects to be cathected by primary love. This difference between 'giving primary love' and 'offering oneself to be cathected by primary love' may be of fundamental importance for our technique not only with regressed patients, but also with a number of difficult treatment situations.

To describe the same role from a different angle, i.e. using different 'words': the analyst must function during these periods as a provider of time and of milieu. This does not mean that he is under obligation to compensate for the patient's early privations and give more care, love, affection than the patient's parents have given originally (and even if he tried, he would almost certainly fail). What the analyst must provide – and, if at all possible, during the regular sessions only – is sufficient time free from extrinsic temptations, stimuli, and demands, including those originating from himself (the analyst). The aim is that the patient should be able to find himself, to accept himself, and to get on with himself, knowing all the time that there is a scar in himself, his basic fault, which cannot be 'analysed' out of existence; moreover, he must be allowed to discover *his* way to the world of objects – and not be shown the 'right' way by some profound or correct interpretation. If this can be done, the patient will not feel that the objects impinge on, and oppress, him. It is only to this extent that the analyst should provide a better, more 'understanding' environment, but in no other way, in particular not in the form of more care, love, attention, gratification, or protection. Perhaps it ought to be stressed that considerations of this kind may serve as criteria for deciding whether a certain 'craving' or 'need' should be satisfied, or recognized but left unsatisfied.

The guiding principle during these periods is to avoid any interference not absolutely necessary; interpretations particularly should be scrutinized most meticulously, since they are felt more often than not as unwarranted demand, attack, criticism, seduction, or stimulation; they should be given only if the analyst is certain that the patient *needs* them, for at such times *not giving* them would be felt as unwarranted demand or stimulation. From this angle, what I have called the dangers of ocnophilic interpretations may be understood better; though the patient is in need of an environment, of a world of objects, such objects – foremost among them the analyst – must not be felt as in any way demanding, interfering, intruding, as this would reinforce the old oppressive inequality between subject and object.

I hope this clinical description will help the reader to understand why so many analysts have quite so many different terms to describe it. Some of these terms were enumerated at the end of Chapter 24. All of them had the following features in common: there was the suggestion that no oppressive or demanding object should be present; that the environment should be quiet, peaceful, safe, and unobtrusive; that it should be there and that it should be favourable to the subject, but that the subject should be in no way obliged to take notice, to acknowledge, or to be concerned about it. Once again, these common features are the exact characteristics of what I called primary objects or primary substance.

To provide this sort of object or environment is certainly an important part of the therapeutic task. Clearly, it is only a part, not the whole of the task. Apart from being a 'need-recognizing' and perhaps even a 'need-satisfying' object, the analyst must be also a 'need-understanding' object who, in addition, must be able to communicate his understanding to his patient.

Chapter 26

Bridging the gulf

In Chapter 14, I spoke of the deep gulf separating the 'child in the patient' from his grown-up analyst and stated that a patient regressed to the level of the basic fault is, as a rule, unable to bridge it on his own. I posed there the question as to which part of this task should be undertaken by the analyst and which must be left to the patient. The first answer to the problem, how to bridge the gap, is the standard one: by understanding what the patient needs from the analyst. This understanding need not – and at times definitely must not – be conveyed to a regressed patient by interpretations but by creating the atmosphere that he needs. This entails tolerating and respecting the patient's analytic 'acting-out' and, in particular, in not urging him to change without any delay his non-verbal ways of expression into the verbal Oedipal form. In the previous Chapter, I have tried to summarize what I think should be done by the analyst. If my ideas will prove correct, they may explain the many difficulties that follow inevitably if an analyst, seduced by his patient's sufferings, tries to do more.

In particular, when dealing with these states, the analyst should bear in mind that on the whole he should try to avoid penetrating defences or undoing splits by incisive and correct interpretations since these might be felt by his regressed patients as disbelieving the justification or validity of their grievances, recriminations, and resentment. Instead, the analyst must sincerely accept all complaints, recriminations, and resentments as real and valid, and allow ample time to his patient to change his violent resentment into regret. This process must not be hurried by interpretations, however correct, since they may be felt as undue interference, as an attempt at devaluing the justification of their complaint and thus, instead of speeding up, they will slow down the therapeutic processes.

True, some patients feel that life is not worth living without their grievances and their hate or, the other way round, without receiving full compensation for all their grievances – and the hate associated with them. Any interpretation that tries to shed a new light on the grievance is felt by those patients as if the analyst was trying to devalue the grievance. Any such attempt is felt as a threat of taking away their justification for existence; they really feel that they have nothing else to live for.

Roughly the same is true about the so-called persecutory anxieties which cannot profitably be analysed unless the patient is helped to feel that the analyst is with him in unreservedly accepting the justification for the complaints, and grants his patient a sufficiently long, in some cases very long, period of violent aggressiveness followed by mourning and regret about the original fault or failure and all the losses caused by it.

Provided the analyst is able to fulfil most of the requirements sincerely and unreservedly, a new relationship may develop which will enable the patient to experience a kind of regret or mourning about the original defect and loss which led to the establishment of the fault or scar in his mental structure. This mourning differs fundamentally from that caused by the loss in reality of a beloved person or that caused by the damage to, or destruction of, an internal object, characteristic of melancholia. The regret or mourning I have in mind is about the unalterable fact of a defect or fault in oneself which, in fact, has cast its shadow over one's whole life, and the unfortunate effects of which can never fully be made good. Though the fault may heal off, its scar will remain for ever; that is, some of its effects will always be demonstrable.[1]

---

[1] As already anticipated in my paper 'New Beginning and the Paranoid and Depressive Syndromes' (1952), this mourning is connected with the giving up of a narcissistic picture of oneself which originally may have been developed as an over-compensation of the basic fault. It was similar over-compensation that led us to think that a fully terminated analytic treatment would enable the patient not to resort any more to unnecessary inhibitions or repressions. This idealized picture means that after a properly terminated analysis no patient can have any more fault in his personality. This ideal case may be, more or less closely, approximated at the Oedipal level but it is unrealistic to expect the same at the level of the basic fault. The basic fault cannot be removed, resolved, or undone; it may perhaps heal off, leaving a scar, which means that the fact that it existed in the past remains discoverable for ever. The process of mourning discussed here is about giving up for good the hope of attaining the faultless ideal of oneself; a successful treatment must lead to the acceptance of the fact that one had a basic fault and to a realistic adaptation to this fact.

The period of mourning must be allowed to run its course which, in some patients, may be exasperatingly long. Although this process cannot be hurried, it is most important that it should be witnessed; since it belongs to the area of the basic fault, apparently it is impossible to go through this mourning by oneself; it can be done only in the framework of a two-person relationship, such as the analytic situation. If the analyst can provide a sufficiently long, unhurried period for this mourning, and maintain the necessary primitive atmosphere by his tolerance and non-interfering interpretations, the patient begins to cooperate in a somewhat different way from before, as if he had become willing and able to re-assess his position *vis-à-vis* his objects and of re-examining the possibility of accepting the often unattractive and indifferent world around him.

None of the details of the therapeutic attitude outlined here are essentially different from what the analyst adopts when dealing with patients at the Oedipal level, and even the topics worked with are usually the same; but there *is* a difference, which is more a difference of atmosphere, of mood. This difference affects both patient and analyst. The analyst is not so keen on 'understanding' everything immediately, and in particular, on 'organizing' and changing everything undesirable by his correct interpretations; in fact, he is more tolerant towards the patient's sufferings and is capable of bearing with them – i.e. of admitting his relative impotence – instead of being at pains to 'analyse' them away in order to prove his therapeutic omnipotence. Neither does the analyst succumb to the other temptation to influence the regressed patient's life by his sympathetic 'management' so that the environment should make no more unbearable demands on him – another kind of omnipotent response. Nor is he intent on providing his patient with 'corrective emotional experiences' in the sense in which a doctor would treat a state of deficiency – a third form of omnipotent response. In fact, if the analyst feels the slightest inclination to respond to his regressed patient by any sort of omnipotent behaviour, this should be recognized at once as a sure diagnostic sign that the work has reached the area of the basic fault. I wish to stress most emphatically that any such inclination in the analyst must be evaluated as a symptom of the patient's illness, but on no account be acted upon – a thing easier to advise than to do.

Some remarks now about 'gratifying the patient's needs or cravings'. In the classical form of technique this demand is not accepted as a possibly valid need which has to be responded to, but only as a desire to be understood. Some modern techniques commend that the analyst should consider satisfying some of his patient's needs in the analytic situation, over and above understanding them, for instance by permitting some 'acting-out'.

Here several problems confront us. We must ask when this satisfaction should happen, what sort of satisfaction should be allowed, and how the satisfaction should take place.

Let us start with a clinical example. A patient of mine reported that in her childhood she was prone to temper-tantrums. These were very painful events, both for her and for the whole family. Soon, however, her mother found a way to cope with these fits. She picked her daughter up and held her tight, firmly but not violently; my patient remembers that she felt this sympathetic restraint as reassuring and safe and it took only a few minutes for her to calm down. In this case the temper-tantrums may be considered as a kind of demand, and the mother's handling of them as a kind of response.

Let us suppose that something of this kind might happen in analysis. Should the analyst do as much as this mother did and, if so, by what means? Should he try to contain his patient by interpretations, by some symbolic action, or even in reality by using his hands? In which cases should the 'child in the patient' be treated as a child, and in which as an adult? Before anybody gets indignant about the possible insinuation, let me recall that in any case the setting of the analytic situation is a kind of 'holding the patient tight'. After all, the patient is asked to lie down on a couch and not to get up from it, the whole of which cannot but be felt as a restraint. Coming back to our problem, I would call the classical analytic setting a restraint by symbolic action on the part of the analyst, and I would like to add that through this symbolic action a kind of relationship develops between analyst and patient that is mutually satisfactory, up to a point.

Moreover, the classical procedure is a convincing example of a symbolic action by the analyst prior to any interpretations: by asking our patients to lie down, we symbolically restrain them before any need for interpretations or action has arisen. This example also shows another important aspect of the satisfaction of a need by the analyst in the analytic situation. As we know, there are in general two kinds of satisfactions. One group, although satisfactory in themselves, act also as a further stimulus, increasing the over-all excitement. A familiar example of this kind are the various fore-pleasure mechanisms used in love-making. The other group of satisfactions have a soothing and calming effect. They act by removing irritating or exciting stimuli from the patient's consciousness, and so help him towards the state which I described as a quiet tranquil well-being and which is the best basis for a good understanding between the individual and his environment.

If one may generalize from this example, then we arrive at yet another answer to one of our questions. The kind of satisfaction that is compatible with the analytic situation is one that does not excite the patient; on the contrary, it reduces the over-all tension and leads in this way to the establishment of a better understanding between him and his analyst. If one examines the classical analytical setting in detail, one will find that there are quite a number of satisfactions of this kind inherent in it. To mention a few: the quiet, well-tempered room, a comfortable couch, unexciting environment, the analyst not interrupting the patient unnecessarily, the patient being given full opportunity to speak his mind, and so on. On the whole, this kind of satisfaction might be described also as looking-after, or even as a kind of psychological nursing.

Obviously all this starts right at the beginning of an analysis. Some analysts are firmly convinced that the limits set by Freud's technical recommendations must remain absolute for ever, and any technique going beyond them must not be called analytic. In my opinion, they are too rigid. May I repeat once more that an analyst in certain cases, in particular with a regressed patient, may go further towards satisfying some demands in order to secure the existence of a therapeutic relationship.

He must, however, respect certain conditions. The first is that by his action he should not court the danger of becoming an 'omniscient and omnipotent object'. The second is that he must be sure that the result of the gratification will not cause a further increase of excitement in the patient, but will lead to the establishment of the 'tranquil quiet well-being' and to a better, safer understanding between the patient and himself. A further condition is that he sees his way to avoid the development of a malignant form of regression.

The more one gets the impression that the regression is aimed chiefly at gratification by an outside object, the more the analyst should be on his guard. In particular, if the patient's possibilities in the world of objects are only limited, the greater will be the danger of developing addiction-like states.

This, I found to be a rather important criterion. Apparently it works in two directions: influencing the patient's future but also shedding some light on his past psychopathology. If there are not many reliably good objects in the external world, the danger of developing highly intense, delusional (Margaret Little, 1938, 1961) transference is very great and the prospect of balancing it with something of equal importance and intensity in the outside world rather poor. On the other hand, the absence of good objects means also that the patient, because of his neurosis, has only a limited capacity to perform the 'work of conquest' (Balint, M., 1947) necessary to change an indifferent object into a participating partner; this indicates a fairly serious basic fault in his mental make-up and character.

If, however, good outside objects, or even partners, are present, some risks might be taken by the analyst, as happened in my case with the somersault. On the other hand, if the outside world is poor in acceptable partners, it is better to bear in mind Freud's advice and to beware of the patient's cravings.

However, if symptoms of the other type of regression are prevalent in the clinical picture, that is of a regression aiming at recognition, in my opinion the prospects are fairly good. True, the analyst must be prepared for some testing times, especially with regard to his sincerity. What these patients cannot tolerate is not receiving the truth, the whole truth, and nothing but the truth from their analyst. As a rule they are hypersensitive anyhow; they may react with pain and withdrawal to any show of insincerity, even to one which is comprised under the general heading of conventional forms of good manners.

If the analyst succeeds in avoiding all these attractive pitfalls, the patient, partly in response to the analyst's increased tolerance, exhibits an otherwise hidden, quiet determination to see things through, to take things in – so to speak on approval – in order to be able to understand them or merely in order to have a look at them.

With this the patient gradually emerges from his regression. This may not be the final move, it may even be followed by relapses, but it is always one step forward on a long road. Thus what I have described in this Part is neither the end nor the whole story. It means,

187

however, always the establishment of a new relationship between the patient and some part of his world which has hitherto been barred by the gulf created by his basic fault, and, in consequence, one step towards a better integration of his ego.

As I have just said, what I have compressed in this Part is not the whole story either. I can even point out some of the missing chapters. First, I have not said anything about the function of repetition, of acting-out, in analytic therapy or, in other terms, I have not defined when, how far, and under what conditions, repetition may become a therapeutic agent. Another chapter would deal with the ways potentially open to a patient to change his internal world which largely determines his relationship to external objects. A parallel chapter would discuss the technical means available to us analysts for helping our patients to achieve this change. And lastly, a very important chapter indeed would deal with the functions of interpretations. I mean here the classical interpretations, in the periods *between* successive regressions. The technical problem I have in mind is how to integrate the two important tasks that have to be achieved by the same interpretations. The one is the creation and maintenance of an atmosphere in which certain therapeutically important events may take place; and the second is to enable the patient to realize what his own and what his analyst's contributions have been to the creation of this atmosphere; how these two determined each other on the one hand, and the final outcome on the other. I hope it has become clear that whatever atmosphere is created, it leads to certain interpretations and excludes others; and on the other hand, certain interpretations create a particular atmosphere, while avoiding these interpretations will create one that is totally different.

Bibliography

ALEXANDER, F. (1956) Two Forms of Regression and their Therapeutic Implications. *Psychoanal. Quart.* Vol. 25. Reprinted in *The Scope of Psychoanalysis*, Basic Books, New York, 1961.

ARLOW, J. (1963) Conflict, Regression and Symptom Formation. *Int. J. Psycho-Anal.* Vol. 44, p. 12.

BALINT, ENID (1963) On being Empty of Oneself. *Int. J. Psycho-Anal.* Vol. 44, p. 470.

BALINT, MICHAEL (1932) Character Analysis and New Beginning.

— (1934) The Final Goal of Psycho-analytic Treatment.

— (1935) Critical Notes on the Theory of the Pregenital Organization of the Libido.

— (1937) Early Developmental States of the Ego. Primary Object-love.

— (1948) On Genital Love. *Int. J. Psycho-Anal.* Vol. 29.

— (1949) Changing Therapeutical Aims and Techniques in Psychoanalysis.

— (1951) On Love and Hate.

(The above papers are included in Balint, Michael (1952).)

— (1952) *Primary Love and Psycho-Analytic Technique.* First edition: Hogarth Press, London; Liveright Publishing Co., New York. Second edition: Tavistock Publications, London; Liveright Publishing Co., New York, 1965.

— (1955) Notes on Parapsychology and Parapsychological Healing. *Int. J. Psycho-Anal.* Vol. 36.

— (1956) Pleasure, Object, and Libido. *Brit. J. Med. Psychol.* Vol. 29, p. 162.

— (1957) *The Doctor, His Patient and the Illness.* Pitman, London; International Universities Press, New York. Second edition 1964.

— (1958) The Three Areas of the Mind. *Int. J. Psycho-Anal.* Vol. 39, p. 1.

— (1959) *Thrills and Regressions.* Hogarth, London; International Universities Press, New York.

— (1960) The Regressed Patient and His Analyst. *Psychiatry* Vol. 23, p. 231.

BIBRING, EDWARD (1936) Versuch einer allgemeinen Theorie der Heilung. *Int. Zeitschrift für Psa.* 1937, Vol. 23, p. 18.

BIBRING, EDWARD (1954) Psychoanalysis and the Dynamic Psychotherapies. *J. Amer. Psychoanal. Ass.* Vol. II, p. 745.

189

Bibliography

BION, W. R. (1962) *Learning from Experience.* Heinemann, London.
— (1963) *Elements of Psychoanalysis.* Heinemann, London.
BOWLBY, J. (1958) The Nature of the Child's Attachment to his Mother. *Int. J. Psycho-Anal.* Vol. 39, p. 350.
BREUER, J., and FREUD, S. (1895) *Studies on Hysteria.* Standard edition Vol. II.
CLYNE, M. B. (1962) *Night Calls.* Tavistock Publications, London; Lippincott, Philadelphia.
DEUTSCH, HELENE (1937) Don Quixote and Don Quixotism. *Psychoanal. Quart.* Vol. 6, p. 215.
DOI, TAKEO (1962) Amae – A Key Concept for Understanding Japanese Personality Structure. *Psychologia (Kyoto)* Vol. 5, 1.
— (1963) Some Thoughts on Helplessness and the Desire to be Loved. *Psychiatry* Vol. 26, p. 266.
EISSLER, K. (1953) The Effect of the Structure of the Ego on Psychoanalytic Technique. *J. Amer. Psychoanal. Ass.* Vol. I, p. 104.
FENICHEL, O. (1945) *The Psychoanalytical Theory of Neurosis.* Norton, New York.
FERENCZI, S. (1919) Technical Difficulties in the Analysis of a Case of Hysteria.
— (1921) Further Development of the Active Therapy in Psychoanalysis.
— (1924) On Forced Phantasies.
— (1926) Contra-Indications to the Active Psychoanalytic Technique.
(The above are reprinted in *Further Contributions*, Hogarth Press, London, and Basic Books, New York, 2nd Edition, 1950.)
— (1924) *Thalassa: A Theory of Genitality*, English Edition, *Psychoanalytic Quarterly*, New York, 1934.
— (1928) The Elasticity of Psychoanalytic Technique.
— (1930) The Principle of Relaxation and Neo-Catharsis.
— (1931) Child Analysis in the Analysis of Adults.
— (1932) Confusion of Tongues between the Adults and the Child.
— (1932) Notes and Fragments.
(All the above reprinted in *Final Contributions*, Hogarth Press, London, and Basic Books, New York, 1955.)
FREUD, A. (1936) *The Ego and the Mechanisms of Defence.* Hogarth Press, London (English Edition, 1937).
— (1963) Regression as a Principle in Mental Development. *Bull. Menninger Clinic* Vol. 27, p. 126.
FREUD, S. (1894) Neuro-Psychoses of Defence. Standard Edition Vol. III.
— (1895) *Studies on Hysteria.* Standard Edition Vol. II.
FREUD S. (1895) Manuscript 'H' – In *The Origins of Psycho-analyse.* Imago Publishing Company, London, 1950.

190

Bibliography

FREUD, S. (1896) Aetiology of Hysteria. Standard Edition Vol. III.

— (1900) *The Interpretation of Dreams*. Standard Edition Vol. IV and V.

— (1905) Fragment of an Analysis of a Case of Hysteria. Standard Edition Vol. VII.

— (1905) *Three Essays on Sexuality*. Standard Edition Vol. VII.

— (1907) Delusions and Dreams in Jensen's *Gradiva*. Standard Edition Vol. IX.

— (1909) *Five Lectures on Psycho-Analysis*. Standard Edition Vol. XI.

— (1909) Analysis of a Phobia in a Five-Year-Old Boy. Standard Edition Vol. X.

— (1909) Notes upon a Case of Obsessional Neurosis. Standard Edition Vol. X.

— (1910) *Leonardo da Vinci and a Memory of his Childhood*. Standard Edition Vol. XI.

— (1911) Psycho-Analytic Notes upon an Autobiographical Account of a Case of Paranoia (Dementia Paranoides). Standard Edition Vol. XII.

— (1912) The Dynamics of Transference. Standard Edition Vol. XII.

— (1913) *Totem and Taboo*. Standard Edition Vol. XIII.

— (1914) On Narcissism: An Introduction. Standard Edition Vol. XIV.

— (1914) Remembering, Repeating and Working-Through. Standard Edition Vol. XII.

— (1914) On the History of the Psycho-Analytic Movement. Standard Edition Vol. XIV.

— (1915) Observations on Transference-Love. Standard Edition Vol. XII.

— (1916/17) *Introductory Lectures on Psycho-Analysis*. Standard Edition Vols. XV and XVI.

— (1917) A Metapsychological Supplement to the Theory of Dreams. Standard Edition Vol. XIV.

— (1918) Lines of Advance in Psycho-Analytic Therapy. Standard Edition Vol. XVII.

— (1920) *Beyond the Pleasure Principle*. Standard Edition Vol. XVIII.

— (1923) Two Encyclopaedia Articles. Standard Edition Vol. XVIII.

— (1923) *The Ego and the Id*. Standard Edition Vol. XIX.

— (1925) An Autobiographical Study. Standard Edition Vol. XX.

— (1926) *Inhibitions, Symptoms, and Anxiety*. Standard Edition Vol. XX.

— (1937) Analysis Terminable and Interminable. Standard Edition Vol. XXIII.

— (1940) *An Outline of Psycho-Analysis*. Standard Edition Vol. XXIII.

FROMM, E. (1963) *The Dogma of Christ and Other Essays on Religion, Psychology and Culture*. Routledge, London, 1963.

GILL, M. M., and BRENMAN, M. (1959) *Hypnosis and Related States*. International Universities Press, New York.

Bibliography

GRECO, R. S. with PITTENGER, R. A. (1966) *One Man's Practice.* Tavistock Publications, London; Lippincott, Philadelphia.

GREENACRE, PHYLLIS (1952) Pre-genital Patterning. *Int. J. Psycho-Anal.* Vol. 33, p. 414.

— (1953) *Trauma, Growth and Personality.* Hogarth Press, London.

— (1960) Regression and Fixation. *J. Amer. Psychoanal. Ass.* Vol. VIII, p. 703.

HARTMANN, HEINZ (1956) The Ego Concept in Freud's Work. *Int. J. Psycho-Anal.* Vol. 37.

HILL, LEWIS B. (1955) Psychotherapeutic Intervention in Schizophrenia. Univ. of Chicago Press, Chicago.

HOFFER, WILLI (1959) Reconsideration of Freud's Concept – 'Primary Narcissism'. Paper read to the British Psycho-Analytical Society in June, 1959.

JONES, ERNEST (1927) The Early Development of Female Sexuality. Reprinted in *Papers on Psycho-analysis*, Baillière, Tindall and Cox, London. 4th Edition 1938.

— (1953) *Sigmund Freud.* Vol. I. Hogarth Press, London.

— (1957) *Sigmund Freud.* Vol. III. Hogarth Press, London.

KANZER, MARK (1955) The Communicative Function of the Dream. *Int. J. Psycho-Anal.* Vol. 36, p. 261.

KHAN, M. M. R. (1962) Dream Psychology and the Evolution of the Psychoanalytic Situation. *Int. J. Psycho-Anal.* Vol. 43.

KLEIN, MELANIE, *et al.* (1955) *New Directions in Psycho-Analysis.* Tavistock Publications, London; Basic Books, New York.

KLEIN, MELANIE (1957) *Envy and Gratitude.* Tavistock Publications, London; Basic Books, New York.

KNAPP, P. (1959) See below: Panel Discussions (1959) on Criteria for Analysability.

KRIS, ERNST (1935) The Psychology of Caricature. Reprinted in *Psychoanalytic Exploration in Art.* International Universities Press, New York.

— (1952) *Psychoanalytic Explorations in Art.* International Universities Press, New York.

LAMPL-DE GROOT, J. (1963) Symptom Formation and Character Formation. *Int. J. Psycho-Anal.* Vol. 44, p. 1.

LASK, A. (1966) *Asthma: Attitude and Milieu.* Tavistock Publications, London; Lippincott, Philadelphia.

LEWIN, BERTRAM D. (1958) *Dreams and the Uses of Regression.* International Universities Press, New York.

LITTLE, MARGARET (1957) 'R'. The Analyst's Total Response to his Patient's Needs. *Int. J. Psycho-Anal.* Vol. 38.

— (1958) On Delusional Transference. *Int. J. Psycho-Anal.* Vol. 39, p. 134.

LOCH, WOLFGANG (1963/4) Regression. *Psyche* Vol. 17, pp. 516–545.

LOEWENSTEIN, R. (1958) Remarks on Some Variation in Psycho-analytic Technique. *Int. J. Psycho-Anal.* Vol. 39, p. 202.

MAIN, T. F. (1957) The Ailment. *Brit. J. med. Psychol.* Vol. 30.

PANEL DISCUSSIONS (1957) Technical Aspects of Regression during Psychoanalysis. *J. Amer. Psychoanal. Ass.* 1958, Vol. VI.

— (1957) Technical Aspects of Transference. *J. Amer. Psychoanal. Ass.* 1958, Vol. VI.

— (1959) Criteria for Analysability. *J. Amer. Psychoanal. Ass.* 1960, Vol. VIII.

— (1960) Panel on Analysability. *J. Amer. Psychoanal. Ass.* Vol. VIII, pp. 86–95.

— (1963) Panel on Analysability. *Bull. Philadelphia Ass. Psychoanal.* Vol. 13, pp. 36–39.

— (1966) Severe Regressive States during Analysis. *J. Amer. Psychoanal. Ass.* Vol. 14, p. 538.

RANK, OTTO (1924) *Don Juan-Gestalt.* Int. Psa. Verlag, Wien.

REICH, ANNIE (1953) Narcissistic Object Choice in Women. *J. Amer. Psychoanal. Ass.* Vol. 1, p. 22.

RICKMAN, JOHN (1951) Number and the Human Sciences. In *Psycho-analysis and Culture.* International Universities Press, New York. (Reprinted in *Selected Contributions on Psychoanalysis.* Hogarth Press, London, 1957.)

SEARLES, HAROLD F. (1961) Sources of the Anxiety in Paranoid Schizophrenia. *Brit. J. med. Psychol.* Vol. 34, p. 129.

— (1963) The Place of Neutral Therapist Responses in Psychotherapy with the Schizophrenic Patient. *Int. J. Psycho-Anal.* Vol. 44, p. 42.

— (1963) Transference Psychosis in the Psychotherapy of Chronic Schizophrenia. *Int. J. Psycho-Anal.* Vol. 44, p. 249.

SPITZ, RENÉ (1946) Anaclitic Depression. *The Psychoanalytic Study of the Child* Vol. 2.

STANTON, A. H., and SCHWARZ, M. S. (1954) *The Mental Hospital.* Basic Books, New York.

STRACHEY, JAMES (1961) Editorial notes to Freud's *The Ego and the Id.* Standard Edition Vol. XIX.

WEISS, EDUARDO (1957) A Comparative Study of Psychoanalytical Ego Concepts. *Int. J. Psycho-Anal.* Vol. 38, p. 212.

WINNICOTT, D. W. (1949) Hate in the Counter-Transference. *Int. J. Psycho-Anal.* Vol. 30.

— (1951) Transitional Objects and Transitional Phenomena. (Reprinted in 1958 as Chapter 18 in *Collected Papers*, Tavistock Publications, London; Basic Books, New York.)

Bibliography

WINNICOTT, D. W. (1958) *Collected Papers.* Tavistock Publications, London; Basic Books, New York.

— (1958) The Capacity to be Alone. *Int. J. Psycho-Anal.* Vol. 39, pp. 416–420. Reprinted in *The Maturational Processes and the Facilitating Environment*, Hogarth Press London, 1965.

ZETZEL, E. (1956) Current Concepts of Transference. *Int. J. Psycho-Anal.* Vol. 37, p. 372.

Special bibliography on oral dependence and related states

Oral dependence

ALEXANDER, F. (1950) *Psychosomatic Medicine*. Allen & Unwin, London; Norton, New York, pp. 102–104 and 133–134.

MASSERMAN, J. (1951) Some Current Concepts of Sexual Behavior. *Psychiatry* Vol. 14.

MEERLOO, J. (1952) Artificial Ecstasy. *J. Nerv. Ment. Dis.* Vol. 115, pp. 246–266.

GRUNBERGER, B. (1953) Oral Conflicts and Hysteria. *Rev. Franc. Psa.* Vol. 17.

FRIEDMAN, L. J. (1953) Defensive Aspects of Orality. *Int. J. Psycho-Anal.* Vol. 34.

KLEIN, MELANIE, et al. (1955) *New Directions in Psycho-Analysis*. Tavistock Publications, London; Basic Books, New York.

Average expectable environment

HARTMANN, H. (1939) *Ego Psychology and the Problem of Adaption*. International Universities Press, New York, 1958.

Need-satisfying object

FREUD, A. (War years and 1963) Concept of Developmental Lines. *Psychoanal. Study Child* Vol. 18.

Extra-uterine matrix

MAHLER, M. (1952) On Childhood Psychosis and Schizophrenia. *Psychoanal. Study Child* Vol. 7.

Good-enough environment

WINNICOTT, D. W. (1941) The Observation of Infants in a Set Situation. In *Collected Papers*. Tavistock Publications, London; Basic Books, New York, 1958.

Ordinary devoted mother

WINNICOTT, D. W. (1949) The Ordinary Devoted Mother and her Baby. In *Collected Papers*.

Bibliography

Primary maternal preoccupation

WINNICOTT, D. W. (1956) Primary Maternal Preoccupation. In *Collected Papers.*

Holding function

WINNICOTT, D. W. (1960) The Parent-Infant Relationship. In *The Maturational Processes and the Facilitating Environment.* Hogarth Press, London, 1965.

Basic unity

LITTLE, MARGARET (1960) On Basic Unity. *Int. J. Psycho-Anal.* Vol. 41.

Facilitating environment

WINNICOTT, D. W. (1963) Casework and Mental Illness AND Theory of Psychiatric Disorder. In *The Maturational Processes and the Facilitating Environment.* Hogarth Press, London, 1965.

Protective shield

KHAN, M. (1963) The Concept of Cumulative Trauma. *Psychoanal. Study Child* Vol. 18.

Mediator of the environment

SPITZ, R. (1965) *The First Year of Life.* International Universities Press, New York.

Index

Index

205